Introduction
to
Marx and Engels

Dimensions of Philosophy Series

Norman Daniels and Keith Lehrer, Series Editors

Introduction to Marx and Engels: A Critical Reconstruction,
Richard Schmitt

FORTHCOMING

Philosophy of Science, Clark Glymour

Knowledge, Keith Lehrer

Contemporary Continental Philosophy, Bernd Magnus

Philosophy of Social Science, Alexander Rosenberg

Philosophy of Physics, Lawrence Sklar

About the Book and Author

In this clear and jargon-free exposition, Richard Schmitt provides the best introduction to the philosophical Marx and Engels now available for students. For professionals he sketches an original and much-needed synthesis of two competing ways of interpreting the fragmented and often apparently contradictory aspects of Marxian thought. By taking seriously the role of dialectic in Marx's thought and by exploring more fully what Marx meant by "human nature," Schmitt does justice to the humanist view of Marx that "human beings make their own history" as well as to the opposing view that human history is inexorably shaped by socioeconomic forces.

The creative tension of the dialectic between human freedom and historical materialism is fruitful, throwing light upon Marx's understanding of social class, determinism, and the "contradictions" of capitalism. Throughout his insightful discussion of these notoriously difficult theories, Schmitt remains at a level entirely appropriate for the beginning student of Marx and Engels.

Richard Schmitt teaches philosophy at Brown University. He has written extensively for journals and has published two books: *Martin Heidegger on Being Human* (1969) and *Alienation and Class* (1983).

Introduction
to
Marx and Engels

A Critical
Reconstruction

Richard Schmitt

Westview Press • Boulder and London

Dimensions of Philosophy Series

Copyright © 1987 by Westview Press, Inc.

Published in 1987 in the United States of America by Westview Press, Inc.; Frederick A. Praeger, Publisher; 5500 Central Avenue, Boulder, Colorado 80301

Library of Congress Cataloging-in-Publication Data
Schmitt, Richard, 1927–
  Introduction to Marx and Engels.
  Bibliography: p.
  Includes index.
  1. Marx, Karl, 1818–1883. 2. Engels, Friedrich,
1820–1895. 3. Communism. I. Title.
HX39.5.S266 1987   335.4   87-8213
ISBN 0-8133-0425-3 (hc)
ISBN 0-8133-0426-1 (pbk.)

Printed and bound in the United States of America

The paper used in this publication meets the requirements of the American National Standard for Permanence of Paper for Printed Library Materials Z39.48-1984.

10   9   8   7   6   5   4   3   2   1

Contents

PART THREE
THE THEORY OF SOCIETY

Preface

KARL MARX WAS, as Engels said at his graveside, "before all else a revolutionist." Because his mind was powerful and his voice eloquent he is still, a hundred years after his death, an inspiration to revolutionaries. Wherever people are impoverished and oppressed, they turn to his writings. But not only revolutionaries take him seriously; his work is equally important for people who tend to be anything but revolutionary. Any social theorist of stature still feels the need to come to grips with Marx's ideas. The Marxist intellectual tradition remains an important source of inspiration and challenge in the social sciences because Marx was more than just a "revolutionist." He was a revolutionary of a new type, a *scientific* revolutionary.

Moral idealists with a vision of a better world have made revolutions in the past. But society is too complex to be transformed on the basis of good intentions alone. This is why revolutionaries have often brought about very different effects from those they had intended. Since they had only a rudimentary understanding of the workings of society and of historical transformations, their actions were blind. Their hope of reshaping society according to their plan was as unrealistic as the attempts to control natural processes by people who have no scientific knowledge of nature.

The development of social science, particularly economics, at the end of the eighteenth century ushered in a new era, one in which human beings could understand the workings of their own society and the processes of social change. Marx foresaw that such knowledge would be enormously liberating because it would allow people much more control over their social conditions, just as the development of natural science had proved liberating in relation to natural forces. Armed with a reliable understanding of the workings of their society, they could set about transforming it to meet their needs.

To have understood the liberatory potential of social and natural science is one of the great contributions of Marx and Engels. But they were insufficiently aware that science could also serve mass regimentation and extermination. In addition, their own social theory was not as complete or defensible as they had hoped: Their expectations for social change remain unfulfilled and, in certain cases, monstrously distorted.

An introductory book is not the place for a thorough critique of Marxian thought, but the major shortcomings of that thought must be pointed out. In this book I will concentrate on providing a defensible interpretation of the writings of Marx and Engels, but I will not hesitate to indicate the most obvious places in which their thought is fragmentary or implausible.

Social science does not make all things possible, as social change is limited by human nature, by the limits of human capabilities. It follows that a good way to approach social change is by reflecting on human nature. Following that, we will ask about the relations of individual to society and then, more concretely, look at the economics and sociology of capitalist society. Finally, we shall examine Marx and Engels' thinking about actually effecting change in capitalist society.

Nowhere did Marx and Engels present their thoughts in systematic form. Their views on history, economics, and social change come down to us in texts that range from incomplete systematic works (*Capital*), polemics (*The German Ideology, The Poverty of Philosophy*), and political programs (*The Communist Manifesto*), to private notebooks (*The Economic and Philosophical Manuscripts*), newspaper accounts of current affairs (*The Civil War in France*), and letters. The reader would need to collect relevant passages from all these writings in order to reconstruct them into one unified whole. Grasping the thought of Marx and Engels is therefore not just a matter of reading the texts with sufficient care, although that is, of course, extremely important. But no amount of careful reading alone will produce a uniquely correct reconstruction. It is disingenuous to accuse interpreters of Marx who give an interpretation different from one's own of being careless readers. The different texts need to be assembled into a coherent whole, and more than one such reconstruction is plausible.

Reconstructions depend on the historical and political circumstances of the readers, their interests, and their philosophical presuppositions. Reconstructions, moreover, must reckon with the history of the inter-pretations of the thought of Marx and Engels. From the very beginning, their writings have never been far from political controversy. Recon-structions of their work necessarily carry the imprint of definite political stances and programs. Contemporary reconstructions of their thought are developed against the background of the history of the socialist and communist movements since the last century, and against the different interpretations that have become identified with different tendencies, political parties, and regimes.

Because this book is primarily intended for readers new to the works of Marx and Engels, I cannot give a full exposition of alternative readings and connect them to their respective intellectual and political backgrounds. But at various points I will mention prominent interpretations differing from my own in order to alert the student to the complexities of the issues and to encourage the curious to explore further the thought of Marx and Engels.

Ways of disagreeing about Marx and Engels are legion, but most of the prevailing interpretations fall into one or another of two classes. I want to contrast these two classes of interpretations here in the most schematic fashion in order to give some indication of the broad controversies about the texts. These are ideal types only; many interpreters of Marx would have good grounds for dissociating themselves in particular respects from one or the other. Nevertheless, the general tendencies of interpretation characterized here are fundamental, and grasping them will make it easier for readers to orient themselves in the multitude of controversies surrounding the interpretation of Marx's and Engels' writings.

The first of these—which I will call the "traditional" reading— takes Marx's preface to his *Contribution to the Critique of Political Economy* as its central text:

> In the social production of their life, men enter into definite relations that are indispensable and independent of their will, relations of production which correspond to a definite stage of development of their material productive forces. . . . The mode of production of material life conditions the social, political and intellectual life process in general. It is not the consciousness of men that determines their being, but, on the contrary, their social being that determines their consciousness.[1]

The interpretation presented in this book takes a different text as central:

> Men make their own history, but they do not make it just as they please; they do not make it under circumstances chosen by themselves.[2]

The differences are subtle; both passages agree that human beings affect the conditions of their lives; both stress the extent to which those conditions react on human existence. But the emphasis of the first is on the effects of material circumstances on human thought and, hence, on human action. The second passage seems to make more room for an independent human contribution to history. The first passage leads us to see ourselves as largely shaped by our external circumstances. The second passage presents those circumstances as the framework within which human beings shape their own history, a framework that, moreover, is itself affected by human choices.

These different emphases will make themselves felt throughout this book. My interpretation begins with a discussion of Marx and Engels' conception of *human nature* and their insistence on the possibility of genuine human freedom (Chapter 1). Traditional Marxism is skeptical of Marx's views on human nature. My interpretation emphasizes those passages in which Marx and Engels stress the social nature of human existence. Accordingly, I insist that the prevailing concept of the *individual* is a social creation (Chapter 2), and that *classes* are self-created in the course of their *history* (Chapter 12). Human self-interpretation—by groups, not by individuals—is central to my interpretation of Marx. He learned that from Hegel and expressed that insight in the Hegelian jargon of the *dialectic*, which many traditional interpreters reject or pass over in embarrassed silence (Chapter 5). The concept of *ideology* takes on very different meanings in different writings of Marx and Engels, but its root meaning is that of an articulated human self-understanding, not of "false consciousness," as the traditional interpretation would have it (Chapter 6). In my interpretation, Marx regards human beings as potentially free because they are able to think about themselves and thus are capable, collectively, of understanding and directing their lives. Abridgment of that freedom is what he means by alienation. *Alienation* thus is not merely a psychological condition (Chapter 15).

Quite predictably, traditional Marxism tends to view economic processes as impersonal sequences of events that take place behind people's backs, whereas my reading stresses the importance of human participation and understanding in *economics* (Chapter 8). The implication is that the failure of some of Marx's *economic predictions* is not as damaging to the political program as traditional Marxism thinks (Chapter 11).

Finally, the two interpretive tendencies have different *political implications*. In my reading, the revolution will bring about a new order emerging from a new understanding of what it means to be human— an understanding not just in the heads of leftist intellectuals but in the practices of the majority as well. The *revolution* will consist not merely of taking state power but of transforming human nature as well (Chapter 18).

Such a change in human outlook and activity clearly requires more time than that considered necessary by traditional Marxism for the advent of revolution. My view thus departs from traditional Marxism in its sense of how long it will take to change the world from capitalism to a more humane social order and what the respective role will be of the Marxists, socialists, and communists on the one hand, and of the majority of people on the other (Chapter 14).

Marx's and Engels' expectations for social change remain unfulfilled because their social science was defective. A reconstruction of their writings, especially one that is to serve as an introduction, must at least indicate the most obvious places in which their understanding of capitalist society and revolution fell short of reality. To be useful, a reconstruction must be critical.

My understanding of Marx derives from many sources. Associates in various political projects taught me a great deal, as did many friends, both within and outside of the Radical Philosophy Association, and the Marxist Activist Philosophers. I owe particular thanks for reading portions of this manuscript to Bruce Brown, Lisa Feldman, and David Schweickart, as well as to an anonymous reader for the publisher. Their comments have been extremely helpful. Spencer Carr, acquisitions editor for Westview, has been unfailingly supportive.

Lucy Candib has shared the writing of this book, as she shares most everything else—particularly the enduring confidence that we can remold this world of oppression and exploitation into one in which mutual respect and concern animate the relations among free human beings.

Notes

1. Karl Marx, *A Contribution to the Critique of Political Economy* (New York: International Publishers, 1970), p. 20.

2. Karl Marx, *The 18th Brumaire of Louis Bonaparte* (New York: International Publishers, 1963), p. 15.

Abbreviated References

CI   *Capital*, Vol. I (Marx)
CII   *Capital*, Vol. II (Marx)
CIII   *Capital*, Vol. III (Marx)
CGP *Critique of the Gotha Program* (Marx)
CM   *Manifesto of the Communist Party* (Marx and Engels)
CSF   *Class Struggles in France* (Marx)
CW   *The Civil War in France* (Marx)
EPM *Economic and Philosophical Manuscripts of 1844* (Marx)
18th   *The 18th Brumaire of Louis Bonaparte* (Marx)
GI   *The German Ideology* (Marx and Engels)
G   *Grundrisse* (Marx)
OF   *The Origin of the Family, Private Property and the State* (Engels)
SUS   *Socialism: Utopian and Scientific* (Engels)
T   *The Marx-Engels Reader* (Tucker, editor)
WLC *Wage Labor and Capital* (Marx)

Introduction

KARL MARX WAS BORN in Trier, Germany, on May 5, 1818, the descendant of a long line of rabbis. His uncle was then the chief rabbi of Trier. Marx's father, Heinrich, had converted to Christianity when new legislation, which excluded Jews from government service, threatened his livelihood as a lawyer. Neither his family nor Marx himself identified themselves as Jews. Marx's wife, Jenny, came from a Protestant family in the Prussian civil service.

Sent to the university, first at Bonn, then in Berlin to study law, Marx immersed himself in philosophy and earned a Ph.D. in 1841 in the hope of obtaining a teaching position at the University in Bonn. But he and his friends spent a good deal of their energy attacking religion and criticizing the autocratic political institutions of Prussia—criticisms that, unfortunately, were fully justified. At that time, Prussia was ruled by an absolute monarch whose power was not limited by a constitution, let alone by popularly elected representatives. The freedoms of speech and religion were not guaranteed. The government exercised strict censorship on publications and on what was taught in the state-run schools. Under those circumstances, Marx and his friend Bruno Bauer, who attacked religion and argued for democratic rights for all citizens, had no chance of getting a teaching job in any Prussian university.

Throughout his life, Marx supported himself by his writing. For two brief periods, in 1844 and again in 1848, he was the editor of a paper; later he earned some money as correspondent for the *New York Herald Tribune* and a number of other publications. For most of his life he also depended on financial help from his friends, primarily Friedrich Engels. Even with this help, he lived in extreme poverty for many years. The biographer of Marx's daughter Eleanor writes: "Mrs. Marx, who was also often unwell, spent a good deal of her time running to the pawnbroker

1

to pledge the linen and plate, her own and her family's personal belongings and attire, and all such household objects as were not immovable."[1]

Marx's poverty was, to be sure, aggravated by his inability to use wisely the money he did have, as well as by the need to keep up a minimal middle-class front. In the main, however, Marx was the victim of the illiberal government of his native Prussia, which made it impossible for him to take up any of the careers to which he was suited—as teacher, lawyer, or journalist—and, instead, forced him to leave Germany. France and Belgium gave him temporary refuge but then expelled him, at the urging of the Prussian government. Only England, where he lived after 1850, allowed him, and his fellow German political refugees, a place in which to work and scrape together a living as best as they could.

Married in 1841, Marx and his wife, Jenny, had six children. Only three reached adulthood. The letters that Marx and Jenny wrote to friends reporting the death of the other three children remain heartbreaking. Marx and Jenny were genuinely devoted to each other, notwithstanding the fact that he had an illegitimate son. It was also a very unequal relationship. Jenny transcribed her husband's virtually illegible hand into neat versions of his voluminous writings, went to meetings and collected articles for him, and supported his political and scholarly work in other ways—all in addition to bearing him six children and caring for them, often under very hard conditions. She died in 1882. Marx followed her within the year.

Marx and Engels first met in 1842, when Marx was 24 and Engels 22. Marx was the editor of a newspaper, Engels already a journalist with something of a reputation. Born into a fairly well-to-do business family of staunch Protestant persuasion, Engels had not gone to university but was self-educated. In many respects, Marx and Engels were very different men: Whereas Marx was mercurial, Engels was even-tempered; whereas Marx was careless with money and his appearance, Engels was an astute businessman and a person of fine taste who cared for his appearance; whereas Marx was a family man, Engels, though capable of deep and lasting attachments—for twenty years he had lived with Mary Burns and was deeply shaken when she died—never married or had children. Whereas Engels had the greater facility as a writer, Marx was clearly the deeper thinker. Both were gifted polemicists, but Marx's prose style at its best is unmatched by anything that Engels wrote.

As already mentioned, Marx depended heavily on Engels' financial support. At times, that support put Engels himself in serious straits, but he always came through for his friend. But Marx also owed a good deal to Engels intellectually. As a young man, Marx was still fighting mainly philosophical battles when Engels, because he was in the family textile business, which took him traveling to England, had begun to study economics and had gained a very clear grasp of the condition of working people. Occasionally, Engels provided intellectual and financial support at the same time. Marx was commissioned to write for the *New York Herald Tribune* when he was still somewhat unsure of his English. His first set of articles was written for him by Engels but published over Marx's name. Their friendship was a source of continued strength for both men.

Although Marx was very frosty at their first meeting in 1842, by 1844 he had read a piece by Engels entitled "Outline of a Critique of Political Economy," which made a deep impression on him. When they met again, they spent ten days together in conversation, and from that time on they were allies and close friends until Marx's death in 1883. They wrote two books together in the next two years, of which the *German Ideology* is of major importance in their thinking. The *Communist Manifesto* of 1847 was written by Marx, but its ideas were demonstrably those of both men.

Both were also seriously involved in radical politics. In the period of the 1847–1848 revolutions, both of them returned to the continent from England, and Engels actually took part in some of the fighting in Germany. They were both active in the First International, an international socialist organization founded in 1864, in which Marx soon came to occupy a position of leadership and to which he devoted the bulk of his time for the next six or seven years.

In his later years, Engels, besides working full-time in his family business in Manchester in order to keep the Marx family and himself going, spent much energy publicizing Marx's ideas. He also developed them in directions probably different from those that Marx would have chosen. Their thinking diverged, it seems, but as neither gave any indication that they were aware of that divergence, we possess no authoritative account of the relationships between their later works. How one interprets the differences between the two men depends on how one reads those later writings. As a consequence, the precise relationship between Marx and Engels as thinkers has become a source of controversy between interpreters. Some see one unified body of doctrine—namely, the thought of Marx-and-Engels; others, in an equally untenable position, see Marx as the deep, humanistic thinker and Engels as the shallow, positivistic popularizer. In fact, the work of neither thinker is of one piece. Marx had more than one opinion on a large range of issues, and these different opinions are not always consistent. The views of the later Engels clearly have their roots in some of the positions held by Marx. It is also true, however, that Engels tended to develop only one side of Marx's very complex thought and not always the side that proved, in the long run, to be the most defensible one. But to ascribe all the errors in the Marxist tradition to Engels, as some readers have done,[2] is to exaggerate Marx's genius into infallibility and seriously to underestimate the contribution of Engels.[3]

Notes

1. Yvonne Kapp, *Eleanor Marx*, Vol. I (London: Lawrence and Wishart, 1972), p. 27.

2. One example of that reading is Norman Levine, *The Tragic Deception: Marx Contra Engels* (Oxford and Santa Barbara: Clio Books, 1975).

3. Readers interested in a more detailed discussion of the relationship between Marx and Engels will find a more balanced account in Terrell Carver, *Marx and Engels: The Intellectual Relationship* (Bloomington: Indiana University Press, 1983).

PART ONE

The Conception of Human Nature

1

Human Nature

MARX AND ENGELS STUDIED social transformations—the processes of historical change from feudalism to capitalism, and from capitalism to socialism and, eventually, communism. According to them, history is human history inasmuch as it is shaped, within limits, by human beings:

> Human beings make their own history, but they do not make it just as they please. (18th, T 595)[1]

Humans are the sort of creatures who shape their own lives and hence affect their own history. The character of human history flows from the character of human nature. It is with human nature that we must begin our reconstruction of the thought of Marx and Engels.

They developed their conception of human nature in their earliest work by asking: What is distinctive about human beings that differentiates them from animals? Many thinkers have raised that question, but Marx and Engels' answer was significantly different from that given by many others.

It is usually thought that human beings are distinguished as human beings by very specific abilities, such as reason or the use of language; by specific practices, such as religious worship; or by specific motivations and patterns of action, such as greed, competitiveness, and the persistent tendency to put their own individual needs and desires above those of any other person. Human nature, in this conception, is defined by very specific traits. In addition, it is taken to be unchangeable throughout history.

The conception of human nature plays a very important role in the thought of Marx and Engels,[2] but theirs is a radically different conception from that held by most other philosophers.[3]

> Men can be distinguished from animals by consciousness, by religion or anything else you like. They themselves begin to distinguish themselves from animals as soon as they begin to *produce* their means of subsistence. (GI, T 150)

Marx and Engels chose a characteristic different from that specified by other philosophers, who defined consciousness, or religion, as the essence of human beings. Marx and Engels chose as essential the fact that humans produce. But if we read beyond the passage quoted, we begin to see that this choice has rather unusual implications:

> By producing their means of subsistence men are indirectly producing their actual material life. The way in which men produce their means of subsistence . . . is a definite form of activity of these individuals, a definite form of expressing their life. . . . As individuals express their life, so they are. (Ibid.)

This paragraph goes through a number of steps:

1. In producing the particular goods that a group needs, its members produce the particular ways in which they go about meeting their material needs; they produce "their actual material life." Thus the fact, for example, that people farm not only yields them farm products but also determines their worklife to be that of farmers.

2. But this worklife determines their entire way of life. Farmers are different from city people not only because they farm, rather than working in offices or factories, but also for reasons aside from the sort of work they do. Country life, as a whole, is different from city life.

3. People who live differently are different people: "As individuals express their life, so they are."

The upshot of this set of steps is that human beings not only produce things but they produce themselves as well, and as different people produce in very different ways, different people make themselves into different people. Thus people are very different from one another, although they are all humans. But many other philosophers would say that too. What is distinctive about the conception of human nature held by Marx and Engels is a further claim—namely, that *human beings make themselves be who they are.* The differences between human beings are produced by these human beings themselves. Central to human nature, then, is this ability of human beings to determine who they will be.

The interpretation of the preceding passages varies according to the meaning one attaches to the verb "to produce." Some interpreters use the term in a rather restricted sense as meaning "producing with tools."[4] In that sense of the word it would not make sense to talk about human beings producing their way of life or producing themselves. I interpret Marx as extending the meaning of that verb beyond its customary sense of making objects of some kind or causing them to be made, to speaking of human beings producing their way of life, and even producing themselves. It is important to notice the extraordinary use of the word "produce" in order to be aware that, so far, it is not at all clear what this process of human self-production looks like. Several chapters will be required to explicate this conception.

We can take a first step toward its clarification by examining the concept of "species being," first used by Marx in the notebooks he wrote in Paris in 1844 (initially published in Berlin in 1932, as *The Economic and Philosophic Manuscripts of 1844*). These notebooks are preliminary works. They were not written for publication and, as a consequence, are difficult to read. In addition, their terminology is foreign to modern readers. They therefore require careful interpretation. Consider this passage from the portion of the notebooks called "Alienated Labor":

> Human beings are species beings, not only because in practice and in theory they adopt the species as their object . . . but also because they treat themselves as the actual, living species. . . . The animal is immediately identical with its life-activity. It does not distinguish itself from it. It *is its life-activity*. Human beings make their life-activity itself the object of their will and of their consciousness. (EPM, T 75–76)

Marx here distinguishes human beings from animals. Animals *belong* to a species, but human beings *are* "species beings." Human beings do not merely belong to the human species; they also make the species "the object" of thinking and action. An animal simply is what it does. The life activity of human beings is something they think about before engaging in it:

> Admittedly animals also produce. They build themselves nests, dwellings, like the bees, beavers, ants, etc. But an animal only produces what it immediately needs for itself or its young. . . . It produces only under the dominion of immediate physical need, whilst human beings produce even when they are free from physical need. . . . (EPM, T 76)

Animals build their dwellings and do whatever else they do compelled by need; human beings act even when they are not compelled by need, but because they first thought about the action and then chose to perform it. Later in the first volume of *Capital*, Marx makes that point much more explicitly:

> A spider conducts operations that resemble those of a weaver, and a bee puts to shame many an architect in the construction of her cells. But what distinguishes the worst architect from the best of bees is this, that the architect raises his structure in imagination before he erects it in reality. (CI, T 344)

These passages can be, and have been, read in different ways. Some commentators say that Marx distinguishes animals from human beings by the fact that human beings plan their actions before they perform them, whereas animals act from instinct.[5] As this interpretation does not tell us what Marx means by "species being," however, it is incomplete.

Other commentators rest their interpretation on Marx's insistence that human beings create their own needs: "The satisfaction of the first need . . . leads to new needs; and this production of new needs is the first historical act"(GI, T 156). Human beings are species beings because they are able to change themselves—for instance, by creating new needs.[6]

What Marx means by "the production of new needs" is not further explained in that passage, but elsewhere he speaks of it in very modern terms:

> Under private property their significance [viz. of human needs] is reversed: every person speculates on creating a *new* need in another, so as to . . . place him in a new dependence and to seduce him into a new mode of *gratification* and therefore economic ruin. (EPM, T 93)

If we connect these passages with those cited earlier in which Marx and Engels stress the importance of human beings producing themselves, in the course of producing whatever they need to live, and with it their way of life, then we see that they claimed not merely that human beings act intentionally or that they create new needs for themselves but, more generally, that *they make themselves be what they are*. And that very general process is itself at least partially intentional.

The underlying thought seems to be the following: Human beings live in very different ways, depending on the different ways in which they go about producing what they need, and depending on what, in fact, they need, which varies widely among different societies. Beyond this great mutability there is only one common characteristic of human beings that we could designate as human nature—namely, that the changes in human ways of life are created by human beings themselves.

The question: What is peculiarly human? is answered very differently by different groups of people because they live very different lives. But since they themselves made their way of life what it is, we may well say that human beings determine what it means to be human—that is, what it is that makes their lives human lives.

It is characteristic of human beings that they are able not just to change themselves but also to determine what it means to be human. They do this by creating the way in which they live, and that, in turn, they accomplish by determining how they will go about meeting their material needs. This self-creation is done as a consequence of thinking and planning. Human beings go about meeting their material needs not driven by instinct but as a result of choosing to meet those needs and choosing how to go about meeting them. They therefore also determine what it means to be human by virtue of their intentional actions.

It is important, however, to be clear on this point: Marx did not claim that people deliberately define "human being" to be this or that. He claimed that people solve their day-to-day problems by thinking about them, developing solutions, and then actively seeking those solutions. These intentional actions often have consequences that were not intended. In many historical situations, the definition of "human being" was not intended but was an unintended consequence of other intentional actions. One must not read Marx and Engels as claiming that human beings explicitly and deliberately set about defining "human being." The definition of "human being" is the result, more often than not the *unintended* result, of intentional actions. As we shall see in Chapter 5, Marx and Engels also believed that it will be possible for human beings to define "human being" deliberately, and that they will then, and only then, be actually free.

As species beings, understood as beings who define their own nature, human beings are free (EPM, T 75). Although the word "free" has many different senses, and although Marx does not explicitly define his use of the word in this context, it is easy enough to infer from the context what he has in mind. Animals are "compelled" by need or by instinct. Human beings act and produce even where there is no need pressing upon them. To the extent that they are free from compulsion, therefore, they are free because they have control over their lives. Creatures governed by instinct are, in that sense, not in control and are therefore not free. But neither are creatures who are controlled by want, by ignorance, by an environment that is not controllable because it is not understood. The ability to make choices is not sufficient for human freedom—making a poorly informed choice does not increase control over one's life. Only to the extent that these choices rest on reliable information, on knowledge about the situation in which the choices are made, can the persons making those choices be said to be free. (We shall return to Marx's concept of freedom in Chapter 15.) Human beings always have the capacity for self-determination, although there are many situations in which they are unable to exercise it. These are situations in which they do not fully understand their circumstances, and hence even their most carefully made choices have unforeseen consequences, or situations in which they are able to make informed choices but are unable to act on those choices due to economic or political pressures. In such situations, their human freedom is only a potentiality that actual conditions prevent from being made a reality. Thus the manuscript entitled "Alienated Labor" (which we will discuss in more detail in Chapter 15) argues that in a capitalist society, human beings are unable to exercise this potentiality for self-definition and are therefore alienated because they are, in fact, unfree.

Marx and Engels in contrast to many philosophers, claim that human beings have in common only very general characteristics such as the *potentiality* for freedom—for defining what it means to be a human being—or the inclination to think before acting. But given this capacity, human beings in different societies will, in practice, act in very different ways and will display very different kinds of motivations. Human nature—that is, what differentiates us from animals—does not consist of specific traits but concerns our ability to change our traits and thus to define our human nature in new and different ways by changing our circumstances.

I began this chapter by saying that Marx and Engels studied the process of social transformation. They were interested in human nature because that "nature" sets limits on the sorts of changes that are possible. For instance, a person who believes that all human beings are selfish, in whatever sense of that term, will think that it is impossible to create a society in which persons do not act selfishly. For thinkers interested in social change the limits placed on such change by human nature is of great interest. Hence Marx and Engels' insistence that human nature is very flexible extends the range of what sorts of social changes are humanly possible.

There are two important restrictions on this conception of the determination by human beings of what it means to be human: (1) Human beings are *capable* of acting according to plans, but they do not always do it; and even when they do, they rarely, if ever, are aware of all the consequences of their actions. (2) Human beings do not determine the meaning of being human each for him- or herself. They do that collectively.

This last point will occupy our attention in the next chapter. The next three chapters will make much clearer what Marx and Engels meant by their claim that human beings define what it is that makes them human. Finally, the remainder of the book will show the important implications of this view.

Notes

1. All quotations from Marx and Engels, unless otherwise stated, have been taken from Robert C. Tucker, ed., *The Marx-Engels Reader*, 2nd ed. (New York: W. W. Norton, 1978). References to this book, abbreviated "T," appear in parentheses along with the appropriate page numbers; preceding each such reference will be an abbreviation indicating the name of the work by Marx and/or Engels in which the quotation was originally found.

2. This is a controversial reading of Marx and Engels. See the third section of Chapter 3.

3. For a good discussion of the sense in which Marx and Engels can be said to have had a conception of human nature, see Allen E. Buchanan, *Marx and Justice* (Totowa, N.J.: Rowman and Allenheld, 1982), Chapter 2 and especially footnote 27.

4. Jon Elster, *Making Sense of Marx* (Cambridge: Cambridge University Press, 1985), p. 64.

5. John McMurtry, *The Structure of Marx's World-View* (Princeton, N.J.: Princeton University Press, 1978), Chapter 1.

6. Buchanan, *Marx and Justice*, pp. 27–28.

For Further Reading

Vernon Venable, *Human Nature: The Marxian View* (New York: Meridian Books, 1966), Chapters 2, 5 and 6.

2

Against Individualism

IN THE PRECEDING CHAPTER, I ascribed to Marx and Engels the thesis that human beings produce themselves by defining, in different ways, what a human being is. That is an attractive thesis, but we must also realize that a part of its attraction lies in its vagueness. It is attractive to some people because they interpret it in ways that Marx would certainly have rejected. I shall begin this chapter by mentioning some clearly mistaken readings, an understanding of which will lead us to a more adequate interpretation of human self-creation.

"Human beings create themselves" is often read as "Men and women, *individually*, make themselves what they are." This is believed to mean that persons who are successful may rightfully take pride in their success because they themselves made that success happen. Conversely, persons who suffer are thought to have brought that suffering on themselves. This thesis ascribes a great deal of responsibility for the course of their lives to individual men and women and, accordingly, denies that the society at large has much responsibility for the plight of the unfortunate.

Whatever the merits of that thesis, it is not what Marx and Engels had in mind. They devoted a good deal of energy to arguing that in a capitalist economy, working people, the poor, and the unemployed suffer even though they are as intelligent and work as hard as people who are much better off. Unemployment, according to Marx and Engels, is a creation of employers (as a class) intended to hold down wages. A certain level of poverty is encouraged for the same purposes. Hence they do not want the claim about human self-creation to be read as applying to individual human beings, making them responsible for being either paupers or captains of industry.

Another misreading of Marx and Engels' thesis claims that we can do anything we want as long as we "believe in ourselves." According to this interpretation, we create ourselves individually, not just by working hard, saving money, and displaying enterprise but by being confident, thinking positively, and, perhaps, trusting in God. This view, as presented by psychologists, ministers, and Eastern sages, is not the view of Marx and Engels either.

When they say that *we* human beings create *ourselves*, the "we" does not refer to you and me as distinct and separate individuals. Marx and Engels insisted that "individuals . . . do not make themselves" (GI, T 164) because human beings do not merely create themselves, each separately—for example, as individual successes or failures; rather, they collectively create a "mode of cooperation"—a social system:

> The production of life . . . now appears . . . as a social relationship. By social we understand the cooperation of several individuals. . . . It follows from this that a certain mode of production . . . is always combined with a certain mode of cooperation (GI, T 157)

in which different people do different jobs, have different roles, and make different contributions. Human beings live in organized societies that assign different roles to different persons. The society functions insofar as the performances of these different roles are coordinated in satisfactory ways. But such a system must always be created cooperatively, even if this means that one person gives the orders and the others take them. One person by him- or herself cannot create a social system. The very nature of such a social system requires that it be created cooperatively. Thus human beings do not create the meaning of "human being," each separately for him- or herself. Each acts to make a contribution to a social setting in which they live together and which shapes each one to be human in the characteristic ways of this group.

But, you will say, groups are collections of individual persons and those persons act only as individuals. Sometimes persons act on behalf of or as representatives of groups, and then we might say, for short, that the group acted. But that would be an inaccurate way of saying that some identifiable individual acted, perhaps as a representative of other individuals who, together, form a group. Human beings—not social groups—act and have needs, desires, and thoughts.

There is no reason to think that Marx would have disagreed with that. In fact, he was very explicit in rejecting any view that held social groups, or society as a whole, to be "persons" who act, think, and desire:

Just as society itself produces *human beings as human beings*, so is society *produced* by them. . . . What is to be avoided above all is the reestablishing of "Society" as an abstraction vis à vis the individual. (EPM, T 86)

Human beings are intrinsically social; whatever they do is social. But that does not mean that there are two separate entities, individuals such as Marx and Engels *and* the society to which they belong. Instead, Marx and Engels are members of the society. Marx and Engels act, as members of the society; the society does not.

What is at issue here? The Hegelians against whom Marx and Engels were arguing in the late 1840s tended to treat society as if it were a superperson. More important, following Hegel himself, they talked about the state as if it were another superperson that acted, decided, and so on. Since then, others have talked about "the people" or "the nation" as if they were such superpersonal subjects, and some politicians today talk about "the working class" in the same way. This view that social entities, societies, states, and nations are superpersons is called "collectivism."

All of this may appear to be just a conflict about words, but in actual practice the political rhetoric that ascribes the characteristics of persons to social entities has, from the days of Hegel to the present, served political regimes that suppress individuals and their freedoms. It is easy to see how that happens: If the "nation" needs me to go to war, what value can my pacifism or the fact that my family needs me have in the face of the need of the whole people? If the "state" demands something from me, how can I resist? To the extent that the political rhetoric that elevates social groups or institutions to the role of persons is accepted, the needs, beliefs, and moral stances of individuals pale to insignificance beside those of the state, the people, and humanity. Collectivism often provides the political rhetoric for oppressive regimes that violate individual integrity.

So far, everyone agrees. But there is considerable disagreement about the implications of the rejection of collectivism. It is frequently thought that a rejection of collectivism commits one to "individualism," an outlook that first gained currency in the early seventeenth century. Individualism is exemplified by the theory of the state of nature from which individuals were said to emerge in order to form organized societies. According to John Locke, individuals first formed society by means of a social contract, when they discovered how inconvenient it was to live without organized society, in the state of nature. The theory of the state of nature implies that persons can be fully functioning persons outside a social context. Hence what they think and do can be explained without reference to a social setting. If one puts this in more modern terminology, one arrives at a contemporary formulation of individualism—namely, that "all social phenomena . . . are in principle explicable in ways that involve only individuals."[1]

If we ask why groups are as they are, the answer will, in the end, be about individuals. Individualism breaks down the actions of groups into the actions of separate individuals. If we ask why any given individual is what he or she is, or does what she or he does, then the answer is either that this individual chose this action independent of anyone else or that others did something to induce this individual to act. According to individualism we may explain the actions, beliefs, motivations, and desires of individuals by reference to social systems, or traditions, or shared ways of life only if we are unable to explain those aspects of individuals by reference to other individuals. Explanations by reference to nonindividual factors, such as traditions or socioeconomic systems, are scientific stopgap measures to which we resort only if we cannot explain the behavior of one individual by that of others. Claims that the social context explains individual behavior are at best incomplete explanations; at worst they are mistakes.

Individualism Is Incomplete

Marx rejected individualism:

The individual and isolated hunter and fisherman, with whom Smith and Ricardo begin, belongs among the unimaginative conceits of the 18th century. . . . The human being is in the most literal sense a *zoon politikon* [social animal], not merely a gregarious animal, but an animal which can individuate itself only in the midst of society. (G, T 222–223)

As opposed to this traditional individualism, Marx insisted that human beings are social animals, not just because they like to be with others— inasmuch as they are sociable—but because they can be *persons* only in a social context. What differentiates different groups is precisely their definition of what it means to be human, and one part of that is surely a definition of what it means to be a person, what it means to be a child or to be a mature adult. The definition of a person changes throughout human history and so, therefore, does the connection of persons to their social setting.

In the past, the connections between individuals and their social contexts were evident to everybody. Individualism became popular only with the rise of capitalist society, because that society attenuated the connections between individual and social whole. Society is now organized differently; individuals are relatively independent of the social context. The individual who is what he or she is, largely independent of his or her social setting, is a modern phenomenon.

> The more deeply we go back into history, the more does the individual, and hence also the producing individual, appear as dependent, as belonging to a greater whole: in a still quite natural way in the family, and in the family expanded into the clan; then later in various forms of communal society arising out of the antitheses and fusions of the clans. Only in the 18th century, in "civil society," do the various forms of social connectedness confront the individual as mere means towards his private purposes, as external necessity. (G, T 222–223)

The term "civil society" refers to the capitalist economy, the sphere of private economic activity, competition, and pursuit of profit and wealth. In this particular social setting, individuals are indeed distinct from each other because each is in competition with the other. Family ties, social connections, and traditions are for the individual so many "means towards his private purposes" to be used and manipulated. They are no longer what that person is.

> In this society of free competition, the individual appears detached from the natural bonds, etc., which in earlier historical periods make him the accessory of a definite and limited human conglomerate. (G, T 222)

Marx was quite explicit: Individualism is false. But in some periods it has been more plausible than in others. In a society such as ours, where family and social ties are weak, where competition reigns and mobility both within and between societies is great, individual identities may well appear untouched by the society. In feudal societies, where there was little mobility, where relations between feudal lord and serf were in a significant sense personal relations, where farming in many localities was done collectively, individualism was sufficiently implausible that no one thought to assert or defend it. The conception of the individual person, which is widely accepted in our present society, is itself a historical phenomenon; it is one way in which groups of people define what it means to be a human being.

Marx, at times, put this conception of the dependence of the identity of individual persons on their social setting in very strong terms:

> But the human essence is no abstraction inherent in each single individual. In its reality it is the ensemble of social relations. (T 145)

Thus states the "6th Thesis on Feuerbach," one of a set of notes in which Marx first articulated his disagreements with Feuerbach. Most likely he overstated his position, which received a more moderate formulation in the *German Ideology*:

> We do not mean it to be understood . . . that, for example, the rentier, the capitalist, etc., cease to be persons; but their personality is conditioned and determined by quite definite class relations. (GI, T 199)

Every person is unique, including, of course, also the capitalist; but in order to be a successful capitalist one needs to be competitive, aggressive, and dedicated to the work of making money. Anyone without those personality traits will fail. Hence the particular personality traits found most often among capitalists are determined by what they do, by the social setting in which they spend their lives.

Individualism ignores the fact that what it means to be an individual is essentially determined by the social setting in which persons live and that, for the same reason, being an individual person has had significantly different meanings throughout history.

> The difference between the individual as a person and what is accidental to him [or her] is not a conceptual difference but a historical fact. (GI, T 194)

The concept of a person changes through history. The concept we have in capitalist societies of persons as individuals whose actions, beliefs, desires, and so on, suffice to explain all human behavior—this itself is a historical phenomenon that requires explanation. In order to explain why individualism appears so plausible to people in our day, we need to talk about its appropriateness to a capitalist society and about the ways in which the capitalist system affects how people think, including how they think about themselves. Individualism overlooks its own history. For that reason, individualism is incomplete.

Individualism Is Misleading

Although Marx and Engels agree that social groups do not literally speak, because they do not have bodies to speak with, nor, for the same reason, do they literally act in other ways, the actions of individuals do involve in their causation the society to which those individuals belong. If capitalists are particular kinds of persons because they are capitalists, then their typical patterns of action are partly shaped by the society in which they live, in which it is possible to be a capitalist.

Thus, while it remains true that only individual persons act, in a literal sense, it is equally true and important that their societies act through them and that when it comes to explaining social phenomena, we need to talk not only about individuals but also about the social settings that shape them.

Individualists deny that groups shape individual actions in these complex ways. They therefore interpret the view taken by Marx and Engels as a defense of collectivism because it rejects individualism.[2] But that interpretation is seriously misleading. Marx agreed, of course, that collectives do not act in the sense in which individuals act; however, he criticized individualism for concealing the fact that actions are not the products of the agent alone but require as necessary conditions complex social settings. When we explain the behavior of people in a capitalist society in part by the fact that they live in a capitalist rather than a feudal or slave society, we are not treating social systems as superpersons. We are saying something much more modest: People's beliefs and actions are shaped in significant ways by the practices characteristic of their societies. Persons living in competitive societies that value individual initiative are likely to think of themselves in much more individualistic terms than persons living in a society where collective action and responsibility shape daily practices.

In Chapters 4 and 5 we shall discuss in much greater detail the ways in which social settings affect the actions and thoughts of individual persons. We shall see that nothing said so far implies that human choices are necessitated by social contexts, or that human beings are not free agents. Then, in Chapter 19, we will explore Marx and Engels' conception of communism—a conception that gives an important place to the development of the individuality of all persons. The individualism rejected by Marx and Engels is quite distinct from the ethical appreciation of individual worth. Marx and Engels affirm without reservation that individual persons are very valuable in their own right.

But first we need to say more about history, in the course of which human beings determine what a human life is.

Notes

1. Jon Elster, *Making Sense of Marx* (Cambridge: Cambridge University Press, 1985), p. 5.

2. This is Elster's view. He therefore believes that Marx is sometimes an individualist and sometimes a collectivist. But that interpretation of Marx is

determined by Elster's own philosophical presuppositions—by his individualism—not by Marx's texts.

For Further Reading

Shlomo Avineri, *The Social and Political Thought of Karl Marx* (Cambridge: Cambridge University Press, 1970), Chapter 3.

3

History

THE WORD "HISTORY" refers both to past events and to our reconstruction of past events. In this chapter history will be discussed in both senses.

History as the Transformation of Human Nature

Our conception of human nature affects our view of what the past was like. For the individualist, who hopes to explain human history by reference to the actions of individual persons, the history of groups becomes the history of its members and, more likely than not, that of its more illustrious members. The individualist, therefore, finds in history primarily the acts of kings, princes, tyrants, and saviors. History, as the reconstruction of the past, reports on the acts of individuals.

If we adopt Marx's position that human beings *as groups* define what "human being" is, history begins to look quite different. History now comes to be the process of human self-creation or, as Marx puts it, of human self-transformation. In the discussion of individualism in the preceding chapter, we saw some examples of that process of self-transformation. Here are some others:

> Only when tribes hunt upon it does a region of the earth become a hunting domain; only cultivation of the soil posits the land as the individual's extended body.[1]

Hunters live very differently from farmers. Roving bands of hunters have an outlook on the world very different from that of sedentary farmers. They differ in their day-to-day practices as well as in their religious beliefs. Thus, when hunting grounds are transformed into farmland and hunters become farmers, a genuine transformation of what it is to be human takes place. A whole new range of possible ways of being a human being comes into the world.

With capitalism, competition, and social mobility arises a new conception of the person as a separate individual, relatively independent of her or his social setting. In a feudal society,

> a nobleman always remains a nobleman, a commoner always a commoner. . . . The accidental nature of the conditions of life for the individual appears only with the emergence of the class, which is itself a product of the bourgeoisie. This accidental character is only engendered and developed by competition and the struggle of individuals among themselves. (GI, T 199)

In a feudal society, what a person was consisted in part of his or her social station. Social mobility was thereby restricted, for a person could not change that social condition and still be the same person. People have remained in the same circumstances for generations because those conditions have defined who they were. In a capitalist society, by contrast, the person becomes quite separate from his or her social or class position. If a tycoon goes bankrupt he is still the same person. He may find the transition to working difficult, but his personal identity is unchanged.

Just as the connection between personal and social roles is different under capitalism from that in a feudal society, so it is with the relationship between persons and their work:

> The limited commerce and the scanty communications between the individual towns, the lack of population and the narrow needs did not allow of a higher division of labor, and therefore every man who wished to become a master [of some craft] had to become proficient in the whole of his craft. Thus there is found with medieval craftsmen an interest in their special work and in proficiency in it, which was capable of rising to a narrow artistic sense . . . every medieval craftsman was completely absorbed in his work . . . to which he was subjected to a far greater extent than the modern worker whose work is a matter of indifference to him. (GI, T 178)

The medieval craftsman "was completely absorbed in his work"; to the modern worker, work is "a matter of indifference." The role that work plays in defining a person's identity is different under capitalism from what it was in a feudal society. Under capitalism, neither what one does nor where one comes from is a defining characteristic of a person as it had been under feudalism; the nature of being a person changed with the rise of capitalism.

But what, then, is a person's identity? Under capitalism, money figures in extensively:

> That which is for me through the medium of *money*—that for which I can pay (i.e., which money can buy)—that am *I*, the possessor of money. . . . I am *stupid*, but money is the real mind of all things and how then should its possessor be stupid? Besides, he can buy talented people for himself, and is he who has power over the talented not more talented than the talented? (EPM, T 103–104)

In a capitalist society, where anything you might want can be bought, the identity of a person is determined by money. Marx elaborated that thought in great detail in "The Power of Money in Bourgeois Society," a section of the *Economic and Philosophic Manuscripts*.

Not only the very definition of a person but also the nature of moral codes have changed:

> During the time that the aristocracy was dominant, the concepts honour, loyalty, etc., were dominant; during the dominance of the bourgeoisie, the concepts freedom, equality, etc. [played the central role] (GI, T 173)

Needs are similarly subject to historical change: Hunger is hunger,

> but the hunger gratified by cooked meat eaten with a knife and fork is a different hunger from that which bolts down raw meat with the aid of hand, nail and tooth. (G, T 230)

Discussions about basic human needs tend to be very abstract. The need for food is always embedded in the concrete practices concerned with providing, preparing, and eating food. In any given setting, people are not simply hungry; they are hungry for particular foods prepared and served in very specific ways. Away from home, people will go for a considerable while with little food rather than eat strange food under conditions that seem unappetizing to them. They are "not hungry."

The idea that human beings define themselves goes hand in hand with the idea that human beings are historical beings. This is not to say merely that human beings live under changing conditions but, as Marx said in *The Poverty of Philosophy*, that

> all history is nothing but a continuous transformation of human nature.[2]

Human beings are historical in that *being human itself* has a history and changes throughout history. That is, the concept of humanity changes. History consists of more than the deeds of individual persons, particularly the high and mighty, the princes and the popes; it consists of more than the complex process in which the circumstances surrounding the life of men and women have changed. It is now the process in which human beings repeatedly define and redefine what human beings are.

But as we saw before, this process of redefinition is not a deliberate one. Human beings do not gather together periodically to consider what it has recently meant to be human, and to change that definition, in the way in which Parisian designers get together annually to redefine what it means to be "well-dressed." The redefinitions of human nature flow indirectly from the changed ways in which people solve their very concrete material problems and from the needs that arise as a consequence of the development of new techniques and the attendant changes in social organization. That is, human beings resolve the problems they find in their day-to-day activities and try to keep their ways of living unchanged. But the implications of these attempts to solve problems are rarely understood at the time.

> The ends are intended, but the results which actually follow from these actions are not intended, or . . . they ultimately have consequences quite other than those intended.[3]

Human beings transform what "human being" is not simply by engaging in philosophical discourse about the meaning of being human but in the course of solving their daily problems. The concrete problems are solved intentionally; the attendant definitions of human nature may well be unintended.

Implicit in the disagreement between Marx and the proponents of individualism is a disagreement about the study of and the writing about history. The individualist insists that we must always try to explain events by providing accounts of individual persons and their behavior and thought. Marx counters that we cannot understand the contributions of individuals unless we also understand the effects of the socioeconomic system on them. History must study the acts of individuals as well as the effects of the social settings on these acts. It must also study the transformation of entire social systems.

Here, then, is Marx and Engels' conception of human nature: At any particular historical stage, human beings have certain specific material needs that they meet in particular ways and with very specific forms of social organization. As the ways change in which needs are met, the needs themselves as well as the forms of social organization change.

One result of those changes is that human nature itself changes. Because these changes in human nature are the result of the actions of human beings in meeting their needs in new and different ways, we may well say that human beings, in this historical process, have redefined what it means to be human.

On what evidence did Marx and Engels base this view of human nature? They derived it, they claimed, from the study of history (GI, T 164).

The Uses of the Study of History

If human nature were universal and unchanging, we would need only to examine ourselves to see what it means to be human. Any one of us could serve as the model human. But if "human being" changes its meaning, then to know what it means to be human we need to study history or other cultures. It is not enough to think about the nature of human beings or, as Marx says, "to speculate" about it. We need to study actual historical events and transformations in order to discover our own human nature.

> Where speculation ends—in real life—there real, positive science begins.
> . . . When reality is depicted, philosophy as an independent branch of
> knowledge loses its medium of existence. At the best its place can only
> be taken by a summing-up of the most general results, abstractions which
> arise from the observation of the historical development of human beings.
> Viewed apart from real history, these abstractions have in themselves no
> value whatsoever. (GI, T 155)

We can now understand the repeated criticism leveled in the *German Ideology* against Marx's erstwhile German associates that they have never "quitted the realm of philosophy" (GI, T 148). "Philosophy" and "speculation," as Marx uses those terms, refer to the endeavor to understand the general features of the world by thinking alone, without doing any empirical study. It rests neither on historical investigations nor on interpretations of documents and evidence; it moves exclusively in the realm of thought. But human concepts are not valid for all times and places because they are themselves human creations; and like all human creations, they are subject to historical change. Hence the analysis of concepts alone yields only a diagnosis of our own world. If we construe all different cultures in the light of our own understandings, we do not produce profound insights into the nature of reality; we only display our own parochialism.

That was the view that Marx and Engels developed in 1845, while they were writing the *German Ideology*. Earlier, Marx had certainly agreed with the view, then prevalent in Germany, that philosophy was a discipline separate from empirical work (see Chapter 15) and had its own sources of evidence—a view still widely held among philosophers today. After 1845, philosophy became the most theoretical layer of the social sciences. The subject matter of philosophy (e.g., what it means to be human) remained unchanged, but the source of knowledge was now quite different. Philosophy lost its independent domain and, instead, became dependent on knowledge of history.

This changed conception of philosophy has important implications for Marx's and Engels' own views. The support for their conception of human nature cannot come from abstract philosophical reflection but must derive from reflection about history, about the tremendous diversity of human cultures, and about how the differences between them both affect what it means to be human and, at the same time, are the results of the actions of the members of those cultures. But these detailed studies of history were never written down by either Marx or Engels. It is obvious, for instance, that Marx's view of history was deeply influenced by the French Revolution, but he never wrote at length about it. He and Engels regarded the English Civil War in the seventeenth century as a battle of the rising bourgeoisie for power in English society. This, at best, is a controversial reading of that episode in history. Nowhere have Marx and Engels worked out their account of that period. The only writing of history they can be said to have done consists of Marx's accounts of contemporary events in France, such as his *18th Brumaire of Louis Bonaparte* (1851–1852) and *The Civil War in France* (1871) and in Engels' *The Origin of the Family, Private Property and the State* (1884). In other words, by their own standards, what they provide for us in, for instance, *The German Ideology*, is no more than the summary of the results of historical study. The detailed evidence is not provided. The best they do is to give us a very brief survey over history (e.g., GI, 176ff). They have asserted their view but not proved it.

Some Alternative Interpretations

I have begun this book with a discussion of the conception of human nature because it will prove important for understanding other parts of the thought of Marx and Engels. Some readers have argued, however, that the conception of human nature does not play a significant role in the works written after 1845 because Marx and Engels surrendered their previous philosophical position while writing the *German Ideology*, which was written in that year, and moved toward a genuinely scientific one. This interpretation is associated with the work of the French philosopher, Louis Althusser.[4]

As we saw at the end of the preceding section, Marx, in part inspired by Engels, moved after 1844 from the discussion of philosophy to the study of history and economics. Although in his earlier philosophical work he was content to analyze concepts, he now demanded that one study the actual history of actual people and the workings of actual economies. "The premises from which we start . . . can thus be verified in a purely empirical way" (GI, T 149). The mature Marx was definitely doing science. Althusser believes that this scientific enterprise is incompatible with the "humanism" of Marx's early works.[5]

The term "humanism" was used by Marx (EPM, T 84) to characterize his views in 1844, when he was 26 years old. In the notebooks he wrote during that year, he developed the view (discussed in the present chapter and in the two preceding ones) that human beings determine what "human being" is and that history is nothing but the history of human self-transformation. Althusser regards that view as "voluntarist"—that is, as making human history entirely the product of human intentional activity.[6]

Althusser's views have been widely attacked. Both Althusser and his critics claim to base their interpretations on a careful reading of actual texts. In some cases, opposite readings of Marx are supported by quotations from the same text. Thus Michel Henri attacks Althusser and quotes from the preface to *A Contribution to the Critique of Political Economy* (T 3), the very same text to which Althusser appeals to bolster his views.[7] But the issue here concerns not just the careful reading of texts. All the careful reading of texts in the world will not yield the one uniquely correct reading of Marx and Engels. Attempts to prove Althusser wrong by showing that the concepts prominent in the early writings—such as alienation and species being—still figure in the later work are relevant to Althusser's claims, but they do not suffice to prove him mistaken. Given the fragmentary character of the writings of Marx and Engels, a *reconstruction* of their thought is needed, and more than one plausible reconstruction is possible.

Althusser is correct in his claim that Marx and Engels, in their later works, insist that there are laws of history (one such law is that the capitalist economy develops in ways that can be investigated scientifically). These laws do not bow to what human beings want or choose. The history of capitalism has a structure and a momentum of its own that cannot be changed at will by the intentional actions of human beings. But is that view inconsistent with the claim that "human beings make their own history"? The reading that I have given of Marx's humanism— the insistence that human beings change their social settings and thus themselves in the course of intentional action—does not deny that their actions have unintended consequences. Hence it is consistent to argue that human beings shape their worlds and that these worlds are subject to laws discoverable by science. Althusser apparently interprets the humanism of the early Marx in a different way.

Notes

1. Karl Marx, *Grundrisse* (Harmondsworth: Penguin Books, 1973), p. 493.
2. Karl Marx, *The Poverty of Philosophy* (New York: International Publishers, 1971), p. 147.
3. Frederick Engels, *Ludwig Feuerbach and the Outcome of Classical German Philosophy* (New York: International Publishers, 1941), p. 48.
4. Louis Althusser, *For Marx* (New York: Vintage Books, 1970), p. 227.
5. Ibid., p. 12.
6. Michel Henri, *Marx: A Philosophy of Human Reality* (Bloomington: Indiana University Press, 1983), p. 10; Althusser, *For Marx*, p. 32.
7. Althusser, *For Marx*, p. 12.

For Further Reading

Vernon Venable, *Human Nature: The Marxian View* (New York: Meridian Books, 1966), Chapter 7.

4

Historical Materialism

In the social production of their life, human beings enter into definite relations that are indispensable and independent of their will, relations of production which correspond to a definite stage of development of their material productive forces. The sum total of these relations of production constitutes the economic structure of society, the real foundation, on which rises a legal and political superstructure and to which correspond definite forms of social consciousness. The mode of production of material life conditions the social, political and intellectual life process in general. It is not the consciousness of human beings that determines their being, but, on the contrary, their social being that determines their consciousness. At a certain stage of their development, the material productive forces of society come in conflict with the existing relations of production. . . . Then begins an epoch of social revolution. (T 4–5)

Together with some sentences from the *Communist Manifesto*, this is no doubt the most famous passage ever written by Marx. It introduces many of the central terms in the Marxist conception of history, as well as some of the best-known and most controversial theses of Marx and Engels.

Let us look at some of the important terms. Every society has its own *forces of production* and its *relations of production*. The forces of production are the raw materials, tools, and workers that actually produce goods. The relations of production—specifically, the relations of ownership and control—are the ways in which the production process is organized. The forces of production produce the goods. Ownership of the forces of production and of the goods finally produced is determined by the relations of production. The relations of production are also called the *economic structure*. Together, forces of production and relations of production constitute the *mode of production*. In addition, the society is differentiated into its *base* and its *superstructure*. The base consists of the relations of production which are also known as the economic structure. The superstructure, in its turn, consists of the legal system, the political system, and, more generally, the forms of social consciousness.

Any society is thus divided into three levels: the forces of production, the relations of production (these two together constitute the mode of production), and the superstructure. These concepts are used for a variety of purposes by Marx and Engels. One such purpose is to state what they mean by "materialism."

Marx and Engels were both influenced in their intellectual development by Hegel, who was then the most influential philosopher in Germany. But early on they rejected Hegel's idealism, substituting for it a view called "historical materialism," or just simply "materialism."

In the common sense view of the world, there are minds and mental entities such as thoughts or beliefs, and there are material things such as human bodies or planets. But the theological view of the world—which holds that everything is created by a Supreme Being who is, moreover, not material—creates difficulties. How did god go about creating the world? Traditional paintings show god blowing breath into Adam's nostrils, suggesting that god created the first human out of clay much like a child making sandcastles at the beach. Theologians, however, believed that this picture did not do justice to god's perfection. God does not first imagine something and then, subsequently, enter into the actual process of material creation. God thinks and the thought is itself the creative act. Accordingly, mind—specifically the divine mind—is given priority in the universe: Material objects are only ideas in the divine mind. Hence all things, whether material or mental, as we commonly understand those words, are in a deeper sense mental, because they are no more than divine ideas. This view is called "idealism," and it was taken over by Hegel from a long tradition of Christian thinkers.[1] Marx and Engels' materialism is opposed to this idealism.

But there are several versions of materialism that need to be distinguished from each other. Engels distinguishes his and Marx's materialism from the "shallow and vulgarized form" of materialism which asserted that

> the material, sensuously perceptible world to which we ourselves belong is the only reality. . . . Matter is not a product of mind but mind itself merely the highest product of matter.[2]

Their view, instead, is that "the *ultimately* determining element in history is the production and reproduction of real life" (T 760). Materialism, as Marx and Engels used the term, refers to a view about the forces shaping history. They are "material" forces—namely, the "production and reproduction of real life"—rather than ideas, thoughts, values. The fundamental causes of historical events are to be sought in the activities of human beings, through which they produce their daily needs and perpetuate—Marx and Engels would have said "reproduce"—their society. In the language of the passage quoted earlier, that view breaks down into two separate theses:

1. that the "social being determines . . . consciousness," and
2. that relations of production "correspond" to a definite stage of development of the forces of production.

The first thesis asserts that thinking is shaped by the way people go about producing what they need and, hence, that historical change, even if it appears to result from the ideas of people, really is the consequence of the way they produce goods and maintain their society. The second thesis asserts that the development of the productive forces is an indispensable condition for changes in production relations.

We shall begin with a discussion of the first thesis. It has been interpreted in a variety of ways that open it to serious criticism. In the first two sections of this chapter, I will discuss some of these interpretations and their defects. In the third section I will provide a more defensible interpretation of materialism. And in the final section I will discuss the second thesis briefly.

Economic Determinism

Human thinking is shaped by material conditions; the base determines the superstructure. We saw a number of examples of that in the preceding chapter: In a tight-knit rural society such as that of the feudal world, a person's identity was closely linked to social status and work. In a capitalist society, where mobility from place to place and job to job is essential to the functioning of the economic system, people think of themselves in very different ways. One's identity is much less tightly connected to family, status, and work. Today we may talk about the psychological influence of family on the personality. Family influence is a very personal and private matter. But the concept of personal identity does not include family or status or work as it did in the past, when one identified oneself *publicly* as the "son or daughter of . . . ." or as "hailing from the village of. . . ." Similarly, values change with changed economic practices: In a competitive society, one approves of competition among people; members of other societies do not.

Most people would accept the idea that material circumstances and ideas interact in complex ways, such that ideas sometimes produce material conditions, and that those conditions sometimes give rise to ideas. According to Marx and Engels, however, what we think arises from the way we produce and reproduce. But, once again, precisely what they are trying to say is not entirely clear. They use various terms to describe the relationship between production and thought—namely "determine," "condition," and "cause." But these terms are by no means synonymous. Which of these words conveys most accurately what Marx and Engels had in mind?

The most common interpretation of historical materialism asserts that all ideas are the effects of the processes of material production. Material production is said to be the *cause* of all sorts of mental events. This view is frequently labeled "economic determinism." It maintains that the economy (the base) determines or is the cause of the superstructure.

Economic determinism has incited a great deal of criticism. Reader after reader has pointed out that the base is not independent of the superstructure: Economic processes such as the production, transport, and sale of goods require clear ownership of all the goods involved in these processes. Who owns the factories and raw materials, the final products of production, the trucks, and the stores must be generally known so that the right people can get paid the right amount and everybody can receive his or her share in the transaction. The operation of capitalism presupposes a functioning legal system that determines property rights. The legal system, a part of the superstructure, is indispensable for the functioning of the process of production, the base. The process of production cannot proceed without these superstructural elements.[3] But given the usual understanding of the word "cause," the base cannot be the cause of the superstructure so long as the former is dependent on the latter. For "A is the cause of B" is usually read as "A is necessary and sufficient for B under condition C." If the powder is dry and you hold a lit match to it, it will explode. Given the requisite antecedent conditions—the powder is dry—a lit match is the necessary and sufficient condition for the explosion. But there are lit matches without explosions; the cause is independent of the effect. If the base is the cause of the superstructure, it cannot be dependent on it. But the account that Marx and Engels give of society suggests very strongly, so the critics insist, that base and superstructure are intimately related. The base therefore cannot be the cause of the superstructure.

The criticism is valid. It does not prove, however, that Marx and Engels were mistaken in their materialism. Instead, it suggests that their materialism is different from economic determinism. Such a suggestion gains plausibility from the fact that economic determinism—the view that the base is independent of the superstructure and is its cause—is clearly inconsistent with the views described in the preceding chapters. For if the changes in economic processes are independent of human thought, and if the transformation of human nature is a consequence of changes in the processes of production, then human nature changes independent of human thought. But then it is false to assert, as Marx did, that human history is the history of human self-definition, because human history turns out, instead, to be the process in which production, unaffected by human thinking, defines what "human being" is.

More seriously, economic determinism just doesn't make any sense. There are no impersonal economic processes: Production, exchange, and distribution are undertaken by human beings who think about what they are doing and act in the light of that thought. Any picture of an economic process that unfolds unaffected by human thinking lacks meaning. Marx never tired of insisting on that:

> To be a slave, to be a citizen, are social characteristics, relations between human beings A & B. Human being A, as such, is not a slave. He is a slave, in and through society. (G, T 247)

Slavery is a mode of production, but it is also a social system. Modes of production that consist of the forces and the relations of production cannot be characterized in exclusively economic terms. Similarly, capitalism is not just an economic system but an entire society that includes an economic system. As noted earlier, it also includes a legal order, a complex network of social roles, traditions, values, and so on. Both slavery and capitalism are definable only by reference to an entire set of social relations that include both base and superstructure.

It seems clear that the meaning of "causation" used by the critics is not Marx's and that, therefore, "economic determinism" is not what Marx and Engels were talking about.

Can we interpret the relationship between base and superstructure in a way that avoids these difficulties? I shall provide an affirmative answer in the section after next.

Base as Limit and as "Ultimately Determining Factor"

In the *Grundrisse* Marx raises a question about the materialist conception of history: What is the connection between the world outlook of the Greeks and their level of technology?

Is the view of nature and of social relations on which the Greek imagination and hence Greek [mythology] is based possible with self-acting mule spindles and railways and locomotives and electrical telegraphs? What chance has Vulcan against Roberts & Co., Jupiter against the lightning-rod, and Hermes against the Credit Mobilier? . . . What becomes of Fama alongside Printing House Square? (G, T 245–246)

Why do we no longer worship the gods of the Greeks? Notice that Marx does not say that Greek economic conditions were the cause of Greek mythology. His claim is much more modest—namely, that Greek mythology would make no sense in modern times. A god, Jupiter, whose power is exhibited by the use of thunder and lightning is a shabby god indeed, once those natural phenomena have been understood and once lightning has become less of a menace due to the invention of lightning rods. Human beings who can set off the atomic blasts of Hiroshima and Nagasaki will not be impressed by a little thunder and lightning. The same applies to the other personages in the Greek pantheon. The goddess of reputation, Fama, cuts a poor figure against the newspapers coming out of London's Printing House Square, and Hermes, the god of commerce, is overshadowed by the enormous power of the worldwide banking network of Paris' Credit Mobilier.

All mythology overcomes and dominates and shapes the forces of nature in the imagination and by the imagination; it therefore vanishes with the advent of real mastery over them. (G, T 246)

The existence of mythology is understandable in cultures that have little control over nature. Thus the existence of mythology is explicable by the low level of economic productivity of the Greeks. This again is a very modest claim. Marx does not maintain that the specific content of Greek mythology can be derived from their system of production.

What, then, is the connection between base and superstructure? The passage cited clearly asserts that the base sets certain limits on what will make sense to people in a given culture. The level of productivity restricts what ideas will have meaning for or appeal to people in that society. Greek mythology is not alive for us in a technological age. The base is not the cause of the superstructure, but it does set its limits.

Some readers of Marx and Engels interpret their historical materialism in this way. The economic base "sets the limits within which super-structural phenomena must stay to survive."[4]

That interpretation seems very plausible. But is it complete? The suspicion lingers that Marx and Engels wanted to claim that the base not only limits what will be in the superstructure but also exerts some other influences:

> The ideas of the ruling class are in every epoch the ruling ideas. . . . The ruling ideas are nothing more than the ideal expression of the dominant material relationships, the dominant material relationships grasped as ideas. (GI, T 172–173)

Here the ideas of a period are not seen as limited by the material conditions; rather, they reflect those conditions. Is this once again the infamous economic determinism?

After Marx died, Engels felt the need to protest that neither he nor Marx had intended to defend economic determinism. They had always understood that much as the base determines the superstructure, the superstructure in turn determines the base. All they had ever wanted to say was that the base was the "ultimately decisive" factor (T 760). Hence the doctrine attributed to Engels is that the base determines the superstructure "in the last instance." But that qualification does not resolve the problem of economic determinism: If there is any problem with claiming that the material base causes the superstructure, then that problem exists just as much if we banish this causal process to "the last instance."

Base and Superstructure

We can resolve this impasse by examining what is meant by "base" and "superstructure." That examination will, at the same time, clarify the sense in which the base might be thought of as the cause of the superstructure.

Usually the term "base" is interpreted as the "economic realm," whereas "superstructure" is taken as the "sphere of law, politics, and ideology." By the "economic realm," moreover, is meant impersonal economic processes that unfold independent of human wishes and desires, and independent of human thinking and understanding. Base differs from superstructure in that the former is material and distinct from human consciousness, whereas the latter is the product of human consciousness. Clearly Engels often thought about base and superstructure in those terms, for he described the problem addressed by materialism as the "relation of thinking to being." As Engels understood materialism, it asserts the primacy of nature over mind.[5] Base and superstructure are matter and mind, respectively.

Very early in his career, Marx understood that this was not the materialism he wanted to defend:

The chief defect of all hitherto existing materialism . . . is that the thing, reality, sense perception, is conceived only in the form of the object, or of *contemplation*, but not as *human sensuous activity, practice*. (T 143)

Matter, the base, is not to be understood only as something outside and distinct from human beings to be "contemplated." By matter, Marx means also what human beings *do*—that is, he refers to their material activities or "production and reproduction." But those, like all human activities, are thinking activities, because it is the essence of human beings to think about what they do. The distinction between base and superstructure is not one between matter that does not think and thinking that is not material. The base consists of human activities, or what in the passage cited at the beginning of this chapter was called "social being." But what, then, is the superstructure?

Thinking is different from self-conscious thinking. People think, feel, and desire a good deal without always being aware of their thoughts, feelings, or desires. These are brought into awareness only with a good deal of effort. When people act, they understand what they are doing even if they have trouble describing their action. It is often an effort to put into words what they understand inarticulately. What applies to individual also applies to groups: Genuine intellectual effort is required to describe their common practices. Like individuals, a group of people who have developed a coherent way of life can, if they make a sincere effort, put their understanding of it into words. They explicitly formulate the rules they have been following thus far—a process that yields systems of moral rules (e.g., the Ten Commandments; legal systems, which codify the previously existing practices; and political theories, which put into words and defend practices that have been around for awhile).

The practices that constitute the base may well be understood— people generally know what they are doing—without having been put into words. At some time in the history of a group, the practices are put into words, described, codified, and defended—and these descriptions, codifications, and defenses form the superstructure. *The base is what we do; the superstructure is how we talk about it.*[6]

Talking about what we do is not an idle pastime; indeed, it serves important purposes. When our accustomed ways of doing things do not seem to work as well as they used to, we need to think about what it is we are doing, and how we can do better. The effort to articulate our inarticulate understanding of ourselves serves to solve problems. The descriptions we give play a definite role; they maintain and protect our existing practices. But this is not to say that we always correctly describe these processes. The superstructural descriptions sometimes serve their function by misrepresenting our practices to ourselves. Then the superstructure plays its role by deceiving us about our daily practices. Superstructure becomes "ideological," as we shall see in Chapter 6. The systems of rules we articulate also serve to socialize new generations, to defend particular practices, to help us decide what needs to be done in heretofore unfamiliar situations, and so on.

Understood in this way, it seems eminently plausible that the base determines the superstructure: Our practices determine how we describe and justify them.

An example may help clarify this. The capitalist, Marx wrote in *Capital*,

> shares with the miser the passion for wealth. But that which in the miser is mere idiosyncrasy is, in the capitalist, the effect of the social mechanism, of which he is but one of the wheels.[7]

There have always been some people who wanted more and more money. But in most societies that trait was an aberration. Such people were called "misers" and were the butts of jokes or of disapproval. But under capitalism, values have changed. What was before a despised characteristic of a few odd people is now not only the rule among capitalists but is required. It is the job of the capitalist to make as much money as possible and to save and reinvest it. What has changed, above all, is economic practice. The goal of the capitalist is to increase his or her capital, to create more wealth. That practice, the base, produces new rules of conduct, new value judgments, a new outlook on the world, a new superstructure. "The ruling ideas [viz. the superstructure] are nothing more than . . . the dominant material relationships [viz. the base] grasped as ideas" (GI, T 172–173).

It makes sense, then, to say that the base determines the superstructure: People talk about their lives in the way they do because their daily practices are what they are. But the relationship is not a causal one in the sense in which the lit match is the cause of the explosion. In the latter situation, we can predict the explosion, if we know the conditions. In observing how people act, we can venture some guesses about their ideologies, but we cannot make firm predictions.

Forces and Relations of Production

The superstructure changes in response to changes in the base. But why does the base change? We come now to the second proposition asserted in the passage from the "preface" with which this chapter began—namely, that relations of production "correspond" to the forces of production. The general claim being made here is clear:

The way in which the production process is organized changes in response to the means by which production is carried on. New technologies, for instance, require new work organizations:

> These social relations into which the producers enter with one another, . . . will naturally vary according to the character of the means of production. With the invention of a new instrument of warfare, firearms, the whole internal organization of the army necessarily changed; the relationships within which individuals can constitute an army and act as an army were transformed and the relations of different armies to one another also changed. (WLC, T 207)

Medieval armies fought hand to hand with sword and halberd. That required a close formation in which soldier stood close to soldier and moved in one body. But, such a military formation is the worst possible one once people start shooting at each other from a distance. Firearms lead to trench warfare—a form of war that would have been impossible when wars were fought with swords. This seems to be a clear example of the way in which changing tools—weapons in this case—changed the organization of an activity. Marx and Engels want to claim that the transformation of the tools in the production process brings about different organizations of that process in an analogous fashion.

This general claim is, however, subject to two distinct interpretations. On the one hand, there are a number of variants of a view called "technological determinism"; on the other hand, there is the "mode of production" view.

Technological determinism asserts that changes in the production process are the ultimate source of historical movement. Human beings, in pursuit of greater efficiency and productivity, improve the existing means of production and create entirely new ones. As a consequence, the relations of production are also altered. In its most plausible version, this view asserts that relations of production function to promote the development of the forces of production and that they therefore change when they no longer fulfill that function.[8]

Technological determinism does not, of course, deny that the concrete historical processes of change exhibit other factors. Changes in the relations of production, for instance, are due to the changes in the relative power of different classes. Marx points out that money lending and trade produced some large capitals at the beginning of the capitalist era, but

> the money capital formed by means of usury and commerce was prevented from turning into industrial capital, in the country by the feudal constitution,

in the towns by the guild organization. These fetters vanished with the dissolution of feudal society.[9]

But this dissolution was accomplished by brute force:

[the methods] all employ the power of the state, the concentrated and organized force of society, to hasten, hothouse fashion, the process of transformation of the feudal mode of production into the capitalist mode. . . . Force is the midwife of every old society pregnant with a new one. (CI, T 436)

Political power is an important lever of change in the relations of production. According to technological determinism, however, it must be explained by the state of the forces of production. The final explanation of the changes in the relations of production always cites the changes in the forces of production.

The alternative view of this process of change—the mode of production view—claims that political factors, e.g., the ability of the rising capitalist class to use force to dissolve feudal production relations, cannot be explained entirely by reference to the constellation of forces of production.[10] Political power is an independent factor in the explanation of historical change. It is not merely the effect of changes in the forces of production.

Materialism and Science

It turns out that materialism asserts that ideas are not the ultimate causes in historical change because they themselves can be explained only in connection with the underlying mode of production. In the transformation of modes of production, in turn, forces of production play a central role.

In the Marxist literature, however, the term "materialism" occurs in a rather different context. Materialism is often regarded as the doctrine that the world is as it is independent of human thinking. What the world is like is discovered by science.[11]Two claims are being made here. The first is an epistemological one, that what we believe about the world is not true just because we believe it. "Thinking does not necessarily make it so." Some philosophers believe that this epistemological position presupposes a metaphysical one—namely, that the world investigated by science exists independent of human thinking. It is clear that Marx and Engels subscribed to the first of these two theses, that what we believe is not true just because we believe it. But did they also accept the ontological thesis that the objects in the world are independent of human thinking? Certainly there are passages in which it seems as if they did: Marx cites with approval the description of one reviewer of the first volume of *Capital*:

> Marx treats the social movement as a process of natural history, governed by laws not only independent of human will, consciousness and intelligence, but rather, on the contrary, determining that will, consciousness, and intelligence. (CI, T 300)

Such passages as this create the impression that Marx and Engels asserted the independence of the social world from all human thinking on the grounds that human thought is the product of impersonal, social, quasi-natural forces. But a problem is created for our interpretation when we recall my earlier argument that, according to Marx and Engels, social forces were the creations of human beings.

In other passages, Marx talks very differently. In *Capital*, for instance, he deplores the fact that no study has been made of the history of technology:

> Darwin has interested us in the history of Nature's Technology, i.e. in the formation of the organs of plants and animals, which organs serve as instruments of production for sustaining life. Does not the history of the productive organs of man . . . deserve equal attention? And would not such a history be easier to compile since, as Vico says, human history differs from natural history in this—that we have made the former, but not the latter?[12]

In what follows, Marx makes it clear that this proposed history of technology could certainly be done scientifically. Thus he envisaged the possibility of scientific treatments of objects made by human beings. The epistemological thesis does not seem to imply the metaphysical one.

The difficulty is that Marx and Engels had very little to say about the concept of science. From their scattered comments we see that by "science" they meant, first, a body of statements whose truth is independent of what human beings believe, want to be true, or imagine. Second, science states "laws" of the phenomena it investigates—that is, "tendencies working with iron necessity towards inevitable results" (CI, T 296). Finally, Marx added that science uncovers a reality that is concealed by the surface appearances. He cited as an example the differences between the light we see and what physics tells us about light (CI, T 321). But these texts do not suffice to answer the question at issue here—namely, whether Marx and Engels subscribed to metaphysical materialism. We need to leave that question open.

Notes

1. For a more detailed discussion of idealism, see Chapter 5.

2. Frederick Engels, *Ludwig Feuerbach and the Outcome of Classical German Philosophy* (New York: International Publishers, 1941), p. 25. It is clear, however, that Engels himself at times defended such a "vulgar" materialism (see the third section of this chapter). A third kind of materialism is mentioned in the fifth section.

3. See, for instance, John Plamenatz, *German Marxism and Russian Communism* (London: Longman's, 1954), p. 25.

4. John McMurtry, *The Structure of Marx's World-View* (Princeton, N.J.: Princeton University Press, 1978), p. 167.

5. Engels, *Ludwig Feuerbach*, p. 21. This conception of materialism has recently been defended by Sebastiano Timpanaro in *Materialism* (London: New Left Books, 1980).

6. Derek Sayer agrees that the base/superstructure distinction is not a distinction between thinking that is not material and matter that does not think, but he goes on to identify the base with what is essential in any social system and the superstructure with its phenomenal manifestations. See Sayer, *Marx's Method* (Sussex, England: Harvester Press, 1979), Chapter 1 and Chapter 4, section 1.

7. Marx, *Capital*, Vol. I (New York: International Publishers, 1967), p. 592.

8. The best exposition of this view is G. A. Cohen's *Karl Marx's Theory of History* (Princeton, N.J.: Princeton University Press, 1978), particularly Chapter 6.

9. Marx, *Capital*, Vol. I, p. 751.

10. This view is presented by Richard W. Miller in *Analyzing Marx* (Princeton, N.J.: Princeton University Press, 1984).

11. Materialism in that sense is discussed by David-Hillel Ruben, in *Marx and Materialism: A Study in Marxist Theory of Knowledge* (Sussex, England: Harvester Press, 1977).

12. Marx, *Capital*, Vol. I, p. 372, footnote 3.

For Further Reading

Melvin Rader, *Marx's Interpretation of History* (New York: Oxford University Press, 1979), Chapter 1.

5

The Dialectic

THE DIALECTIC IS the most obscure aspect of Marx's and Engels' writings. Many commentators either ignore it or reject it outright as an unfortunate hangover from Marx's interest, as a very young man, in Hegel's philosophy. But Marx himself tells us that he used a dialectical method:

> My dialectic method is not only different from the Hegelian, but its direct opposite. To Hegel . . . the process of thinking . . . is the demiurgos [creator] of the real world. With me, on the contrary, the ideal is nothing else than the material world reflected by the human mind. (T 301)

Hegel's dialectic is idealist; Marx's is materialist. In order to understand Marx's dialectic, we need to look at Hegel's first.

Hegel's Dialectic

Hegel's dialectic served a very specific philosophical purpose—namely, to reconcile religion, specifically Christianity, with science as it was rapidly developing. In the past, very basic questions about nature had been given religious answers: What is the origin of the universe? God created the heavens and the earth in six days. What keeps the planets in their precise orbits? God maintains the universe from moment to moment. What accounts for the different kinds of plants and animals? God created them each of their own kind. And so on. But the work of Kepler, Galileo, and Newton provided an alternative answer to the question about the planets. This answer was based on observation and did not presuppose the existence of a deity. The origins of the earth

43

and the multitude of species of plants and animals were soon to be accounted for in similarly nonreligious terms. It was clear to Hegel that the harmony between the knowledge of nature and religion, which had lasted for a long time, was about to collapse. Science and Christianity were coming into conflict.

Hegel's philosophy was dedicated to restoring this harmony between scientific knowledge and religion in addition to preserving the supremacy of the divine in the universe. Science is incompatible with the conception of a transcendent god who creates the world. In order to effect the reconciliation of science and religion, Hegel denied that god is the creator in a literal sense, or a god beyond this world. Instead, he considered all of creation a manifestation of god. Both nature and human history are stages in god's development. Hegel's god, instead of being an uncreated creator, creates the world and himself at the same time. God is coming into existence, and the different episodes in natural and human history are episodes in god's development.

But this reconciliation still must deal with some major problems: God is infinite, the world in which we live is finite. God is perfect, much in our world is defective. God is good, but there is a great deal of pain and evil and ugliness in our world. These striking contradictions between the divine nature and the human world, let alone the animal world, are reconciled through several claims that Hegel makes:

1. The world is not completely identical with god, but it is divine insofar as it is a manifestation of the divine.
2. The world changes and, in its changes, god develops.
3. The development proceeds through a complex set of stages.
4. Each stage represents one aspect of the divine nature, but, insofar as it represents only one aspect, it is incomplete and hence defective.
5. Each stage is therefore replaced by a new stage that develops what was lacking in the preceding stage.
6. The stages, as they follow one another, are in opposition to each other, for each provides what was lacking in the preceding one. At the same time, each succeeding stage develops and preserves what was of value in the preceding one.
7. Successive stages are therefore opposed to one another and identical at the same time.

Successive stages are not just similar but identical. This claim, more than any other, gives readers of Hegel trouble. And, finally,

8. Oppositions between two stages are resolved in a new stage that preserves what is worth preserving in the two preceding ones, and surrenders what should be surrendered.

These theses summarize the historical process in which god comes to be. That process is Hegel's dialectic. Hegel's god, like the traditional Christian god, is immaterial—pure mind. The only development he can undergo is therefore of a spiritual kind: As god develops, he grows in knowledge. But since god is identical with all there is, god is not only the subject of knowing but also the object. The knowledge that god acquires in the process of development is self-knowledge. In coming to be, god attains self-consciousness.

The dialectic describes the pattern of divine development. It therefore also describes the pattern of the history of the world. And since divine development is spiritual, the dialectic also describes the pattern in which thought develops. The dialectic is therefore a thought process in which god comes to know the divine nature and thereby actualizes it. In that knowledge, which, at the same time, is a creation of the entire universe, the divine comes to be and know itself. God is that whole. Philosophy, which recapitulates this entire process in human terms, is a form of divine self-knowledge.

The stages in the development of god, the stages in history, are stages in the process of god coming to know himself. Each such stage represents a particular partial view of the divine nature. Conflict in history is conflict between different partial views of the world, and historical change occurs when one view of the world is replaced by another. Different stages of history differ from one another because they represent different worldviews.

It is this aspect of Hegel's dialectic that, as we shall see, seemed important and correct to Marx. The dialectic is conceived as a process of struggle between opposite views that are nevertheless connected, because each is merely a partial view of a larger truth or reality. Out of these struggles emerges something new that combines what was true and worth saving in the two opposites and discards what deserved to be lost. Hegel's favorite example of this is the history of the development of freedom. Different historical periods develop different forms of free institutions. In the early periods, which were very primitive—Hegel's example is the oriental despot who has unrestricted power over the lives and property of all his subjects—freedom was accorded to only very few members of a society. Their freedom was fairly absolute, and arbitrary. These early cultures were replaced, not without struggle, by new institutions that included more people among the free; freedom became embedded in more complex institutions, such as legal systems and political institutions that involved certain guarantees of individual liberties. Insofar as these institutions were very different from each other, they were, in the terminology of the dialectic, contradictories. But as developments of the same set of ideas, they were also identical.

Dialectic and Formal Logic

Hegel's goal was to reconcile modern science with the religious view of the world. In religion, a powerful god explains the existence and persistence of all sorts of natural phenomena. Science provides more satisfactory explanations of the same phenomena without assuming the existence of a god. Hegel attempts to deal with that problem by regarding the scientific view of the world as one more perspective, one more stage in the history of god. Such an explanation is acceptable from the dialectical point of view, but not from the point of view of natural science. The story of the creation is not an earlier scientific hypothesis, later replaced by the theory of evolution in biology and the big bang theory in cosmology. The story of creation is not science at all; it is a religious myth. Even less acceptable to the scientist would be the view that natural science is itself a limited view of the world that, from a different perspective, could be seen as one very partial manifestation of the divine history—for on that account science would be an imperfect version of a religious view of the universe.

The problem is that natural science cannot be fitted into the dialectic because the explanations it gives are not dialectical. Hegel recognized that and distinguished between the formal logical thinking of science and the dialectical thinking of speculative philosophy.

Formal logic deals with the most basic conditions of intelligible communication. For instance, in order to communicate information (ordinary statements that are intended to be either true or false) to an English speaker, you need to speak English. What is more, you need to speak clearly and directly. If you connect your sentences in an odd way, if you are not being "logical," people cannot understand you. Being logical has to do with not contradicting yourself. It requires that three laws be respected: the law of identity, that of noncontradiction, and that of the excluded middle.

The law of noncontradiction tells us that conversations soon come to an end if we affirm and then deny the same thing. The sentence "Hegel was a dialectical thinker" is contradicted by "It is false that Hegel was a dialectical thinker." If one of these sentences is true, the other must be false. (The law of identity asserts that a statement is either true or false, whereas the law of excluded middle holds that there is no third possibility between a statement being true and one being false. The law of noncontradiction rests on the fact that if you insist on asserting both of these statements, I do not know what you are trying to tell me and the conversation comes to an end.)

In the interest of his reconciliation of the divine and science, Hegel claimed that formal logic is, to be sure, the logic of science; but from the point of view of the whole—that is from the divine point of view— we see that what science regards as distinct and irreconcilably contradictory are in fact only dialectical contradictions, imperfect views that in the future will be reconciled. The concept of contradiction is being redefined here. In formal logic a contradiction consists of two sentences that cannot both be true or both be false, because one is the denial of the other. In the Hegelian dialectic, two contradictories may both be true, because each, being only a one-sided view of divine reality, is only partially true anyway. Hence the law of excluded middle is compromised also because we no longer recognize only true and false statements but also statements that are partially true.

The Materialist Dialectic

Marx rejects Hegel's claim that the world is no more than a manifestation of divine thought. He rejects idealism and endorses materialism. We would therefore also expect him to reject the dialectic, but he does not do that. He finds something extremely valuable in the dialectic. Hegel's dialectic, Marx thought,

is standing on its head. It must be turned right side up again, if you would discover the rational kernel within the mystical shell. (T 302)

What is this "rational kernel"?

From Marx and Engels' materialist point of view there is no deity who creates the world. Hence the dialectic need not reconcile the divine, infinite, and perfect existence with this finite and very imperfect world. Nor need the dialectic reconcile science with the existence of god or god's role in creating and maintaining the universe. Thus there is no reason for them to follow Hegel in claiming that the dialectic is a logic that replaces formal logic; nor is there a reason to accept his redefinition of "contradiction." When Marx and Engels use the term "contradiction," they are referring to oppositions, conflicts, and incoherences of all kinds but not to logical contradictions in the strict sense. In retaining the dialectic, they are not accepting what appears to be Hegel's irrationalism.

Stripped of its theological and logical claims, Hegel's dialectic becomes an account of how thinking, now no longer the thinking of god, develops— not through pure mental activity, but in the course of practical activity, to solve the survival problems of a given group. The material dialectic of Marx describes the process in which human beings develop their ways of life under concrete conditions, in the course of solving concrete problems. Marx acknowledged that he owed this understanding to Hegel:

> The outstanding thing in Hegel's Phenomenology . . . is thus, first, that Hegel conceives the self-genesis of human beings as a process . . . and comprehends objective humans . . . as the outcome of their own labor. (EPM, T 112)

Marx also learned from Hegel that human activity, or labor, is always thinking activity, and that we must differentiate the thinking that is a part of activity from the thinking that reflects about what we do and tries to describe and understand it.

> Our ideas exist, first of all, in action: The production of ideas . . . is, at first, directly interwoven with the material activity and the material intercourse of human beings, the language of real life. (GI, T 154)

Activity is always conscious activity but not necessarily self-conscious. Thought is not self-transparent. Self-awareness is not automatic but is an achievement. The thinking that accompanies what we do is conscious but not always self-conscious. Self-consciousness is achieved only through significant efforts. This insight Marx and Engels also owe to Hegel.

Thinking practice and thinking separated from practice become distinct from one another only in the course of historical development. The distinction is drawn only after humans develop a division of labor between mental and manual work:

> Division of labor becomes truly such from the moment when a division of material and mental labor appears. (The first form of ideologists, *priests*, is concurrent.) From this moment onwards consciousness *can* really flatter itself that it is something other than consciousness of existing practice. (GI, T 159)

The idea that consciousness is separate from what we do arises when a separate class of people appears whose job it is to think while the rest of the community goes about its daily tasks. The priests were the first such class of thinkers.

Thinking, viewed dialectically, thus becomes a historical process. Human beings define what being human is, as I said earlier, not by holding a convention and discussing the meaning of being human but by building social systems.

Human self-creation produces systematic wholes. A particular group's conception of what being human means, developed in the course of their day-to-day practice, has some sort of inner coherence. The different institutions, practices, beliefs, and values that constitute a particular culture are not strung together arbitrarily but form a whole. This systematic aspect of human societies has been interpreted as the claim that "all things are internally related."[1] At other times it has been taken as the assertion that in addition to individuals, there exist entities we call "wholes." But Marx makes much more specific claims:

1. In any given society, certain important aspects are connected with each other in such a way that each depends on the other for its existence. Thus, for example, money becomes capital only in a society in which there exists a pool of people looking for wage labor (G, T 254).

2. In many cases these dependencies are mutual. For instance, a pool of people looking for wage work become proletarians only where there is capital to put them to work. In situations where there is no capital these people looking for work become vagabonds, robbers, and thieves.[2]

3. Social systems tend to reproduce themselves. The members of a particular culture make a concerted effort to preserve their accustomed way of life. Social systems are built and reproduced by solving specific, concrete problems as they arise. That is what Marx and Engels learned from Hegel. The following passage illustrates that process once more:

> The survival of the community as such in the old mode requires the reproduction of its members in the presupposed objective conditions. *Production itself, the advance of population (this too belongs with production), necessarily suspends these conditions little by little; destroys them instead of reproducing them, etc., and, with that, the communal system declines and falls, together with the property relations on which it is based.*[3]

In the long run, the attempts of a given group to maintain its traditions and institutions intact are self-defeating. The attempt to reproduce the community unchanged will destroy it:

> Not only do the objective conditions change in the act of reproduction, e.g., the village becomes a town, the wildnerness a cleared field, etc., but the producers change, too, in that they bring out new qualities, develop themselves in production . . . and develop new powers and ideas, new modes of intercourse, new needs, and new language.[4]

Human beings live in different societies, which, in turn, have different conceptions of what it means to be human in this world. Change occurs insofar as any of these conceptions destroys itself as a consequence of its internal contradictions. In the course of time, these become more and more obtrusive until they finally bring about a fundamental transformation of the society. Human cultures are systems, in the sense defined, but they are not necessarily coherent in all respects. On the contrary, cultures struggle to preserve themselves not only in the face of changed external conditions but also against the stresses and internal tensions within the culture itself. This is illustrated in the earlier passage from *Grundrisse*: "Production itself, the advance of population . . . necessarily suspends these conditions [required for the survival of the group] little by little. . . . " In certain agricultural communities, for instance, having more children is an advantage because it adds to the labor force. At the same time, however, a growing population puts great pressure on the available land and thus calls forth solutions that destroy the established way of life. The existing techniques for survival, which include having large families, sooner or later destroy the traditional ways they were intended to preserve.

The materialist dialectic thus is not a logic superior to formal logic. It is, instead, a very general view of the outlines of past human history. But inasmuch as this human history is the development of thinking practice and its consequences, the pattern of human history is also a pattern of thought—not of the fully articulated, self-conscious thought of individuals, let alone that of a divine individual, but the thinking implicit in the practices and problem solving of human groups. So far Marx agrees with Hegel. But Hegel, who understood that human beings "are the outcome of the labor of human beings" (EPM,T 112), misunderstood the nature of labor and thinking: "The only labor which Hegel knows and recognizes is *abstractly mental* labor [viz. philosophy]" (EPM,T 112). Hence Marx, the materialist, substitutes the process in which human beings solve the problems of meeting their material needs for Hegel's grand panorama of divine thinking.

The Dialectic in Marx and Engels

With his redefinition of "contradiction," Hegel seems to reject what is, in fact, a necessary condition for intelligible conversation. This is, understandably, a controversial position and has earned Hegel a great deal of philosophical opposition. Marx rejects Hegel's idealism but does not discuss Hegel's other claim—that the dialectic is a higher logic.

Since he did not reject this claim explicitly, many of his readers assume that the Marxist dialectic is also offered as a logic to replace formal logic. Some interpreters agree with this rejection of formal logic.[5] Some add that if the dialectic is indeed a logic, one that in some sense supersedes traditional formal logic but is now a logic in the service of materialism, then it must apply everywhere; and thus in this interpretation of Marx's dialectic, nature must also be regarded as dialectical.[6]

But readers of Marx who are uneasy about the rejection of formal logic tend to minimize Marx's interest in dialectic and to treat it as an error on his part, or as a hangover from his university days in Berlin.[7]

Other readers, unhappy with these interpretations, have rejected the idea that the dialectic is a logic in any sense, regarding it instead as an ontology (i.e., a doctrine of the most general features of reality).[8] In this interpretation, the dialectic refers to the fact that societies are organic wholes that develop and sooner or later perish as a consequence of their internal contradictions.

The interpretation of the materialist dialectic of Marx provided in the preceding section is certainly consistent with this latter reading, but adds that the dialectic consists of a theory about the nature and function of thinking in human history.

Notes

1. Bertell Ollman, *Alienation: Marx's Conception of Man in Capitalist Society* (Cambridge: Cambridge University Press, 1971), Chapters 2 and 3 and Appendix.

2. Marx, *Capital*, Vol. I (New York: International Publishers, 1967), Chapter 28.

3. Marx, *Grundrisse* (Harmondsworth: Penguin Books, 1974), p. 486. Italics added.

4. Marx, *Grundrisse*, p. 494.

5. George Novak, *An Introduction to the Logic of Marxism* (New York: Merit Publishers, 1969).

6. This was Engels' view, one also taken up by Soviet readers of Marx. See Friedrich Engels, *The Dialectic of Nature* (New York: International Publishers, 1940). A footnote in *Capital*, Vol. I (p. 309, fn 1), is sometimes cited to suggest that Marx, too, supported the dialectic of nature. That footnote, however, turns out to have been inserted by Engels.

7. See G. A. Cohen, *Karl Marx's Theory of History* (Princeton, N.J.: Princeton University Press, 1978), p. 89.

8. Allen W. Wood, *Karl Marx* (London: Routledge and Kegan Paul, 1981), Part 5.

For Further Reading

Robert Heilbroner, *Marxism: For and Against* (New York: Norton, 1970), Chapter 11.

Sidney Hook, *From Hegel to Marx* (Ann Arbor: University of Michigan Press, 1971), Chapter 3.

6

Ideology

MARX LEARNED FROM HEGEL that human activity is thinking activity, that it involves self-understanding and an understanding of the world in which the action takes place. Such thinking and understanding are not necessarily self-conscious. A good deal of what human beings know and understand is inarticulate knowledge and understanding. To these insights derived from Hegel, Marx added the enormously important view that when we come to put into words what we understand inarticulately about our own practices, we may attempt to be accurate, but we may also, and often do, distort our previously inarticulate understanding. Sometimes we do so intentionally and sometimes we do so in spite of our attempts to be accurate and complete. What we say about our practices, about the ways in which we live, is frequently misleading. Marx develops this idea in his theory of ideology.

It is important to begin by insisting that the term "ideology" in the work of Marx and Engels has a meaning different from that in current English, which treats it as a near synonym of "propaganda" (particularly of a political sort). Ideology usually refers to beliefs that no one would adopt on rational grounds, beliefs that have been instilled in people by force or deception. In political rhetoric, the beliefs of our opponents are therefore often characterized as "ideologies" because they are assumed to be false. Among conservatives, Marxism is a favorite example of ideology in that sense, because it is assumed that no one would take Marxian thought seriously unless duped or coerced. In order to understand what Marx and Engels mean by this word, then, we must put the current sense of it aside.

Marx and Engels use the term "ideology" in a variety of senses; all of which are connected. The variations in the meaning of the word "ideology" are not the result of carelessness on their part; rather, they flow from their general conception of what it means to be a human being.

We cannot understand what Marx and Engels mean by "ideology" unless we take seriously the claim that human beings shape their world. They therefore always understand that world, even if their understanding is not self-conscious and remains inarticulate. For instance, as we noted in Chapter 3, a particular region of the earth becomes a hunting ground only when a group hunts there. They make it into a hunting ground by living in that region. They live on that land, as hunters, and look at it through the eyes of hunters. They interpret the world with the outlook of a hunting people. In *The German Ideology*, Marx and Engels call this inarticulate understanding "practical consciousness" (GI, T 158).

This practical consciousness consists not only of ideas, beliefs, values, and other ways of thinking. Indeed, as the term suggests, it primarily involves patterns of actions, ways of doing things. But since actions are conscious actions, they involve beliefs, hypotheses, and schemes of explanation and classification. Inasmuch as actions are, at the same time, imperfectly self-conscious, these beliefs, hypotheses, and so on, are inarticulate. It requires considerable mental effort to put the guiding beliefs of a given culture into words.

We must distinguish practical consciousness from what I shall call "explicit" ideologies, which, by definition, are put into words. We enter the realm of ideology only when the often inarticulate practical understanding that animates people's daily life is formulated in some way. Marx's examples of explicit ideology are religion, morals, and philosophy (GI, T 154–155), but we can also include the common wisdom of a group by which it guides its own choices. Common sense, if that means the opinions a group accepts as true, is also an example of explicit ideology. It consists of what people invariably say in particular situations and repeat to children at home and in school, until they too accept it as common sense.

Explicit ideology plays a definite role in the functioning of a culture— hence Marx's comments on Greek mythology (G, T 245), cited earlier. The Greeks dominated their world through mythology because they did not have the science and technology to dominate it in a more literal and effective fashion. In similar ways religion serves an important purpose:

Religious suffering is at the same time an *expression* of real suffering and a *protest* against real suffering. Religion is the sigh of the oppressed creature, the sentiment of a heartless world, and the soul of soulless conditions. It is the *opium* of the people. The abolition of religion as the

illusory happiness of human beings is a demand for their real happiness.
(T 54)

Religion plays a role in society and is therefore important. But we can also see that there are better ways of achieving the same result, just as there are better ways of being in control of the environment than mythology. Religion is "illusory happiness" but real happiness is possible.

Religion and mythology are prime examples of what Marx and Engels mean by ideology.

> If in all ideology human beings and their circumstances appear upside down as in a *camera obscura*, this phenomenon arises just as much from their life-process as the inversion of objects on the retina does from their physical life-process. (GI, T 154)

The explicit ideologies, such as religion or mythology, are "inverted" because they fulfill their function by misrepresenting the actual practices and way of life of the society. But the metaphor of "inversion" must not be taken too literally. If we look at Marx's actual criticism of the ideologists, we find that he considers their work incomplete. They provide us with only part of the truth. They distort reality by giving a one-sided account. Ideology is not literally the opposite of the truth but a truncated version of it. Ideology is, to varying extents, avoidable. One can criticize current misrepresentations by showing that they are one-sided, just as Marx did with the work of his contemporary economists. Different ideologies, functioning in different situations and "distorting" actual practices in different ways, serve different purposes with these distortions.

Ideologies formulate our previously unformulated understandings of ourselves, but they do so in a distorted manner. Not all distortions are ideological, however. They may be the product of inattention or ineptitude. The distortions of ideology, by contrast, are not due to carelessness, inattention, or stupidity; they are there for a purpose—namely, to render the world of a particular group intelligible to that group and to justify its common practices. Ideologies arise from human "life processes"; they play a specific role in those life processes. Often that role is very complex. Religion, for instance, is both an expression of human suffering and a protest against it. But it is more than that: It is the "sentiment of the heartless world, . . . the soul of soulless conditions"; it gives meaning to human life that seems devoid of meaning. Finally it both drugs people and provides happiness, albeit an illusory one.

Ideologies are the product of a group's attempt to understand its world. To the extent that such understanding is distorted *and* functions to maintain the world and the practices of that group—to that extent is it ideological.

There is no general answer to the question as to why particular ideologies exist; we need to examine concrete cases to understand the function of different ideologies. Their function is different in different cases, as are the human "life processes" in different cultures. Thus Marx, responding to the criticism that life in the Ancient World was primarily shaped by politics and life in the Middle Ages was shaped by Catholicism, not by "material interests," declared

> it is the mode in which they gained a livelihood that explains why here politics, and there Catholicism, played the chief part.[1]

Only the particular social and economic conditions of Antiquity and Feudal Europe can explain why the Greeks and Romans thought about their social world in political terms, and the Medievals in religious terms, thereby misrepresenting to themselves the economic conditions that shaped their lives. Similarly, the misrepresentations of capitalist society can be understood only from a careful analysis of the capitalist economy. Marx discusses that in the context of "The Fetishism of Commodities" (see Chapter 9).

Marx and Engels also suggest that ideological distortions serve a political purpose—namely, to perpetuate the rule of the current ruling class. A rising class presents its interests as universal human interests. To that extent it represents the society as if it had only one class, as if there were no class oppositions in that society. Such a belief distorts; it is ideological because the distortion serves the specific political purpose of retarding the development of an oppositional class. For it conceals the fact that not everyone in the society has the same interests as the ruling class. To the extent that ideology serves the function of concealing class antagonisms, there will be no ideology in a classless society:

> This whole semblance that the rule of a certain class is only the rule of certain ideas, comes to a natural end, of course, as soon as class rule in general ceases . . . as soon as it is no longer necessary to represent a particular interest as general. (GI, T 174)

Marx's and Engels' views on the functions of ideology appear vague: At times, they seem to have ascribed varying functions to ideology; at others, they seem to have insisted that its function is always political, that in its ideology a ruling class presents its outlook on the world as the outlook of everybody. This vagueness gave rise to different interpretations of the function of ideology: ideology as a one-sided understanding of existing practices, or ideology as a class point of view imposed on the members of a different class.[2]

At a certain time in human history, mental work becomes separated from physical work. Thinking becomes the task of a special group of people, the intellectuals. The explicit formulation of the underlying ideology of a group thus becomes the task of particular people, of

active, conceptive ideologists, who make the perfecting of the illusions of the class about itself their chief source of livelihood. (GI, T 173)

We may call what they produce "literary ideology," which includes not only written philosophy and religion but, as Marx argues, also legal systems (T 188) and the theories that underlie the political system (T 173).

Literary ideologies, in their turn, are of very different kinds: Marx distinguishes, for instance, between economists who, though in error, did an honest and scientific job of trying to unravel the complexities of the capitalist economy, and mere apologists for the system:

Once for all, I may here state, that by classical Political Economy, I understand that economy which . . . has investigated the real relations of production, in contradistinction to vulgar economy, which deals with appearances only . . . proclaiming for everlasting truths the trite ideas held by the self-complacent bourgeoisie with regard to their own world, to them the best of all possible worlds.[3]

Adam Smith and David Ricardo "investigated the real relations of production." Some of Marx's contemporaries, Marx thought, did no more than "proclaim the trite ideas" of the ruling capitalist elite of his day. The latter, to give just one example, took for granted that the capitalist, if successful, makes a profit on his investment. The economic origins of that profit are not investigated by the "vulgar" economists, whereas they were a major concern of Smith and Ricardo.

With this last sense of the word "ideology" we obviously come close to the sense in which that word is used today—namely, in the sense of propaganda, or half-truths known to be such but spread about in order to mislead people who do not know any better.

Not all readers of Marx have recognized all of these different senses of ideology. The word "ideology" is often used to designate all the explicit, conscious beliefs of a group about its world, without drawing any of the distinctions indicated here. Since the concept of ideology carries with it the connotation of "distortion," ideology is often characterized, quite generally, as "false consciousness."[4]

Many have found that concept of ideology to be problematic. They have assumed that the materialism of Marx and Engels commits them to the view that all people living under given material conditions must adopt its ideology, because "life determines consciousness." If that is true, Marx and Engels are also victims of bourgeois ideology, that is, of "false consciousness." But since they also claimed to be doing science, which they distinguished from and opposed to ideology, they seemed to be caught in a contradiction. They appear to have believed that all people in a given culture are inevitably infected by the reigning ideology, *and* that they themselves did science and saw through the ideology of the age. But those two views are inconsistent.[5] Commentators have taken different routes in dealing with this supposed contradiction.

In order to appreciate the different responses to this paradox, we must state its elements with more precision. Interpreters claim that (1) in all class societies, ideology is inevitable. But that is still ambiguous for it means either that (a) there exist no class societies in which ideologies do not play an important role, or that (b) there is no individual, in any class society, who is able to see through the reigning ideologies.

It is clear that point b is a much stronger claim. It may well be that in all class societies many people and their actions are affected by ideology, but there may still be some people who see the ideologies for the distortions that they are.

Furthermore, (2) according to materialism, all forms of thinking in a given society are ideological, and (3) science and ideology are incompatible.

Now, one can assert that ideology is inevitable in class society without also claiming that nobody in the society sees through their misrepresentations. In one version of this interpretation, ideologies are understood as systems of beliefs developed intentionally in order to mislead people. Ideology is then not forced on us by material conditions and thus does not prevent us from doing real science.[6] According to Althusser, ideology is the system of beliefs that are more or less deliberately imposed on a population by the "ideological state apparatuses"—the schools, the churches, and the media. If that is true, then not all beliefs are necessarily ideological and it is up to the individual person whether he or she does genuine science or accepts the ideology. I shall argue the same view below, on very different grounds.

One can also hold that no one in a given society can resist its ideology but deny that all thinking is ideological. Science, in that case, may be nonideological thinking, and thus doing science and being in the thrall of the reigning ideology need not be inconsistent.[7]

One can also deny that science and ideology are incompatible.[8]

Finally, it is possible, of course, to deny that the doctrines of Marx and Engels deserve to be called science. But here one rescues them from the accusation of being inconsistent at the price of degrading the product of their intellectual efforts to the level of "ideology" or "myth."[9] It is not difficult to find support for these different readings in the texts. Clinging to one passage or another may help bolster a particular interpretation of ideology, but it does not help to make sense of Marx and Engels' thought as a whole.

In actual fact, the contradiction ascribed to Marx and Engels does not exist. Materialism does not imply that any member of a culture *necessarily* adopts a given explicit or literary ideology or cannot break out of it. Marx gave the title "Critiques" to successive versions of his economics in order to suggest that he was trying to separate out the ideological distortions from genuine insights in the existing economic theories. He thereby recognized the strong influence of ideology in the self-understanding of capitalist society *and* the possibility of unmasking these ideological distortions. The practices that any *given* group follows, in which it expresses its understanding of the world, shape what they say about that world, because explicit and literary ideologies are formulations of the inarticulate understanding that constitutes practical consciousness. But that does not, of course, imply that our understanding of capitalism *must* be distorted. As we have already seen, some people see through the one-sidedness of a dominant view.

Thus Marx and Engels' claim to be doing science is not incompatible with their theory of ideology. Whether they succeeded in doing genuine science is another matter. They certainly thought they had done so, but since they very rarely discussed what they meant by "science," the solidity of that claim is difficult to evaluate. The controversies that have arisen among commentators about their claim to be doing science cannot be discussed here for lack of space.

A very different problem with the theory of ideology arises with the prevalence of sexism and racism in our society. Sexism and racism consist of certain beliefs and to that extent are ideological, but these beliefs, in their turn, are articulations of certain practices, which are part of our practical consciousness. But what shapes those practices? Marx and Engels seem to believe that the way people go about their daily business is determined by the mode of production. That seems to be what materialism asserts. Hence their ideologies are also shaped by the mode of production. But racism and sexism long antedate capitalism and thus seem to be more properly described as hangovers from an earlier mode of production.[10]

But if we admit that elements of our practical consciousness and our ideology are shaped by earlier modes of production, the explanatory power of materialism is seriously weakened. The attraction of materialism, particularly for the person thinking about social and political change, is that it promises to account for the way people think and act. If we are interested in changing how people think and act, we are also, of course, very interested in knowing what we need to change in order to change people's thinking and action. But if some of what people do and think is really a hangover from an earlier social order, it becomes much harder to be certain of our explanations linking present behavior to capitalism. There is always the possibility that the particular actions or beliefs we are trying to account for are hangovers from an earlier era.

More seriously still, if what people do today is the effect of social structures that have long since been changed, the claim of materialism that changing social structures will change human behavior must be false.

The twin phenomena of racism and sexism thus impose a serious limitation on one's interpretation of materialism, dialectic, and ideology. In the face of practices and beliefs that are clearly not the products of capitalism, we need to recognize that one cannot claim more than that the existing mode of production strongly affects our practices and actions and, hence, that a replacement of that mode of production by another would produce major changes. More specific predictions about the changes in human behavior to be hoped for from an abolition of capitalism need to be based on detailed arguments linking capitalism and specific behaviors. It is, for instance, extremely unlikely that replacing private ownership of the means of production by a genuinely democratic socialism would wipe away sexism and racism—an expectation defended more than once by serious readers of Marx.

These considerations reveal an important area of uncertainty in the views of Marx and Engels about the relationship between the socio-economic structure of the society and the practices and beliefs of the people in it: They have made a strong case that social and economic practices leave their unmistakable mark on all aspects of the culture. That is an important insight, but it is also very general. If we want to know more details about the extent of this effect of socioeconomic structure on the culture as a whole, or about the links, say, between capitalism and particular cultural, political, ideological phenomena, the materialism of Marx and Engels is not terribly helpful.

Notes

1. Jorge Larrain, *The Concept of Ideology* (Athens: University of Georgia Press, 1979), Chapters 1 and 2.

2. Marx, *Capital*, Vol. I (New York: International Publishers, 1967), p. 82, n. 1.

3. Marx, *Capital*, Vol. I, p. 80, n. 2.

4. George Lichtheim, *The Concept of Ideology, and Other Essays* (New York: Vintage Books, 1967), pp. 17—22.

5. William Leon McBride, *The Philosophy of Marx* (New York: St. Martin's Press, 1977).

6. This appears to be the view of Louis Althusser. See Althusser, *Lenin and Philosophy* (New York: Monthly Review Press, 1971).

7. Larrain, *The Concept of Ideology*, Chapter 1.

8. McMurtry, however, denies that science and ideology are incompatible. See John McMurtry, *The Structure of Marx's World-View* (Princeton, N.J.: Princeton University Press, 1978), Chapter 5.

9. Robert C. Tucker, *Philosophy and Myth in Karl Marx* (Cambridge: Cambridge University Press, 1972).

10. This point is persuasively argued by Cedric J. Robinson in *Black Marxism* (London: Zed Books, 1983), Part I.

For Further Reading

Richard Lichtman, "Marx's Theory of Ideology," *Socialist Revolution* 23, no. 1 (1975).

PART TWO

Economics

7

Capitalism

"M. PROUDHON DOES NOT KNOW," Marx wrote in 1847, "that all history is nothing but a continuous transformation of human nature."[1]

> M. Proudhon the economist understands very well that men make cloth, linen or silk materials in definite relations of production. But what he has not understood is that these definite social relations are just as much produced by men as linen, flax, etc.[2]

These quotations are shorthand expressions of the complex conception of human nature discussed in the preceding chapters. Human beings transform themselves in the course of history precisely by creating and recreating definite relations of production. These social relations, Marx continues in the passage cited, are "closely bound up with productive forces." Relations of production and, more generally, economic systems are human creations. They have histories.

The same view is reiterated in *Capital*: "By thus acting on the external world and changing it, he [viz. the worker] at the same time changes his own nature."[3] This general conception of human nature is the starting point of Marx's researches into economics. The chief goal is, clearly, to formulate the laws that govern economic activity in a capitalist society, but that enterprise must be approached through a history of capitalism. Capitalism is a historical human creation, and it will be misunderstood unless we understand how it came to be. We need to discover, first of all, how it developed from the modes of production that preceded it. Capitalism is clearly the result of past development, the product of many economic revolutions, of the extinction of a whole series of older forms of social production. (C, T 338)

Unless we consult the history of capitalism we are liable to focus only on its subsidiary aspects. If we do that, our economics will, similarly, explain only subsidiary phenomena. It will be incomplete and hence "ideological."

The Historical Development of Capitalism

Marx never produced a systematic history of capitalism, but sketches of the history that culminates in the development of capitalist institutions are scattered throughout his major economic writings, particularly *Capital* and *Grundrisse*. A number of changes are repeatedly emphasized in these sketches: transformations of property relations, transformations of the role of money, and transformations of commodity production and the role of labor.

In earlier times, land was communally owned. To be a member of a community was to be one of the owners of the land. The identity of the group consisted of the common possession and cultivation of the land. Before capitalism could arise, this conception and practice of communal property had to be replaced by the individual ownership of land by single individuals. But the relation between people and their tools also had to change. In the medieval guilds,

> labor itself is still half artistic, half end-in-itself, etc. . . . . Attainment of particular skill in the work also secures possession of instruments. . . .
> (G, T 263) The art of really appropriating the instrument, of handling it as an instrument of labor, appears as the worker's peculiar skill, which posits him as the owner of the instrument. (G, T 265)

Ownership of tools was earned by the acquisition of skills. The master craftsman had his tools because he was a master of his craft. Tools were not mere commodities that anyone with enough money could buy.

These artisans produced "commodities"—things that were made in order to be sold. They did not merely produce, say, shoes for their own use but made their livings by making shoes for anyone who could buy them. Yet, although a capitalist society is commodity producing, not all commodity-producing societies are capitalist:

> With the urban crafts, although they rest essentially on exchange and on the creation of exchange values, the direct and chief aim of this production

is *subsistence as craftsmen,* as *master-journeymen,* hence use-value, not *wealth,* not *exchange value as exchange value.* (G, T 275)

In capitalism the goal is to produce profits to be reinvested in more means of production. The goal is therefore to increase one's capital. The medieval guild journeyman, by contrast, wanted to make simply enough to live. Wealth—namely, new capital—was not his goal (for reasons that will be explained in the next section). The development of production of commodities by craftsmen is not by itself sufficient for the development of capitalism. Nor is the accumulation of monetary wealth:

The *mere presence of monetary wealth,* and even the achievement of a kind of supremacy on its part, is in no way sufficient for this *dissolution into capital* to happen. Or else ancient Rome, Byzantium, etc., would have ended their history with free labor and capital. . . . There, too, the dissolution of the old property relations was bound up with the development of monetary wealth—of trade, etc. But instead of leading to industry, this dissolution led in fact to the supremacy of the countryside over the city. (G, T 270)

What made Roman history different from that of England in the sixteenth and seventeenth centuries, when capitalism developed, was the emergence in the latter period, and not in the former, of a workforce of people who had no means of supporting themselves except by hiring themselves out for wages. But this mass of wage workers originated

when, e.g., the great English landowners dismissed their retainers, who had, together with them, consumed the surplus product of the land; when further their tenants chased off the smaller cottagers, etc., then firstly a mass of living labor was thereby thrown onto the labor market, a mass which was free in a double sense, free from the old relations of clientship, bondage and servitude, and secondly free from all belongings and possessions, . . . *free of all property,* dependent on the sale of its labor capacity or on begging, vagabondage and robbery as its only source of income. It is a matter of historic record that they tried the latter first, but were driven off this road by the gallows, stocks, and whippings, onto the narrow path of the labor market. (G, T 271)

Of all the changes mentioned, the rise of "free" labor appeared to Marx to be the central change in the transition to capitalism. The crucial characteristic of that new economic system, according to him, was the presence of two different classes of people in a capitalist society: the owners of the factories, raw materials, tools and machines, and all the other means of production on the one hand, and the workers who did not own any means of production and thus were dependent on *wage labor* for their livelihood on the other.

Why did Marx refuse the title of capitalist to the Roman merchant who accumulated a sizeable fortune in money, or to the medieval craftsman who owned tools and raw materials that he and his apprentices and laborers transformed into commodities? One can, of course, call anything "capitalism" if one so chooses, but the decisive difference between Rome or the medieval economy, on one hand, and capitalism, on the other, seemed to Marx to be the ready availability of wage laborers in the latter and their absence in the former setting. His reasons for that will emerge from a more detailed discussion of capitalism.

At the same time, the existence of wage laborers is not a sufficient condition for the existence of capitalism. Also needed, as we have seen, are money capital and means of subsistence in the form of commodities, because capitalism is a *system*. (See the third section of Chapter 5.)

What Is Modern Capitalism?

We must begin with the concept of capital. Usually we think of that as money, or perhaps as means of production: buildings, machines, raw materials, tools, means of communication, office equipment, laboratories, and so on. Frequently Marx, too, writes as if that is also what he meant by the word "capital." But when he was really careful about his language he used "capital" to refer to a "social relation of production":

> A spinning jenny is a machine for spinning cotton. It becomes *capital* only in certain relations. Torn from these relationships it is no more capital than gold itself is *money* or sugar the price of sugar. . . . *Capital*, also, is a social relation of production. (WLC, T 207)

Means of production are "capital" only *in a very specific setting*—namely, when they are the private property of some members of a society while all the others own no means of production and, in fact, own little beyond their own persons and their ability to work. Means of production become capital only when most people do wage labor precisely because they do not own means of production (CI, T 431ff.).

Wage labor, under capitalism, is "free" in two senses. Workers are free from the serfdom that tied peasants to their land, and from the ties of slavery that tied the slave's person to her or his owner. Unlike the serf or the slave, the modern worker can change employers if one offers better wages or conditions than another; she or he can move to a different town if there is more work there. Serfs and slaves, by contrast, were not free to make those choices. Hence labor *power* under feudalism or slavery was not a commodity traded in a labor market (under slavery the person, not his or her ability to work, is a commodity). Under capitalism, by contrast, labor power is a commodity (G,T 270/1). But workers are also "free of all property." They do not, for instance, own plots of land that would support them and their families, even for awhile, so that they can refuse work if it is badly paid or excessively arduous. Nor do they own wealth that would support them so that they can refuse work that for whatever reason they do not like. The forces of labor are thus also "free" in the sense that they are without any financial reserves and, therefore, must work to live.

Marx notes several background conditions for the existence of "free" labor. One is the "free exchange relation" (G, T 254). If there is to be a labor market in which individual employers and workers contract for work and wages, there must be a legal system that enforces contracts evenhandedly—that is, a legal system that does not apply different rules to the rich and to the poor, to the nobleman and to the commoner. Whatever the actual realities in particular places and times may be, capitalism does establish a legal system for the enforcement of contracts of which the central principle is "equality before the law."

A population of "free" labor also presupposes a commodity economy developed to the point where it can supply food, clothing, and housing to such a working population that cannot supply any of its own needs, because it owns no means of production. Hence the need for rental housing near the factories as well as stores that sell clothes and food, to house, clothe, and feed this propertyless population. Marx noted that as more and more women and children were employed in the English factories in the first half of the nineteenth century,

> domestic work such as sewing and mending [had to] be replaced by the purchase of ready-made articles.[4]

What is the effect of the presence of "free" labor on capital? Capital, in the sense usually considered, is money that is readily convertible into means of production: factories, tools, raw materials. But all of those means are of use only to the extent that labor is available to work and thereby to transform the raw materials into finished products. More important, the acquisition of additional tools or raw materials is of no interest to an owner unless more labor is available. Thus, under medieval guild restrictions on the numbers of apprentices an owner could hire, only a limited number of apprentices were available anyway; moreover, the purchase of more tools or raw materials would have been a waste because workers would not have been on hand to do the work of transforming those additional raw materials into finished products.

The rules of guilds, . . . by limiting most strictly the number of apprentices and journeymen that a single master could employ, prevented him from becoming a capitalist. . . . A merchant could buy every kind of commodity, but labor as a commodity he could not buy. (CI, T 396)

Similarly, in the countryside, acquiring new land was of no advantage unless one also acquired more people to work it. But inasmuch as people were attached to the land under serfdom, there was no reserve force of agricultural labor to be hired to till additional land. There was no market in land; land was not bought or sold. New land was acquired by warfare that, at the same time, provided a workforce to cultivate land newly acquired from among the conquered people.[5]

Once labor becomes a commodity also, the function of the means of production changes drastically: They become capital in the modern sense. The capitalist now

has two objects in view: in the first place he wants to produce a use-value that has a value in exchange, that is to say, an article that is destined to be sold, a commodity; and secondly he desires to produce a commodity whose value shall be greater than the sum of the values of the commodities used in its production. (CI, T 351)

The capitalist wants to produce goods that sell; otherwise, his effort is useless and he squanders his capital. But equally important, he wants to make a *profit*. If at the end of a period of work he just breaks even— that is, he has just enough left to live on after paying for his means of production and his labor—then his effort is wasted. In that situation,

property in raw materials and instruments of labor would be merely *nominal*; economically they would belong to the worker as much as to the capitalist since they would create *value* only insofar as he himself were a worker. (G, T 248)

The purpose of capitalist efforts is to remunerate the worker, to pay for the raw materials used up, to pay the capitalist for his work, *and, in addition,* to produce a return on capital that can be reinvested. The medieval craftsman wanted to earn enough to stay alive and to keep working, but he did not seek "wealth" (i.e., profits over and above what he and his family consumed). Hence, in his case, the fact that he owned tools and raw materials was "merely nominal." It did not make any practical difference, for the livelihood gained by the master was only a reward for his own work. The capitalist, on the other hand, seeks to increase his capital by reinvesting the profits that accrue to capital. His ownership of the capital not only brings him remuneration for his work; it also makes him the owner of the additional proceeds available for reinvestment. The capitalist's motto is

accumulate, accumulate! That is Moses and the Prophets. . . . Accumulation for accumulation's sake, production for production's sake: by this formula classical economy expressed the historical mission of the bourgeoisie.[6]

Capital is different from means of production or money in a society where there is no labor market, because it is only in a labor market that capital can seek to enlarge itself continually. A capitalist society is different from a commodity producing society in which there is no free labor because, again, commodity production cannot yield significant profits for reinvestment unless there is free labor available to be put to work by this new capital. It is for this reason that Marx insists that capital is not just money or machines but a "social relation of production." This is a shorthand way of saying that means of production come to be capital and function to produce profits and accumulation of capital only where there are very specific relations of production—namely, those that obtain in a society with free labor and private ownership of the means of production.

Three other important points must be mentioned to round out Marx's characterization of capitalism:

1. Once capitalists are oriented toward growth, they will attempt to increase profits. The commodities they produce are intended for sale in a market, and profits are increased by selling more commodities. Under ordinary circumstances, they can do that in a variety of different ways— for instance, by lowering prices and thereby capturing a larger share of the total demand for whatever they produce. In any ordinary period, the demand for toothbrushes, for instance, is fairly constant. Barring a sudden panic over bad breath or bad teeth, or a sizeable increase in the population over a very short period, the number of toothbrushes that sell in any given year does not change very significantly. If any given manufacturer of toothbrushes wants to make more money, he or she must capture a larger market share—that is, he or she must sell a larger proportion of the total number of toothbrushes sold. Capitalists, in pursuit of greater profits, compete with each other:

Except in the periods of prosperity, there rages between the capitalists the most furious combat for the share of each in the markets.[7]

They can compete by having "price wars" but also through advertising campaigns, by redesigning products, and so on. The capitalist economy is a competitive one. Capitalists compete with one another and so do workers.

2. But none of that would happen unless people were willing to compete, unless making profits appeared to them to be of paramount importance. Marx notes that not all cultures have valued profit making as highly as do capitalist ones.

> We never find the Ancients investigating which form of land ownership, etc., is the most productive and produces the greatest wealth. Wealth does not appear to be the goal of production. . . . The question is always which form of property creates the best citizens. . . . Wealth as an end in itself appears only with the few mercantile peoples . . . who live in the interstices of the ancient world, as did the Jews in medieval society.[8]

As we would expect on the basis of the discussions in Part One of this book, with changing social relations of production, human beings change also. We have here an example of a change not only in values but also in complex patterns of actions, of choices that people actually make— all of which we refer to in a shorthand way by saying that in a capitalist society people are animated by the "profit motive." Making a profit, getting rich, accumulating capital are important motivations in a capitalist society. They were not so in other societies; in still others they played only a subsidiary role.

But this point about the motivations of the capitalist must be properly understood; it is often misinterpreted as a claim about the personality of individual capitalists. Thus one hears about the "greed" of capitalists— an expression that Marx also used from time to time. Now, as greed is usually regarded as a fault, we end up talking as if capitalism was the effect of the bad character of a class of people, the capitalists. That not only does an injustice to actual capitalists, who most likely are as decent as any other class of individuals, but it also confuses the entire analysis of capitalism because it seems to imply that if we could either improve the moral character of existing capitalists or replace the ones we have with people who are less greedy, then capitalism would be very different and probably be more benign. But this is, of course, not true: Capitalists act as they do because that is what the social system demands of them. A capitalist who refuses to increase his or her capital will not remain a capitalist for long. Imagine that you are employed as the manager of a company. Because you pay unusually high wages or support colleges or orphanages, you do not turn a profit from one year to the next and therefore have no profits from which to pay dividends to the stockholders. You may well be applauded for your enlightened labor management relations and your generous contributions, but you will be fired anyway because you did not do the job you were hired for—namely, to make your company grow.[9]

3. Capitalism is frequently identified with industry and industrial development. Here again, Marx draws on history to clarify the relationship between capitalism and industrial modes of production. It is clear that machines play an essential role in modern capitalism. Not only are they in evidence everywhere, but they are also important tools in the competition among capitalists. In their attempt to undersell competitors, for instance, capitalists will frequently install new machines that cheapen products and thus allow the producer to lower prices. It is equally clear from the history of capitalism, however, that its early phases preceded the development of modern technology. The early capitalist workshops had no more machinery than the medieval artisans' workshops. They managed to produce profits because they employed a much more finely honed division of labor, and because they assembled many workers under one roof and thus improved surveillance over the workers. But soon the productiveness of that form of capitalism was exhausted and machine production began to develop (CI, T 388–403). Capitalism can exist without technology but not for very long. The development of technology is the result rather than the cause of the development of capitalist social relations of production.

Capitalism is characterized by a money economy, commodity production, and private property in means of production. But unlike other social orders with those characteristics, under capitalism the ability to do work (labor power) has also become a commodity. There is a large group of people who have no means of support except wage labor. In such a society the pursuit of profit, the effort to increase one's capital, becomes a central motivation that pits capitalists against each other in a competitive struggle. The great contribution of that system is that it gives impetus to a previously undreamt of productivity as a result of the development of technology and the reorganization of worklife.

Commodity production has existed in other types of societies. But it is only in capitalist society that everything, including labor power, is a commodity. To be sure, not everyone who works produces commodities. Women who keep house and raise children are a prime example. But housework and child raising are also done for money as commodity production. Similarly, virtually all occupations that do not produce commodities have an analogue in commodity production. Capitalist society is therefore a commodity society unlike any other society. It is for this reason that Marx regards the concept of the commodity as the central concept in economics and begins *Capital* with an analysis of that concept.

Notes

1. Marx, *The Poverty of Philosophy* (New York: International Publishers, 1963), p. 147.
2. Marx, *The Poverty of Philosophy*, p. 109.
3. Marx, *Capital*, Vol. I (New York: International Publishers, 1967), p. 177.
4. Marx, *Capital*, Vol. I, p. 385, n. 2.
5. Marx, *Grundrisse* (Harmondsworth: Penguin Books, 1973), p. 487.
6. Marx, *Capital*, Vol. I, p. 595.
7. Marx, *Capital*, Vol. I, p. 453.
8. Marx, *Grundrisse*, p. 487.
9. To complete this argument one would, of course, have to show that the demands of the stockholders, too, were not motivated by personal greed but flowed from the prevailing social practices.

For Further Reading

Martin Nicolaus, "The Unknown Marx," in Carl Oglesby, ed., *The New Left Reader* (New York: Grove Press, 1969).

8

Capitalism and Exploitation

Is CAPITALISM, as characterized by Marx, very different from the ways in which its defenders describe it? There is a good deal of agreement about its central features between Marx, who is fiercely critical of capitalism, and those who accept capitalism. Only Marx regards the descriptions of capitalism offered by its defenders as quite incomplete. What he would have added, however, the defenders of capitalism definitely reject.

A capitalist society is a commodity-producing society. Commodities are made in the expectation that someone will have a use for them and therefore *buy* them. The room that I add onto my house is not a commodity because I do build it not to sell to someone else, but for my own use. But once I manufacture anything for sale, I am producing commodities. That is another way of saying that I produce for sale in a marketplace. To say that a capitalist society is a commodity society is, therefore, to say that products, including the ability to work, are bought and sold in a marketplace. Markets determine prices by supply and demand. To call capitalism a market society is thus to claim that prices are determined by supply and demand. This, too, Marx recognized quite readily. Wages, he wrote for instance, "will rise and fall according to the relations of supply and demand" (WLC, T 206).

Marx, then, had no objection to calling capitalism a "market society." Neither would he have hesitated to describe capitalism as a "free enterprise system." This description implies that under capitalism there are very minimal legal restrictions on going into business. Whereas in feudal society, both farming and the production of consumption goods by artisans were very carefully regulated by law and custom, in a capitalist society, one is legally free to pursue profit in any way one sees fit, short of defrauding others or endangering their safety. Accordingly, people in a capitalist society are socially very mobile: Different generations of the same family may not have the same social status or wealth, and, hence, it is often said that *"anybody* can become a capitalist." Again, Marx agrees:

> The circumstance that a man without fortune but possessing energy, solidity, ability and business acumen may become a capitalist in this manner . . . is greatly admired by apologists of the capitalist system. In a similar way . . . the Catholic Church in the Middle Ages formed its hierarchy out of the best brains in the land, regardless of their estate, birth or fortune.[1]

It is often also said that *"everybody* can become a capitalist." But that, of course, is a false statement. What is true of each individual separately is not true of all of them together. In a footrace where the contestants are equally matched, it might be true that anybody can win. But it is clearly not true that everybody can win. The very fact that one person wins makes it impossible for all others to win. Similarly, the fact that some people are capitalists makes it impossible for others to be capitalists. Capitalism, as we saw in the preceding chapter, exists precisely in those societies where *some* people own and control the means of production and others do not and therefore must do wage labor. Without a large number of available wage laborers, there can be no capitalism. Hence not everybody can be a capitalist.

It follows that a capitalist society is, indeed, a market society and a free enterprise system, but it is also something else: a class society. There is capitalism only where there are two different kinds of people—capitalists who own the means of production and wage laborers who support themselves exclusively by working for a living.

Many people who do not consider themselves followers of Marx would be willing to agree that there are two classes, owners and workers, in capitalist societies. But Marx went even further by characterizing the relationship between employers and workers in a very specific way: *Owners exploit their workers.* Here most readers of Marx part company with him.

The Concept of Exploitation

What does Marx mean by "exploitation"?

> Capital has not invented surplus labor. Wherever a part of society possesses the monopoly of the means of production, the laborer, free or not free,

must add to the working time necessary for his maintenance an extra working time in order to produce the means of subsistence for the owners of the means of production, whether this proprietor be the Athenian nobleman, Etruscan theocrat, civis Romanus, Norman baron, American slaveowner, Wallachian Boyard [a feudal landowner in what is today Romania], modern landlord or capitalist. . . . The comparison of the greed for surplus labor in the Danubian principalities [Romania] with the same greed in the English factories has a special interest, because surplus labor in the corvee [the feudal form of surplus labor] has an independent and palpable form. . . . The necessary labor which the Wallachian peasant does for his own maintenance is distinctly marked off from his labor on behalf of the Boyard. The one he does in his own field, the other on the seignorial estate. Both parts of the labor time exist, therefore, independently, side by side. In the corvee the surplus labor is accurately marked off from the necessary labor. (CI, T 364–365)

In a wide range of cultures that, in other respects, were very different from one another, we find one common component—namely, the fact that some people worked to support other people who did not work. In Athens, slaves worked to support the free citizens, just as slaves worked for the American slaveowners. Feudal lords—"Norman barons and Wallachian Boyards"—were supported by the unpaid labor of serfs. In the former case the slaveowner could make the slave work to support him because the slave was his property. In the latter case, the corvee (i.e., unpaid) labor of the serf was, in the final analysis, enforced by the fact that the feudal lord had a monopoly on military might: He got the serf to work for him by threatening physical violence.[2] In both cases the crucial fact is that slaves or serfs were not rewarded for their work. The work they did for their masters was essentially unpaid, and they did unpaid work simply because they could not avoid doing so. Marx calls this unpaid work "surplus labor."

Both slave and serf were, in Marx's terminology, exploited. A person is exploited when he or she is regularly forced to do work for someone else without getting paid for that work, and when the products of this labor are forcibly appropriated by someone else. Exploitation thus has three aspects: (1) Workers produce more than they receive in wages; (2) the surplus is appropriated by someone else; and (3) this arrangement is imposed on the workers by force. (As we shall soon see, that force takes very different forms in different economic systems.) We shall see below that the coercion by a particular employer of a particular worker presupposes that the *class* of employers has greater power than the class of workers and uses it against them.

Why are workers exploited under capitalism? Because the employer's goal is profit. Profit in turn increases (all other things being equal) when costs go down. If a pair of shoes, at current market prices, sells for $5.00 and costs the capitalist $4.00 to produce and sell, then his profit is $1.00 per pair. If he can lower his cost to $3.75, his profit increases accordingly. One important way of lowering costs is to increase the productivity of labor. One way of doing that is to get workers to produce more pairs of shoes in a working day without increasing wages or increasing other costs. Hence "profits and wages are in inverse proportion" (WLC, T 211). As the wage cost of every pair of shoes goes down, the profit goes up. The capitalist therefore has an interest in getting the worker to do as much work as possible for as little money as possible.

In the shoe industry, for instance, there are large numbers of producers, each competing with the other. One important way of increasing profits is by selling more shoes, and one way of effecting that is to lower one's price. Hence there is a strong incentive to use one's economic power over the workers to get them to produce more without paying them more. Any owner of a shoe factory, even the most benevolent, must be prepared to find that his competitors are lowering their costs and prices. If that happens, our compassionate shoe manufacturer finds himself compelled to increase the productivity of labor and lower wages, however repugnant that may be to him.

Capitalism thus puts workers and employers at odds. The owner is able to and *must*, whether he likes it or not, squeeze as much labor out of a worker as possible in order to increase profits. The worker is therefore exploited because with an increase of productivity, due perhaps to increased speed at work or longer hours, wages do not rise and the worker does more work without getting more pay: He or she does work that is not paid for.

Capitalism and Profits

Under capitalism, as under feudalism and slavery, labor is exploited. That was the claim of the passage cited previously. But that passage makes another very important claim as well: Under feudalism and slavery, exploitation was very obvious—under slavery because the slave did not get paid at all, and under feudalism because serfs did unpaid labor on distinct days (here "surplus labor" had "an independent and palpable form" [CI, T 364]) that was separate from the work they did on their own land to earn their livelihood. But under capitalism, exploitation "is not evident on the surface" (CI, T 365) because the worker strikes a bargain in the labor market in which, on the average at least, no one gets cheated. In certain cases, employers take advantage of workers, but Marx is perfectly willing to concede that sometimes workers also take advantage of employers. On the average, he thinks, the wage bargain between employer and worker is fair in the sense that the laborer gets paid the full value of his or her commodity (labor power), just as other commodities are purchased at their full value.

> The sphere . . . within whose boundaries the sale and purchase of labor power goes on, is in fact a very Eden of the innate rights of man. There alone rule Freedom, Equality, Property and Bentham. Freedom because both buyer and seller of a commodity, say labor power, are constrained only by their own free will. They contract as free agents, and the agreement they come to, is but the form in which they give legal expression to their common will. Equality because each enters into relation with the other, as with a simple owner of commodities, and *they exchange equivalent for equivalent*. Property because each disposes only of what is his own. And Bentham, because each looks only to himself. . . . [Jeremy Bentham was an English philosopher and jurist, 1748–1832.] (CI, T 343; italics added)

The contract between worker and employer is freely entered into, and they "exchange equivalents"; that is, the worker receives full value for what he or she provides for the employer. Yet, at the same time, Marx maintains that labor is coerced into doing work for which it is not compensated. The employer exploits the workers by extracting unpaid work from them.

There appears to be a contradiction here. Marx is fully aware of that. I will discuss the solution he proposes in the third section of this chapter and again in Chapter 10. But in this present section we must examine, in more detail, what he means by the claim that under capitalism, exploitation "is not evident on the surface." According to some interpreters, this means that exploitation is not observed by the average worker but is discovered only by the economic analyst.[3] I shall argue, by contrast, that exploitation is a palpable fact of workers' experience, but one difficult to interpret because workers also strike bargains with their employers in which they do not get cheated.

Marx provides many examples of the experience of exploitation. Parts III, IV, and V of the first volume of *Capital* deal with the ways in which capitalists get their workers to do surplus labor, the resulting struggles, the enormous costs in ill health, overwork, and family disruptions that workers pay for that surplus labor, and the ways in which capitalists turn that surplus labor into profits. These three parts cover roughly half of the 750 pages of Volume I. Much of the material in these pages is taken from British government documents, most of which are reports of factory inspectors. In the course of these extended discussions, Marx notes that over the vigorous objections of the manufacturers, the Factory Acts of 1850 limited the legal work week to 60 hours (CI, T 365–366).

Not all industries were covered by these acts. In the potteries, according to government inspectors, children less than ten years old worked fifteen hours a day (CI, T 386).

These first legal limits on the working day were adopted because some members of society feared for the health of working people. These fears were well justified:

> Dr. Lee, medical health officer for Manchester, stated "that the average age of death of the Manchester . . . upper middle class was 38 years, while the average age at death of the laboring class 17; while at Liverpool those figures were represented as 35 against 15."[4]

But the working day was chiefly limited as a consequence of "a protracted civil war . . . between the capitalist class and the working class."[5] Struggles between workers and employers are endemic to capitalism. What is their origin? One could try to explain the "virtual civil war" in English factories simply as a response to the horrendous working conditions. But that would be an incomplete explanation. Workers have the unmistakable experience of employers trying to raise output without raising wages by increasing the intensity of work, by hiring cheaper labor, or by saving money by not providing hygienic and protective devices for the workers. It seems clear that exploitation, the extracting of products without paying for having them produced, is there for anyone to see.

If exploitation is not directly experienced but only revealed by technical economic analysis, then the workers' struggles can revolve around exploitation only to the extent that economists, or other intellectuals, have persuaded the workers that they are being exploited. But experience refutes that interpretation: Workers do not need the experts' technical analysis of capitalism to engage in struggles against their employers. Economic theory is needed only to show how exploitation is compatible with the fact that the wage bargain is, in some sense, an equitable one.

But what if Marx's economics turns out to be less well-founded than he believed it to be? If exploitation is not directly experienced, the claim that workers are exploited also loses its foundation. According to my interpretation, on the other hand, we can still maintain that exploitation is pervasive, even if we distance ourselves from some of Marx's technical economic claims. I shall discuss this issue in more detail in Chapter 11.

Exploitation and Coercion

Capitalists responded to the passage of the Factory Acts by intensifying the pace of work. Once workers began working fewer hours, they had to work faster and service more machines than before (CI, T 407). With the increased use of machinery, less physical strength was required; hence women and children were recruited into the factories because they could be paid less than male workers (CI, T 404). In all of these ways, employers tried to get the workers to produce a few more products per day without raising wages. Marx sums up these and similar observations about working conditions in England in the first half of the nineteenth century:

> The determination of what is a working day presents itself as the result of a struggle, a struggle between collective capital, i.e., the class of capitalists, and collective labor, i.e., the working class.[6]

The same was true of the agreements reached about working conditions, pay, or the intensity of work. The relations between workers and their employers were a constant struggle in which the workers tried to lessen their burdens and improve their pay and the employers sought to get more work from their employees for lower wages. The victory in the struggle went to the more powerful. Workers were exploited because their employers had more power. This superior power enabled them to force the workers to accept conditions they did not want. In other words, workers accepted wage offers under coercion.

Of course, the employers do not have *all* the power; sometimes the workers win a strike and get the wages and working conditions they have fought for. But as a class, they remain the underdogs. As we shall see in Chapter 17, the capitalists have control over the state, and, with it, coercive power over the police and army. The capitalists control the economy, the jobs, and the distribution and reinvestment of the national surplus. The society is created in their image; the overwhelming share of power is theirs. Even if individual groups of workers have more power than their employers, the class of employers has more power than the class of workers.

But is the labor contract not freely entered into? This apparent contradiction in Marx's account of the relations between workers and employers is resolved by considering different senses of the word "free." Yes, workers under capitalism enter freely into a contract with their employers. They are not compelled by law to work, or to work for a particular person, or to work under specified conditions. They are not slave laborers, nor are they serfs. Hence it is perfectly true that the workers have *chosen* their jobs—chosen them freely in the sense that they were not compelled by the threat of violence to accept them.

At the same time, being "free" in the other sense—that is, in the sense of owning little or no property (and certainly no property that they can use to produce their means of subsistence), no land, no substantial savings that they can invest in order to live off the interest, no capital for starting a business of their own—means that they need to work in order to live. They are thus compelled by the very fact of not owning means of production to work under the best conditions they can get. But if all the jobs available are more or less dreadful as they were in Marx's day, then the worker must take one of these dreadful jobs—compelled by economic need (i.e., by the threat of starvation) even if not by the threat of physical violence. But it is clear that, for the workers, the threat of starving if they do not work is not so different from the threat of physical harm that the feudal lords used against the serfs. The final effect in either case is severe physical suffering. Hence the workers, while free in one sense, are truly coerced in another.

It is an interesting reflection on capitalist ways of thinking that we regard threatening someone with a gun or a baseball bat as an illegal act, whereas threatening someone with poverty or unemployment is regarded as a legitimate move in the marketplace. Yet poverty, malnutrition, poor medical care, and lack of education pose as much threat of physical harm as does the threat with gun or club.

But, someone will object, the worker can always take a different job and is to that extent free. The point is well taken, but due to the competitive pressures on the capitalist, who needs to keep costs down in order to keep profits up, the variations between jobs are minor, for every capitalist is under pressure to get as much work from the worker as possible at the lowest possible cost.

In a capitalist society, workers do not own the means of production. Hence (1) they need to work in order to live, and (2) someone else, the capitalist, controls access to the possibility of work. As a consequence the capitalist—to put it rather dramatically—has the power of life and death over the worker, albeit in a less open way than did the feudal lord or the slaveowner. The worker under capitalism is coerced into working.

> Even the most favorable situation for the working class, the *most rapid possible growth of capital*, however much it may improve the material existence of the worker, does not remove the antagonism of his interest and the interests of the bourgeoisie, the interests of the capitalists. Profit and wages remain as before in *inverse proportion*. (WLC, T 211)

In times of an expanding economy, there tends to be a shortage of workers and hence wages go up, hours go down, and working conditions improve. But even under those conditions, the relationship between worker and employer is a coercive one.[7]

We see once more that Marx's claim that workers are exploited by the owners of the means of production can be argued without recourse to his more technical economic concepts, specifically to his theory of value. We do not need that economic theory to show that the relationship between workers and employers in a capitalist society is a thoroughly coercive and therefore antagonistic one, and that one of the constant sources of friction is the ever-repeated attempt by the capitalist to increase profits by getting the worker to perform surplus labor—that is, to perform work that is not paid for. Marx's technical economic theory is needed once we want to calculate how much surplus labor is performed and the size of the profits made. It is also needed, as we saw in the preceding section, to clarify the confusing aspects of exploitation—namely, that workers both strike an equitable bargain with their employers and do work that remains unpaid.[8]

This interpretation would be rejected by many careful readers of Marx. They would disagree with the preceding account of exploitation because they believe that only the first two conditions of exploitation —that workers produce more value than they receive as wages, and that someone else appropriates the difference—are sufficient for exploitation to occur.[9]

This disagreement over the definition of exploitation has important implications for the critique of capitalism. Exploitation is clearly regarded as objectionable by Marx and Engels. (We shall discuss some of their reasons for that in the following section.) If we define exploitation as the fact that workers produce surplus value or do surplus labor, then capitalism is open to criticism because a part of what workers produce is appropriated by the capitalists. By implication, then, a better society would give to the worker the whole product of his or her labor. But that was not Marx's view:

> Surplus labor in general . . . must always remain. . . . A definite quantity of surplus labor is required as insurance against accidents and by the necessary and progressive expansion of the process of reproduction [of social wealth]. (CIII, T 440)

All societies require surplus labor to store up food and so on for a bad year, expanding populations, or a rising standard of living. Elsewhere, Marx also points out that the producers cannot get all they produce for their own use because someone has to pay for common goods and services, such as roads, hospitals, and schools (CGP, T 528–529). According to Marx, therefore, capitalism is objectionable not because workers do not receive the full product of their work, but because some of what they produce goes to others *whether the workers want them to have it or not.* Marx objects to exploitation because that appropriation is coercive. But capitalism is clearly not completely reprehensible. Its contribution to human welfare and liberation is the fantastic development of human powers of production. "Development of the productive forces of social labor is the historical task and *justification* of capital."[10] But what makes that development of productive forces possible is nothing other than the performance of surplus labor, for it provides the capital for investment in more and more productive machines and forms of organizing the labor process. This is not to say that there is nothing wrong with capitalism—there obviously is for Marx and Engels—or that we may not object to exploitation. The point is simply that the performance of surplus labor and the expropriation of surplus value are objectionable only because they are coerced. In a future society that coercion will be eliminated.

> [Capitalism] gives rise to a stage . . . in which coercion and monopolization of social development (including its material and intellectual advantages) by one portion of society at the expense of the other are eliminated. (CIII, T 440)

Surplus labor will continue to exist in a socialist society, but the product of that labor will not be privately owned by a privileged class; instead, it will be controlled by all. Moreover, the reinvestment or consumption of the social surplus will be decided democratically.

What Is Wrong with Exploitation?

Exploitation does not rest on fraud. Hence one cannot condemn the exploitation of workers for being dishonest.[11] One is thus led to criticize exploitation because it is coercive. But that criticism must be examined more closely. Coercion is not to be condemned in all cases. We force children to be careful when they are in danger; we use force on irrational adults in order to protect them as well as others. The law employs coercion to enforce contracts. Some commentators have thought that the coercion used by employers in the workplace is of that sort.[12] The law might also be used to enforce an obligation to work for all citizens in conditions where such a requirement was democratically adopted by all citizens.

> Marx argues explicitly that exploitation is not illegal: . . . apart from extremely elastic bounds, the nature of the exchange commodities itself imposes no limit to the working day, no limit to surplus labor. The capitalist

maintains his rights as a purchaser when he tries to make the working day as long as possible . . . and the laborer maintains his right as seller when he wishes to reduce the working day. . . . There is here therefore an antinomy of right against right, both equally bearing the seal of the law of exchanges. Between equal rights force decides. Hence it is that in the history of capitalist production the determination of what is a working day presents itself as the result of a struggle.[13]

Contracts between labor and employer leave a lot of details unspecified. Hence each party is justified, according to the *legalities* of contracts, to struggle to obtain as favorable an interpretation of the contract as possible. To the extent that employers have the upper hand because they have greater economic power, they can forcibly impose their conditions on the worker. They can coerce him to work more than he wants for less money than he wants and under less favorable conditions than he wants. In this course of action, the employers are *legally* justified. Exploitation is not illegal. It does not violate "rights of property."[14] Given the accuracy of Marx's dictum that the "ideas of the ruling class are in every epoch the ruling ideas" (GI, T 172), we could hardly expect exploitation to be illegal.

However legal it may be, exploitation is nevertheless not justified. Exploitation cannot be justified as a case of protecting society or protecting workers against themselves, or as an exercise of parental power. Nor is exploitation just a matter of using one's power to enforce a contract. The intensity of the working day, for instance, is not specified in the labor contract. Increasing the worker's output, therefore, is not just a simple matter of enforcing a contract; rather, it is a case of getting the most out of a worker in a respect that the labor contract did not specify.

Exploitation, insofar as it is coercive, is thus open to objections. To begin with, the coercion of an employee by an employer does not seem to be one of the familiar kinds of coercion that we are willing, however reluctantly, to accept as necessary in civilized society. Nor is the performance of surplus labor in a capitalist society decided by majority vote. We vote for representatives who vote for taxes and thus, indirectly, commit ourselves to work a sizeable amount of time to pay for common goods. But we do not vote on the right of corporations to extract surplus value from their workers. Even less do we vote on the disposal of the profits of corporations. The fact that means of production are privately owned implies that the profits of the corporations are also private property and, though produced by all, are to be reinvested by their owners as they see fit. They are not subject to collective, democratic control.

But is there not also something unfair about this distribution of products? It is difficult to put aside the feeling that capitalist societies, even the most affluent ones, misapportion their product, given that many people remain in poverty and near poverty while some have more than they could possibly know what to do with. It is clearly a scandal that there still are large numbers of people in the United States, for instance, who are malnourished, in poor health, ill housed, and undereducated. This maldistribution of resources is connected with exploitation. Because surplus value is appropriated by the capitalists, they use it in ways that are good for capital:

> Capital does not consist in accumulated labor serving living labor as a means for new production. It consists in living labor serving accumulated labor as a means of maintaining and multiplying the exchange value of the latter. (WLC, T 205)

Under capitalism, then, capital ("accumulated labor") is not available to produce what people ("living labor") decide they need. Because capital is privately owned, the people at large have no say over what gets produced. The capitalists are under pressure from their competitors to keep their capitals growing—the pressure "of maintaining and multiplying the exchange value" of capital. They must produce what is profitable, not what people need and want. Thus the misappropriation of national wealth is a consequence of the power relations that underlie exploitation.

Exploitation exists under capitalism, as it did under feudalism. But capitalism conceals what was out in the open for everyone to see under feudalism. Unlike other modes of production, capitalism misrepresents itself. Marx attaches great importance to that self-mystifying characteristic of capitalism. We shall investigate it in the next chapter.

Notes

1. Marx, *Capital*, Vol. III (New York: International Publishers, 1967), pp. 600–601.

2. For an interesting critique of this standard interpretation of Marx's conception of feudalism, see John E. Martin, *Feudalism to Capitalism* (Atlantic Highlands, N.J.: Humanities Press, 1983).

3. Maurice Godelier, "Structure, Contradiction in *Capital*" in Ralph Miliband and John Saville, eds., *Socialist Register 1976* (London: Merlin Press, 1968).

4. Marx, *Capital*, Vol. I, pp. 641–642.

5. Ibid., p. 299.

6. Ibid., p. 235.

7. Another question is whether workers are coerced to remain workers rather than, say, going into business for themselves. On that question, see G. A. Cohen,

"The Structure of Proletarian Unfreedom," in John Roemer, ed., *Analytical Marxism* (Cambridge: Cambridge University Press, 1986), pp. 237–259.

8. Meghnad Desai, *Marxian Economic Theory* (London: Gray-Mills Publishing, 1974), p. 14.

9. See, for example, John Roemer, "New Directions in the Marxian Theory of Exploitation and Class," *Politics and Society* 11 (1982):253–287. On the other hand, Allen E. Buchanan, in *Marx and Justice* (Totowa, N.J.: Rowman and Allanheld, 1982), Chapter 3, finds a more comprehensive sense of "exploitation" in the writings of Marx.

10. Marx, *Capital*, Vol III, p. 259. Italics mine.

11. For an interesting argument that exploitation is not unjust, see Allen W. Wood, "The Marxian Critique of Justice," in Marshall Cohen et al., eds., *Marx, Justice, History* (Princeton, N.J.: Princeton University Press, 1980). For a useful development and critique of Wood's paper, see Nancy Holmstrom, "Exploitation," *Canadian Journal of Philosophy* 7, no. 2 (1977).

12. Jon Elster, *Making Sense of Marx* (Cambridge: Cambridge University Press, 1985), p. 199.

13. Marx, *Capital*, Vol. I, pp. 234–235.

14. Ibid., p. 585.

For Further Reading

Robert Paul Wolff, *Understanding Marx* (Princeton, N.J.: Princeton University Press, 1984), Chapter 4.

9

The Fetishism of Commodities

IN CHAPTER 7 we saw that there is capitalism only where there is a sizable force of people who live exclusively by doing wage labor. Capitalist society is therefore a commodity society in which every kind of thing is produced in order to be sold and whatever kind of thing anyone might want can be purchased. In such a society, which is called a "market society," every kind of thing has a price and all kinds of transactions are, at bottom, exchange transactions. Any particular kind of thing, such as childcare or sexual love, may be a commodity in some instances and not in others.

In Chapter 8, we got a very different view of capitalist society. Here we looked at the relationship between worker and employer. From one perspective, that relationship, too, is an exchange relation, but we saw that the exchange takes place against the background of very unequal power. Whereas in the labor market employer and employee exchange equivalents, in the workplace, during the actual process of production, the worker is exploited because the employer has superior economic power and hence can compel the worker to do surplus labor. What is more, even the equal exchange in the labor market is forced on the employee by the superior power of the employer class.

One could evade this apparent contradiction by denying that exploitation exists. Economically speaking, one might say that capitalist society is a market society, and that is all it is. But in light of the history of a capitalism that was, as we have seen, consistently coercive, as well as in light of the continuing struggle in the workplace where the employer tries to increase profits by getting more work from the workers without paying more, this claim is very implausible.

There exists a more sophisticated bourgeois response to Marx's observation that relations in capitalist society appear to be both exploitative and commodity oriented—both power relations and relations of exchange. Proponents of this view recognize the existing power differences between classes but, unlike Marx, assert that these differences are not *economically* significant. The economist deals exclusively with exchange transactions in the marketplace. Power relations are studied by the political scientist and perhaps the sociologist. Both are separate topics to be investigated by separate disciplines. This separation between the concerns of the political scientist and the economist was, and still is, very popular. Marx, however, insists that the contradiction between commodity and power relations is integral to the capitalist economy; if it is not understood, he claims, the workings of the capitalist economy remain unintelligible. He argues for this view in his discussion of the "Fetishism of Commodities" which he introduced in Volume I of *Capital* (Chapter 1, section 4).

Fetishism and Commodities

Marx begins this part of *Capital* by describing a commodity as

at first sight, a trivial thing. Its analysis shows that it is, in reality, a very queer thing, abounding in metaphysical subtleties and theological niceties. (CI, T 319)

But what makes commodities so peculiar? Marx goes on for a whole page saying that commodities are "mystical" and "enigmatical" before telling us that

a commodity is therefore a mysterious thing simply because in it the *social* character of men's labors appears to be as an objective character stamped upon the product of that labor. (CI, T 320; italics added)

But that explanation of the mysterious nature of commodities needs explaining too.

Human beings work and produce in a specific social order. They work always in coordination with one another. In all societies, even the most primitive ones, there is some sort of division of labor. The goods produced and their distribution—who gets what and in what quantities—reflect the social order in which they are produced. But in a commodity society (i.e., under capitalism), it seems that what is produced, and by whom, and how it is distributed are not the results of the social order as a whole but, rather, depend exclusively on the prices of commodities. In a capitalist economy, capital is privately owned and the competent capitalist will make it grow by making a profit. Capital must therefore be invested where it will be profitable, and such decisions determine what will be produced. The profitability of certain goods, compared to that of others, decides what a society will produce. Profitability, in turn, is connected with the prices at which something can be sold, compared to the costs of producing it. The decision made in a society as to what will be produced is closely tied to prices.

Commodities have intrinsic characteristics. Often these are physical properties such as size, weight, and color but some are nonmaterial properties such as usefulness and efficiency. Prices appear to be intrinsic characteristics. They are not set by particular people but come with the commodity, as one of its characteristics. When a consumer goes to the store to buy something, the commodity has a price. The careful consumer soon finds out that different stores do not charge the same price. But these price variations are not the results of arbitrary decisions by storeowners; rather, the prices are set in accordance with economic necessities, such as the storeowners' costs and the need to make a profit. Prices are determined by market forces. The storeowners merely try to read those market forces as accurately as possible.

Prices determine what is produced, but they also determine the distribution of goods to different people. A person sells his or her ability to work, and the price that ability fetches in a labor market determines what share of the society's product s/he will be able to acquire. The price of a person's ability to work, together with the price of the capital owned or controlled by that person, thus also determines how much power s/he has. The rich are powerful, the poor are not. The owners of oil refineries are rich and powerful, but the person who tells many fine traditional Appalachian folktales, all carefully committed to memory, is likely to be neither rich nor powerful. The relations among persons in society are determined by the prices of commodities, among which capital and labor power are the most important. But what is so remarkable about that?

> The relation of the producers to the sum total of their own labor is presented to them as a social relation, existing not between themselves but between the products of their labor. (CI, T 320)

The relations between people—the questions of who is rich and who is poor and how they relate to each other and, similarly, who has power and who not and how the powerful exercise that power over the weak— are in a capitalist society presented as relations among things. The capitalist world thus appears topsy-turvy because things, which human beings create, seem to determine the relations of human beings in the course of production. The social world of human beings seems to be ordered by commodities, which, after all, are no more than the products of human beings. Marx first approaches this problem by using an analogy from natural science:

> In the same way, the light from an object is perceived by us not as the subjective excitation of the optic nerve, but as the objective form of something outside the eye itself. (T 321)

The world of naive observation is full of incomprehensible facts. We see light, for instance, from a candle, but we also see physical objects. The light enters through the eye and is then perceived. But the table or other physical objects are perceived without entering our eye. We can begin to explain vision once we understand that objects reflect light and, hence, that seeing is a matter of receiving light rays on the retina even when we appear to be seeing an object in space. Our scientific knowledge reconstructs naively observed reality to make it more intelligible, but that does not change what we observe in everyday life.

In a similar way,

> after the discovery, by science, of the component gases of air, the atmosphere itself remained unaltered. (T 323)

We *know* that we breathe a number of gases, but that does not affect the *perceived* reality of the air we breathe. Without that knowledge, however, there is much about the perceived world that we cannot understand. We know that what strikes the retina is reflected light, but that does not affect what we see. There is thus a perceived reality on the one hand and then the reality as reconstructed by science on the other. The former is not illusory in the sense of something to be discarded because science explains that perceived reality, taking it to be real. But it is not fully intelligible unless it is linked to reality reconstructed by science. Thus, there is both a *surface reality* and a *deep reality*.

Neither the surface nor the deep reality that natural science deals with is created by human activity. In the realm of economics, of the production and exchange of commodities, the surface reality appears, in analogous ways, to be governed by markets and the interrelations among commodities. But this market system presupposes the existence of capital, and capital, as we saw in Chapter 7, presupposes the existence of two classes—the owners of the means of production and the workers. Workers are exploited, as we saw in Chapter 8. Accordingly, an explanation of the functioning of the capitalist society requires an understanding both of the market and of the exploitation of workers. If one wants to understand capitalism, one needs to understand how equals exchange for equals in the market, including the labor market, and how that exchange is, in the labor market, a coercive one.

The regularities of the market appear, like regularities in nature, independent of human activity. Prices, for instance, are not really set by buyers and sellers but are determined by the impersonal forces of supply and demand. But the market mechanism *as a whole* is not a natural phenomenon, such as gravity, that exists independent of human activity and choice. On the contrary, the existence of a market system is on the one hand maintained by human activities, and on the other hand constantly contested. The existence of a market in labor is fought over in the workplace, and in labor's attempts to limit the ravages of a free labor market through legislation (e.g., through laws limiting the length of the working day). The application of market forces in other areas of human life is resisted by different groups. Opponents of prostitution want to keep sexual love from being a commodity; proponents of the traditional family object to childcare becoming something to be bought and sold in a market. Various experiments at rent control try to take housing out of the marketplace; government subsidies for different groups put a limitation on market forces.

Human activities and relations seem to be governed by these market forces. But the essence of the deep reality that Marx uncovers is that the commodity society, which appears to function unregulatedly, following autonomous laws, is created and constantly re-created by the actions of human beings. Hence the central metaphor used by Marx is the "fetish"—a metaphor he draws from religion, where

the productions of the human brain appear as independent beings endowed with life, and entering into relation both with one another and the human race. (T 321)

Fetishes are objects of religious worship, made by human beings, that are endowed by their human creators with supernatural powers. But the human beings sometimes forget that the powers they revere in their fetish were, in the first place, bestowed by them. Similarly, the relation between the surface and deep realities of any given society are fetishistic because "human beings make their own history." Nature is independent of human thinking in a way that social relations are not. We create and re-create social relations by acting within them.

The fetishism of commodities thus refers to the fact that the commodities present themselves as a complete reality but are, in fact, not fully understandable unless we uncover a deep reality that explains, though it does not alter, the surface reality of the commodity society. The deep reality that bourgeois economics, even at its best, leaves out of consideration is the historical nature of commodity production. Once we see capitalism as a historical creation arising from the intentional actions of human beings, commodities lose their "mystical" character:

> The whole mystery of commodities . . . vanishes, therefore, so soon as we come to other forms of production. (T 324)

The market is a human creation that, like all human creations, is transitory and historical. The fetishism of commodities conceals the historical nature of capitalism and the need for studying it historically.

Once we study societies historically, we see that every society has the same task. Speaking very generally,

> in all states of society, the labor time that it costs to produce the means of subsistence must necessarily be an object of interest to mankind. (CI, T 320)

Time is always limited. There are always alternative ways of apportioning time, and different societies choose different ones. But societies differ also in the ways in which that choice is made. Most societies make that choice openly. In feudal Europe, the serf worked so many days a week for his lord. The total working time available to the society was thus apportioned in such a way that half the week, say, was used to produce the necessities for the majority of people, and the other half was used to produce necessities and luxuries for a small minority, the nobility. A patriarchal family apportions its time openly also—in that setting everyone has his or her job—but perhaps on the basis of different principles. A "community of free individuals" apportions time in a still different way. Here people get together and decide collectively what they will produce and who will do and get what (CI, T 324–326). In the past, decision making was in the open, but the decisions were made in favor of the persons who had the most power. Under capitalism, social labor time may seem to be apportioned by impartial mechanisms of exchange, but the reality is that a discrepancy of power—economic power in this case—underlies capitalist society. Class struggle is not accidental to capitalist society; it is its very essence. The apparent discrepancy between the class struggle and the exchange society is resolved only when we see capitalist society also as a human creation for the purposes of apportioning labor power in favor of the few at the expense of the many. But we can understand that only if we differentiate the surface from the deep reality of capitalism. The many pages that Marx devotes in *Capital* to a description of working conditions in the England of his day are intended not merely to arouse opposition to capitalism but also to document the pervasiveness of struggle.

We can understand now why Marx believed that we may not limit our study of the economy to a study of markets and leave the discussion of power relations, and the coercion that is endemic in capitalist economic life, to different disciplines. If we truly want to understand our social world, we must study the surface reality of the market in light of the deep reality—the system of social relations created and re-created daily by human beings. We shall return to this topic briefly in the third section of this chapter.

Fetishism and Human Nature

All societies are networks of social relations, but the relations in a capitalist society are different from those in other societies. In a capitalist society human beings, therefore, have characteristics they do not have in other societies. For instance,

> the capitalist epoch is therefore characterized by this, that labor power takes, in the eyes of the laborer himself, the form of a commodity which is his property.[1]

For labor power to be a commodity, workers must think of their own ability to work in that way; they must have certain specific beliefs, but they must also *act* in very specific ways: The medieval artisan possessed specific skills not in the sense of property that he could sell piecemeal but in the sense that his identity as a person consisted of his being a skillful person. As a craftsman he deserved a certain status and respect. He could do very specific things, such as make a certain kind of shoe, and did that well. But that was all that he could do. The modern industrial worker does more or less unskilled work. He hires himself out to anybody who pays well. He sells his time but not himself. His ability to work is quite separate from his person. It is very general. He will do a wide range of jobs as long as they pay. Marx repeats that over and over again: Under capitalism, labor becomes "abstract":

> This abstraction of labor is not merely the mental product of a totality of laborers. Indifference towards specific labors corresponds to a form of society in which individuals can with ease transfer from one labor to another, and where the specific kind is a matter of chance for them, hence

of indifference. . . . Labor itself . . . has ceased to be organically linked with specific individuals in any specific forms. (G, T 240–241)

Labor is abstract, not just in thought but as it is actually done. Because people are no longer identified by the particular work they do—an identification to which we still owe many of our family names, such as Smith, Brewer, Cooper, Taylor—but will do whatever they can get paid for, their relationship to their work is much more distant. What they do is "a matter of . . . indifference" to them; it is "just a job," as we say. To a considerable extent, this phenomenon is the result of mechanization, which in turn is one of the products of capitalism. The worker's relation to a machine is very different from that of the artisan to his tool. Hence not only work but also the worker are now very different.

Not as with the instrument, which the worker animates and makes into his organ with his skill and strength, and whose handling therefore depends on his virtuosity. Rather it is the machine which possesses skill and strength in place of the worker, is itself the virtuoso. . . . The worker's activity, reduced to a mere abstraction of activity, is determined and regulated on all sides by the movement of the machinery, and not the opposite. (G, T 279)

Work is emptied of skill, hence of interest. It becomes a commodity because it is done merely in exchange for money. It loses all intrinsic attraction. Work, and the worker, become alienated. One aspect of capitalism is that labor becomes abstract. The consequences of these transformations for the meaning of being human are obvious.

But capitalism also manifests itself in the transformation of things. We saw much earlier that machines, tools, and so on, are not capital, except under very specific social relations—namely, where there is free labor available. Thus tools that used to belong to a craftsman by virtue of that person's skill now become commodities that anyone can buy, whether they can handle them or not. Land, which was sacred to some people, is now an object of speculation. People own land and houses that they have never seen and have no intention of ever living in. Art that was created for, say, a religious purpose can now become an investment. Trees that were sacred or the dwellings of woodnymphs are now only potential lumber or obstacles in the way of a bulldozer. Thus the relations that human beings have to things, both human products and natural objects, are quite different in the commodity society from what they were in other societies.

Private property has made us so stupid and one-sided that an object is *ours* only when we have it—when it exists for us as capital, or when it is directly possessed, eaten, drunk, worn, inhabited, etc.—in short, when it is used by us. (EPM, T 87)

Human nature is certain to be affected by this very different environment.

Nor are relations between persons unaffected by the commodity society. Human relations become predominantly commercial transactions. One person performs a service; the other pays for it. In the *Communist Manifesto*, Marx and Engels extend that commercial character to marriage:

On what foundation is the present family, the bourgeois family based? On capital, on private gain. (CM, T 487)

Marriage is a commercial transaction like any other—a view that is reflected in the traditional notion that the man is the breadwinner and supports the woman who, *in return*, must stay home and take care of the children. It is not for nothing that we talk about "marriage contracts." Commercial thinking and language have influenced even our thinking about the most personal and emotional relations between people. We think about them in terms of exchanges, of "who does what for whom."

In this way, once again, capitalism shapes not only our world but inevitably, what sorts of persons we are. The way we go about loving other people cannot help but affect who we are.

Not only do our relations to ourselves, to others, and to things increasingly approximate commercial relations but, as a consequence, our conduct begins to obey the impersonal laws of the economy more and more and thus becomes less and less the conduct of free individuals. In treating ourselves and others as if we were exchanging things, we get to be more like things. The circulation of commodities in the society obeys the impersonal laws of economics. They cannot be affected by the wishes or actions of any particular person. To the extent that I become a commodity, inasmuch as I work or exist in relation to other people, my behavior, too, becomes governed by the impersonal laws of the market. It is here that the fetishism of commodities arises: The members of the society begin to consider themselves the pawns in an impersonal game directed by commodities. Market forces and the laws that govern them are the sources of human destiny. Human freedom is reduced to getting what one wants within the limits of this system of commercial transactions. What moves more and more into the background is the fact that this market has been created by human beings over a long time, and thus what seems to regulate our lives can be changed by us because we re-create it daily as we operate in it. The freedom to create one's world knowingly and intentionally—to "make the species one's object," as Marx said early on—is replaced by the freedom to operate rationally in the marketplace, to buy cheap and sell dear. (I shall discuss the opposition between capitalism and freedom in more detail in Chapter 15.)

Marx discusses the fetishism of commodities in order to argue that exploitation, clearly a power relation between persons, is as important to an understanding of economics as are the laws governing prices and the distribution of goods. But an even deeper motivation is his concern with human freedom. Human beings have the capacity to direct their lives rationally, on the basis of explicit thought and the best available information. Human beings are truly free only to the extent that they run their affairs consciously and intentionally, to the extent that that is possible. Capitalism leaves many potential human decisions to impersonal forces and, what is worse, tends to conceal the fact that we could run our economy, and hence our entire society, with much more foresight and deliberation than we do. Capitalism therefore degrades the meaning of human freedom, which becomes a matter of getting as much as one can for oneself, subject only to economic and social forces over which one has no control.

In this interpretation, fetishism is one effect of the capitalist system that leaves the running of the society, in large part, to the impersonal forces of the market. It is therefore intimately connected with alienation, abstract labor, and the denial of human freedom. As a consequence, some interpreters identify alienation and fetishism.[2] Alienation is discussed in more detail in Chapter 15.

Fetishism and Economics

According to Marx, the fact that modern economics first developed in the period of the rise of capitalism was no accident. It had not been possible to formulate such quantitative laws beforehand, because economic behavior was not governed by quantitative laws previous to the advent of commodity exchange.

> Political economy, which as an independent science, first sprang into being during the period of manufacture [i.e., the very earliest capitalist period], views the social division of labor only . . . [as] . . . the means of producing more commodities with a given quantity of labor, and consequently, of cheapening commodities and hurrying on the accumulation of capital. In most striking contrast with this accentuation of quantity and exchange value is the attitude of the writers of classical antiquity, who hold exclusively by quality and use-value. (CI, T 401)

A quantitative science of economics becomes possible only under capitalism. But at the same time, it becomes a requirement:

The correct observation and deduction of these laws, as having themselves become in history [having themselves undergone the process of becoming described earlier], always leads to primary equations—like the empirical numbers, e.g., in natural science. (G, T 252)

Once empirical, quantitative science becomes possible, it becomes also what is needed; and Marx, no less than any other economist, strove to develop a quantitative science of economics.

But the fetishism of commodities threatens to distort this effort. Quantitative laws—equations—are derived from a set of assumptions and definitions. What is going to validate those assumptions and definitions? It is widely held among economists, in practice if not in theory, that a model that allows us to provide a plausible analysis of economic relations is thereby validated. If the equations prove useful, the assumptions and definitions that underlie them are regarded as acceptable. Conversely, if the assumptions yield equations that are not acceptable, then the assumptions must also be rejected.

Following that strategy, many economists reject Marx's concept of exploitation because they have managed to formulate useful equations that do not use such a concept.

Marx found a good deal of bourgeois economics to be acceptable.

The categories of bourgeois economics . . . are forms of thought expressing *with social validity* the conditions and relations of a definite historically determined mode of production, viz. the production of commodities. (T 324; italics added)

But being useful in certain economic calculations and predictions is not enough. By denying that there is exploitation at all, or that it is of any concern to the economist, bourgeois economics provides a one-sided view of our social reality; it becomes ideological.

The discussion of exploitation in Chapter 8 showed that the observed (i.e., surface) reality of capitalist society is incoherent. On the one hand, workers are free agents in the labor market, but on the other, employers coerce workers. Under the sway of fetishism, bourgeois social science tends to try to remove that contradiction by extending the market metaphor to all areas of social life. Politics is described as "bargaining," ideas are "sold," relations are a matter of "give and take," works of art are "consumed," entertainment is an "industry," and what matters in the end is the "bottom line." The tendency is to describe all aspects of human life as market relations. But this description conceals the central importance of power relations. More important, it conceals the fact that this ubiquity of market relations is a *matter of human choice.* The capitalist market is a historical, human creation. Any social science that obscures that fact is inadequate.

With this, Marx committed himself to the development of a quantitative economic analysis in which the fact of exploitation is a central concept. We shall see how he went about that in the next chapter.

Notes

1. Marx, *Capital,* Vol. I (New York: International Publishers, 1967), p. 170, n. 1.

2. Lucio Coletti, "Bernstein and the Marxism of the Second International," in *From Rousseau to Lenin* (New York: Monthly Review Press, 1974), pp. 82ff.

For Further Reading

Shlomo Avineri, *The Social and Political Thought of Karl Marx* (Cambridge: Cambridge University Press, 1970), Chapter 4.

10

The Labor Theory of Value

THE CENTERPIECE OF Marx's economics is the Labor Theory of Value. Marx did not invent this theory. It was the prevailing theory when he began to study economics. Early on he rejected the Labor Theory because he thought that it obscured the existence of exploitation. He began to take it more seriously when he saw that the opposite was true.[1] Subsequently, he adopted and improved it in order to account for exploitation and to measure its extent.

Terminology

Marx begins his major economic work, *Capital*, with a discussion of commodities. Commodities are goods and services produced in order to be sold. Marx distinguishes a number of aspects at the very beginning: Commodities have "use value," "exchange value," "value," and, finally, a "price." Let us begin with this last concept.

Prices determine what one pays for commodities when one buys, or what one receives when one sells. Prices fluctuate depending on supply and demand (WLC, T 206). Suppose you sell 1 pound bags of coffee. If you have ten bags to sell and twelve people want to buy a pound apiece, demand exceeds supply and you will raise your price. If you have more bags than people want to buy, you lower your price in the hope of attracting additional buyers. When supply equals demand, coffee sells at its so-called "equilibrium price."

What your coffee sells for can be expressed in money terms as its price—say, $6.00 per pound (or 3 yen, etc.). But it can also be expressed in terms of the quantities of other commodities for which it could be exchanged. One pound of coffee may thus be equal to 24 candy bars or 1 and 1/5 movie ticket. The ratio in which one commodity exchanges against other commodities Marx calls the "exchange value."

What is the relation between exchange value and price? Early on Marx formulates that relation as follows: Equilibrium price is the expression, in money terms (i.e., in dollars or yen), of the exchange value of commodities (WLC, T 208). We shall see in the next section, however, that the relation between prices and values is more complex.

Now we can ask: why is the exchange value of coffee 24 candy bars rather than 240 or 24 million candy bars? (Or why is the equilibrium price just where it is?) Marx answers: Because this coffee has a certain "value" (CI, T 305). The ratio at which commodities exchange (i.e., their exchange value) is determined by the *value* of each. Saying that, of course, only introduces Marx's terminology; it does not answer the substantive question of what determines the value of a commodity. We will address this question in a moment. But first we need to discuss the first term, "use value."

A commodity will not sell unless someone has a use for it. A commodity that no one wants will not sell and therefore has no value (CI, T 308). What use a commodity has depends on different people's needs and desires and on the physical properties of the commodity. People walking rough terrain may want shoes, but not shoes made of thin paper. The physical properties of the commodity make it usable in certain ways and thus, as Marx says, "limit" its use value (CI, T 303).

What Determines Value?

Marx, following the economic orthodoxy of his day, argued that "the value of a commodity is determined by the quantity of labor expended" (CI, T 351) in producing it. What a commodity is worth depends on how much work is involved in producing it.

This general thesis requires qualification, however.

1. The value of a commodity depends on the productivity of labor. Some people are more productive than others. Suppose one man takes five hours to make a pair of shoes, while his daughter takes only three to make an identical pair. She can therefore sell her shoes for less than her father can sell his. But in actuality, their products will sell for the same price, because no buyers would be willing to pay the higher price if he or she could get the same shoes at the lower price. The shoes that it takes five hours to make will therefore sell for no more than the identical shoes made in three. Only the labor that is necessary, given skillful workers and state-of-the-art production techniques, go into the makeup of the commodity's value.

The introduction of the powerloom into England probably reduced by one-half the labor required to weave a given quantity of yarn into cloth. The handweavers, as a matter of fact, required the same time as before; but for all that, the product of one hour of their labor represented after the change only half one hour's social labor, and consequently fell to one-half its former value. (CI, T 306)

Socially necessary labor time determines the value of commodities. Put abstractly, this amounts to saying that the value of commodities varies with the productivity of labor:

The value of a commodity would, therefore, remain constant if the labor time required for its production also remained constant. But the latter changes with every change in the productiveness of labor. (CI, T 307)

2. But what are equal quantities of labor? Marx's example of exchange value is "one coat is worth 20 yds. of linen." But how can one equate the tailoring that produces the coat with the spinning that produces the linen thread? Is the comparison of quantities of tailoring with quantities of spinning akin to comparing apples to oranges? After all "tailoring and weaving are, qualitatively, different kinds of labor" (CI, T 310).

In order to answer that question, Marx draws a distinction between skilled and simple labor. Tailoring, spinning, and weaving are skilled labor. They are very specific ways of expending "human brains, nerves and muscles" (CI, T 310). But there also exists an expenditure of human energy that is not specific, one that "remains the same under all its modifications" (ibid.)—namely, simple or unskilled labor. Skilled and simple labor are not different ways of looking at work but are different *kinds* of work. In a capitalist society there is a constant tendency to reduce "different sorts of labor . . . to unskilled labor" (CI, T 311).

There are two tendencies at work here. First, new technologies tend to make work less complicated and less skilled. Capitalists have an interest in introducing such technologies because by reducing their costs they also increase the potential for profits. Hence capitalists tend, in general, to introduce new technologies that call for less skilled labor. Second, as labor is a commodity exchanged in a labor market, different levels of skill tend to be regarded as "multiplied simple labor" (CI, T 310). The quantity of skilled labor is measured as multiples of the quantity of simple labor. Skilled and unskilled labor thus become comparable. It is easy to see that both tendencies are aspects of a competitive market society.

This point is important not only for technical reasons but also to bring out, once more, the historical nature of capitalism. The general thesis that the value of a commodity is determined by the value of the labor power required to produce it is ambiguous. "Labor" is always "social labor"—labor in a specific society. It therefore has different meanings in different societies. The skilled labor of the medieval craftsman is a different kind of labor from that of the unskilled industrial factory worker. Hence "value" also has a different meaning, for only in the capitalist society does it take the form of exchange value.

> The labor time expressed in exchange value is the labor time of an individual in no way different from the next individual . . . insofar as they perform equal labor. . . . On the other hand, under the rural patriarchal system, when spinner and weaver lived under the same roof—the women of the family spinning and the men weaving . . . [the] social character [of labor] did not appear in the form of yarn becoming a universal equivalent exchanged for linen as a universal equivalent.[2]

In short, value becomes exchange value only where labor is reducible to simple labor, but that happens only in a capitalist economy.

What Determines Wages?

Marx, along with a number of his contemporaries, saw this difficulty in the Labor Theory: To be told that the value of commodities is determined by the value of the labor power expended in producing those commodities is not helpful. It merely explains that the price of a commodity, when it is neither overpriced nor undervalued, is determined by the wages of the people producing it. But what determines those wages? That question still needs an answer.

Marx distinguishes between "labor" and "labor power." *Labor* is not a commodity; it has use value but no exchange value. *Labor power* is a commodity and has value. It is measured in time. The worker sells his or her ability to work (i.e., so much labor time) to an employer, and that means that he or she will be at the employer's disposal for the period sold. During that time the worker works ("labors") and puts out energy. In the same period, some workers work very hard and others do no work at all. The amount of work put out in a given period of time varies enormously, depending on the state of the class struggle between workers and employers, and all kinds of other factors. The employer, as we saw in Chapter 8, wants to get as much work out of the worker as possible in the period agreed on between them. The worker resists.

This distinction paves the way for an answer to our question: Labor power is a commodity. Its value, like that of all other commodities, depends on how much labor is required to produce it. Thus the value of labor power depends on the labor cost of the goods needed to reproduce labor power. The wage of workers is thus, minimally, what it takes to enable a man or woman who works today to come back to work tomorrow. It also includes the cost of training and education, as well as the cost of producing a new generation of workers when the present one is too old to work. We can find out easily enough what the current average standard of living of workers is. We can express it in terms of the goods consumed by them: food, shelter, clothing, and so on, for themselves and their families. We can then find out how much time it takes to produce that market basket of goods and thus determine the value of labor power (CI, T 339ff.).

The value of labor power is influenced by biological facts about human beings—what it takes to keep a person sufficiently healthy to work for a number of years and what it takes to replace existing workers with new ones—but it is also affected by social conceptions of a decent standard of living. The standard of living varies over time and, with it, varies the conception of what a "decent" standard of living is.

The social norms governing what constitutes a decent standard of living are affected significantly by continuing struggles between workers and their employers. As a consequence of exploitation, there is a constant battle over how much effort workers will expend that they do not get paid for. These struggles occur in the workplace but also in the political arena. Labor gets legislation passed, such as laws to limit the working day or to improve wages and working conditions. This legislation tends to raise the standard of living and with it the value of a given period of labor.

Thus the value of labor power is set by economic, social, and political factors that determine the average decent standard of living of workers and thereby the value of an hour, or a day, of work.

The price of labor power, as opposed to its value, is also affected by fluctuations of supply and demand in the labor market. Labor power is not quite a commodity like all others, because it is not produced by industrial methods. The short-term supply of labor in the labor market is not affected by the over- or underproduction of human beings. But capitalists clearly have an interest in increasing the supply of labor, for that tends to depress wages. As they cannot manipulate the production of new human beings, they turn to manipulating the supply of workers looking for work. One important weapon in the struggle to keep wages low and thus to set the value of labor power as low as possible is what Marx calls the "industrial reserve army." As capitalists employ new and bigger machinery, they are able to produce more commodities with fewer workers. The excess workers are fired and thrown upon the labor market to compete with their fellow workers. Similarly, the division of labor increases the productivity of individual workers and thus reduces the number of workers needed:

The greater division of labor enables one worker to do the work of five, ten or twenty; it therefore multiplies competition among the workers. (WLC, T 214)

Therefore,

taking them as a whole, the general movements of wages are exclusively regulated by the expansion and contraction of the industrial reserve army. (WLC, T 426)

How Is Exploitation Possible?

The traditional Labor Theory of Value, entertained by Adam Smith and defended by David Ricardo, seemed to imply that "the exchange value of the working day is equal [to the exchange value] of the product it yields" (CI, T 355). But if that is true, then the exchange value of the working day—and thus, in money terms, its price (the workers' wage)—equals the total output of the worker for that day. But in that case, where does the capitalist's profit come from?

This is a serious problem for the Labor Theory. It is clear that capitalism seeks profit and that a capitalist who fails to make a profit fails as a capitalist. Profit is what is left over after the capitalist has sold the goods produced and has paid wages as well as the costs of raw materials and overhead. But it appears that, according to the Labor Theory, there is no profit left over because the value of the total product is equal to the value of the day's work embodied in it. That value is contained in the cost of the raw materials, machinery, and buildings as well as in the wage of the worker. If the capitalist can recover no more than those costs upon selling the product, then there is no profit. That objection was well known in Marx's day, but different authors drew different conclusions from it. The so-called Ricardian socialists concluded that profits arose only because capitalists paid labor less than it was worth—in other words, that the actual wage, the *price* of labor power, was less than the value of labor. Labor, they concluded, was systematically cheated and underpaid in order to yield some profits for the capitalist. It also followed from this line of reasoning that labor was entitled to everything it produced. "Labor," asserted the slogan of the Ricardian socialists, "is the source of all wealth."

Marx rejected that argument as well as Ricardian socialism and its slogan. We need to assume, he insisted, that in any exchange economy, equivalents exchange for equivalents. To be sure, some people get overcharged, but every time one person gets more than full value, the other party gets less; thus, on the average, equals exchange for equals. The existence of profits cannot be explained by the claim that the workers are systematically underpaid.[3]

If the Labor Theory of Value cannot account for profits, it needs to be discarded—that was the other response to the problem of profits.

But Marx did not accept that response either. Instead, he argued that, while it is true that the value of commodities produced in one day is *determined* by the value of one day's labor power, the two values are *not equal* because the value of the worker's output for that day consists of the value of the raw materials, the labor expended, *plus* the profit. The cost of reproducing the worker's labor power determines the value of one day of work. The value of the day's *output*, however, pays for wages, raw materials, and so on, plus something extra: surplus value. This is a value the employer does not pay for without, however, cheating the worker. The worker produces goods of greater value than are needed to pay for wages, raw materials, and so on. The difference between the costs and the value of the worker's output is surplus value.

> The fact that a half-day's labor is necessary to keep the laborer alive during 24 hours does not in any way prevent him from working a whole day. Therefore the value of labor power and the value which that labor creates in the labor process are two entirely different magnitudes; and that difference of the two values is what the capitalist had in view when he was purchasing the labor power. (CI, T 357)

The wages consist of the value of labor power—that is, of what it costs to enable to the worker to work for, say, one day. If the worker gets that much, she or he is not underpaid. But it does not take a whole day to produce the wages to pay the worker. The rest of the day is used to produce money to pay for raw materials (and so on) *and* to yield a profit.

Thus the value of the commodity produced is determined by the cost of the time it takes a worker to make that commodity. But not all the commodities produced are needed to pay the workers' wages and so on. The costs of reproducing the worker's capacity to work, and all the other costs of production, are less than the total value of what a worker produces in the course of one day. The employer sees to that.

Having explained profits in this way, Marx also provided an explanation for exploitation and the capitalist's reason for exploiting workers. If profit arises in the difference between the time the worker works to produce his or her own pay and the total working day, then the capitalist will try constantly to decrease the former and increase the latter. The capitalist will constantly try to increase the amount of time the worker works "without pay," thereby increasing the rate of exploitation. But workers do not willingly work harder or longer hours without additional pay; they have to be coerced into doing that. Exploitation is therefore coercive.

Only a capitalist who is a failure as a capitalist because he or she does not make any profit will fail to exploit workers. Under capitalism, therefore, workers are always exploited. Inasmuch as all value is produced by labor and exploitation consists of extracting value that is not paid for, it follows that only workers can be exploited.

In this way Marx explains the source of profits and the possibility of exploitation. Hence it is therefore not difficult to see why he espoused the Labor Theory of Value[4] and tried to develop it. In the process of trying to do that, however, Marx ran into a great deal of difficulty.

Problems with the Labor Theory of Value

The Connection Between Values and Prices

Market transactions are regulated by prices, whereas socially necessary labor determines the values of commodities. Are prices and values connected in some systematic way, and, if so, what is their connection?

The first volume of Capital appears to provide a very simple answer to this question: The quantity of value in any given commodity is equal to the value of the time it takes to make that commodity, given current techniques of production. As prices fluctuate around value—sometimes they are above value, sometimes below—equilibrium prices are equal to values, as Marx argues in Capital. We saw earlier that Marx seems to hold the same view in Wage Labor and Capital.

Marx argues for this claim as follows: Commodities are exchanged because they are different from one another. No one exchanges identical items. But if they are different, how can we compare them? There must be one quality common to both so that we can ascertain that x quantity of one commodity is equal to y quantity of the other. Inasmuch as the commodities are physically different, and different ones are useful to different persons, use value cannot be that common property. Their only common property is that they are both the products of human labor (CI, T 305). Each commodity has a certain value that determines its equilibrium price.

But this argument, though frequently repeated, is not very plausible. Commodities clearly have all kinds of other properties that might count as common qualities; for example, they may require certain quantities of raw materials, or their production may consume a certain quantity of steam or electricity. What is more, the central premise, that two entities must have at least one common property if they are to exchange in a fixed ratio, is never argued by Marx. The premise is clearly not self-evident. In fact, it may very well be false. What many interpreters of Marx have taken to be an *argument* for the equivalence between equilibrium prices and the amount of labor expended in production is dubious at best. But Marx, who labored over his economics for many years and wrote certain parts over and over, neither entertained nor refuted such suggestions.

More important, Marx himself knew all along that the Labor Theory of Value, as stated in the first chapter of Volume I of *Capital*, is false:

Average prices do not directly coincide with the values of commodities, as Adam Smith, Ricardo, and others believe.[5]

By the time he had gotten around to writing the third volume of *Capital*, Marx's claim about the connection between values and prices was much less definite:

Whatever the manner in which the prices of various commodities are first mutually fixed or regulated, their movements are always governed by the law of value. If the labor time required for their production happens to shrink, prices fall; if it increases, prices rise, provided other conditions remain the same.[6]

Here his claim is much more restricted. Increases in productivity (when more commodities are produced in a given period of working time) bring about falling prices; decreases in productivity (when the labor time required to produce a given quantity of commodities increases) produce increasing prices. How specific that connection is—whether it applies, say, to a particular style and size of shoe, or to shoes in general, or only to all the commodities produced at a particular time—remains open. In the passage just above, Marx seems to assert no more than that there is a connection between price increases and decreases and rises and falls in productivity. There is an important connection between what commodities sell for in the marketplace and how long it takes to make them, and it is clear that this connection is very complex.

Why does Marx provide us with such different versions of the Labor Theory of Value? He has often been accused by his critics of being blatantly inconsistent. It is said that by the time he wrote the third volume of *Capital*, he had forgotten what he had written at the beginning of the first. But in light of the fact that he had recognized the problem of the relation between prices and values by 1859—the year of publication of the *Contribution to the Critique of Political Economy* and four years before the publication of Volume I of *Capital*—and stated the problem in Volume I of *Capital* itself, that is an implausible suggestion.

Marx himself explained what he was up to in a letter to his friend Ludwig Kugelmann:

All that palaver about the necessity of proving the concept of value comes from the complete ignorance both of the subject dealt with and of scientific method. Every child knows that a nation which ceased to work, I will not say for a year, but even for a few weeks, would perish. Every child knows, too, that the volume of products corresponding to the different needs require different and quantitatively determined amounts of the total labor of society. That this *necessity* of the *distribution* of social labor in definite proportions cannot possibly be done away with by a *particular form* of social production, but can only change the *mode* of *its appearance*, is self-evident. . . . The form in which this proportional distribution of labor asserts itself, in a social system where the interconnection of social labor manifests itself through the private exchange of individual products of labor, is precisely the exchange value of these products. Science consists precisely in demonstrating *how* the law of value asserts itself.[7]

Marx makes several important points here:

1. He is not proposing to *prove* that value is determined by labor time. Hence it is an error to read the first chapter of Volume I of *Capital* as a proof.
2. Human beings need to work in order to survive.
3. But total available working time can be allotted by different methods. This is a point we saw Marx make in the preceding chapter.
4. In a capitalist society, labor time is apportioned not by the decisions of some or all members of the society but by virtue of market mechanisms (i.e., through the exchange of commodities).
5. The market allots social labor to different efforts through the mechanism of prices, as we also saw in the preceding chapter.
6. Unless the prices of commodities are in some way connected with labor time, it is not conceivable that the exchange of commodities can function to apportion social labor time.
7. The important question, therefore, is this: What is that connection?

Marx struggled throughout his working life to answer that question. We shall see that he was not fully successful. But the question is not hard to understand: Capitalist society conceals social relations among people behind the market relations of commodities. That means not only that social relations are difficult to decipher but, more important, that *social decisions* are left to the workings of market exchanges that, in differently organized societies, are made by members of those societies. Under capitalism, the large number of individual investment decisions of individual investors together determine how the collective labor power of the society will be employed. The question for Marx was how the surface reality of the marketplace is connected with the deep reality of the social division of labor, or how the marketplace assigns who works where, and when, and how much. The task is to connect the surface (the exchange of commodities) with the deep reality (the work that is done in the society to maintain it). In the context of the Labor Theory of Value, that task takes the form of trying to clear up the relation between values and prices.

In the first volume of *Capital*, Marx offers the Labor Theory of Value as a hypothesis that seems useful in providing a complete account of the inner working of capitalism. But one cannot decide whether that hypothesis should be accepted until the complete explanation of the working of capitalism has been supplied. Inasmuch as Marx did not complete his economic model, and his successors did little to supplement his work, his hypothesis remains just that—a hypothesis that shows promise.[8]

The Transformation Problem

One of the important tasks of economics is to provide quantitative accounts. Thus we cannot be satisfied with the vague statement that rises in productivity will bring about a fall in prices. We want a set of equations that will allow us to transform value magnitudes into prices and, perhaps, vice versa. Marx provides such a set of equations in the third volume of *Capital*. The debate over the adequacy of these equations is usually referred to as the "transformation problem."

This transformation problem has given rise to a heated controversy that began shortly after the publication of Volume III of *Capital* by Engels in 1894, (eleven years after Marx's death) and has continued to this day.[9] The positions taken can be roughly classified as follows: (1) Some authors accept Marx's equations.[10] The majority of readers of Marx reject them, however. Among them there are (2) readers globally hostile to Marx and Marxism who take the difficulties with Marx's transformation equations as sufficient grounds for paying no more attention to Marxian economics. (3) Some sympathetic readers, on the other hand, believe that the transformation problem is solvable. Marx, it is said, made some serious errors, but the equations can be stated in ways that are above reproach.[11] (4) Others believe that there exist mathematically correct formulations of the transformation equations but argue that they do not do justice to Marx's sociology.[12] If this is true, then the existing mathematically acceptable transformation equations are not adequate for Marx's purposes—namely, to develop his claims about fetishism and exploitation in precise quantitative terms. (5) Finally, some readers hold that one can say all that is important in Marx's economics without introducing the Marxian conception of value, that is, without the Labor Theory of Value. One therefore does not need to bother about the transformation problem.[13]

As we saw earlier, the very fact that capitalist society regulates the apportioning of social labor power by means of the market mechanism makes it possible to have thoroughly quantitative economic analyses. But once those analyses become possible, we need to produce them if we want to understand the capitalist economy. Contrary to the opinion of some readers of Marx that his numerical examples are not very important, the interpretation offered here implies that without adequate quantitative analyses, the Marxian account of capitalism is incomplete. To the extent that it remains incomplete, its adequacy remains in question.

Whether the Labor Theory of Value should be accepted remains an open question. Marx's development of this theory was fragmentary and not always correct. Not much has been added to his economics since then. The Labor Theory thus remains as an ingenious and interesting suggestion that awaits careful development if it is to become as illuminating as Marx believed it to be.

Notes

1. Ernest Mandel, *The Formation of the Economic Thought of Karl Marx* (New York: Monthly Review Press, 1971), Chapter 3.

2. Marx, *A Contribution to the Critique of Political Economy* (New York: International Publishers, 1970), pp. 32–33.

3. Marx, *Capital*, Vol. I (New York: International Publishers, 1967), pp. 156ff.

4. Ronald Meek provides a different explanation of why Marx adopted the Labor Theory of Value—namely, that it is implied in the historical materialist method. See Meek, *Studies in the Labor Theory of Value* (New York: Monthly Review Press, 1956), Chapter 4.

5. Marx, *Capital*, Vol. I, p. 166, n. 1; p. 220, n. 1; and p. 307.

6. Marx, *Capital*, Vol. III, p. 177.

7. Marx, "Letter to Ludwig Kugelmann, July 11, 1868," in S. W. Ryazanskaya, ed., *Marx-Engels: Selected Correspondence* (Moscow: Progress Publishers, 1975).

8. This is also Erik Olin Wright's interpretation of the Labor Theory of Value. See Wright, *Class, Crisis and the State* (London: Verso, 1978), Chapter 3.

9. For a lucid summary of the major contributions to this controversy, see Meghnad Desai, *Marxian Economic Theory* (London: Gray-Mills Publishing, 1974).

10. See for instance, Ernest Mandel, *Marxist Economic Theory*, 2 vols. (New York: Monthly Review Press, 1971).

11. Paul M. Sweezy, *The Theory of Capitalist Development* (New York: Monthly Review Press, 1942).

12. Desai, *Marxian Economic Theory*, Chapter 12.

13. This view is widely defended today. A very good exposition of it may be found in Geoff Hodgson, *Capitalism, Value and Exploitation* (Oxford: Martin Robertson, 1982).

For Further Reading

M. C. Howard and J. E. King, *The Political Economy of Marx* (Burnt Mill, England: Longmans, 1975), Chapters 4, 5, and 6.

11

The Predictions

We have seen over and over again that Marx considers the present from a historical perspective. His questions always begin with the origins of the present in the past. His central assumption is that human affairs are mutable, that they never remain the same however hard we may try to keep our world the way it is.

This is true not only of the historical periods that preceded ours; it applies equally to the present. This society will no more remain unchanged than did earlier ones. Hence Marx was interested not merely in how capitalism works but also in how it changes. In Chapter 7 we saw how feudalism changed into capitalism. It is time now to consider how capitalism will change in the future.

Marx's predictions have played an important role in the last 125 years. The political movements that took their inspiration and, to varying extents, their theories from the writings of Marx and Engels were obviously more directly interested in those predictions for the future, and for the possibilities of social and political change, than in the vicissitudes of feudalism or early capitalism. Members of these movements, as well as their enemies, have come to accept an account of Marx's predictions that runs roughly as follows:

The central drive of capital is for expansion by means of the reinvestment of profits. Hence every capitalist tries to increase profits. That increase can be accomplished by several means. For instance, the capitalists can keep wages as low as possible. Or they can improve their position relative to their competitors by increasing productivity and decreasing costs. That is done by using newer and bigger machines or by manufacturing on a larger scale. Thus capitalists are bound to try to keep their wages as low as possible, to improve their technological capabilities, and to create larger and larger companies.

While all of these strategies work to raise profits, they also have other, less desirable consequences. The pressure for keeping wages low results in the progressive impoverishment of workers. That in turn limits the purchasing powers of those workers and thus tends to give rise to crises of underconsumption when there is not enough demand for consumer goods. As a result of the lack of demand, business failures, recessions, and depressions occur.

At the same time, the transformation of the capitalist production process into larger and more mechanized forms transforms the working class. Workers learn to work together because it is only together that they have any product—it takes many men and women to produce one automobile, for instance—and only together that they will be able to exert any power against capital.

The constant drive for increased productivity through mechanization tends to drive up the ratio of capital invested in machinery to capital invested in wages (organic composition of capital). There is an ever greater sum invested in machines per worker. As a consequence, the amount of profit each worker produces goes down. The decrease in the rate of profit makes capitalists reluctant to invest and thus leads to stagnation in the economy.

The lowering of the rate of profit has disastrous effects on businesses that are marginal already. The number of bankruptcies increases and, with it, the danger of general economic crisis.

The push for larger firms tends to substitute the monopolistic price fixing of the large corporations for the competition of the marketplace. As a result, less efficient enterprises are preserved. Capitalism thus loses the advantage of the competitive economy, which weeds out inefficient producers. More and more of them remain in business, thus contributing further to stagnation and low productivity. Capitalism becomes unable to fulfill its historical role of increasing human productivity.

The capitalist marketplace is, in the words of the Marxian tradition, "anarchical": Every individual seeks to increase his or her profit, but there is no plan governing the market as a whole. Thus the individual capitalist's drive for profits has, in the aggregate, the opposite effect of what was intended: There are more and more severe economic crises at shorter and shorter intervals. As each individual capitalist strives to increase profits, the overall effect of all these efforts is a series of recurring and ever more serious business crises. It becomes increasingly apparent that the capitalist economic system is no longer functioning properly. The working class gets poorer and poorer, but it also gets better organized. When it becomes clear that the inevitable breakdown of capitalism is imminent, a proletarian uprising and socialist revolution ensue.

This reading of Marx seems clearly supported by some of his most eloquent statements:

> As soon as this process of transformation [viz. from feudalism to early capitalism] has sufficiently decomposed the old society from top to bottom . . . that which is now to be expropriated is no longer the laborer working for himself, but the capitalist exploiting many laborers. This expropriation is accomplished by the immanent laws of capitalistic production itself, by the centralisation of its capital. One capitalist kills many. . . . Along with the constantly diminishing number of magnates of capital, who usurp and monopolise all advantages of this process of transformation, grows the mass of misery, oppression, slavery, degradation, exploitation; but with this too grows the revolt of the working class, a class always increasing in numbers and disciplined, united, organized by the very mechanisms of capitalist production itself. The monopoly of capital becomes a fetter on the mode of production. . . . Centralisation of the means of production and socialisation of labor at last reach a point where they become incompatible with their capitalist integument. This integument is burst asunder. The knell of capitalist private property sounds. The expropriators are expropriated. (CI, T 437–438)

The capitalist's drive for profits has these consequences:

1. The immiseration of the worker.
2. The falling rate of profit.
3. The concentration of capital.
4. More and more severe economic crises.
5. A more united and better organized proletariat.
6. The final breakdown of capitalism.
7. The proletarian revolution.

The traditional Marxist account of these developments regards all of them as certain. The immiseration of the proletariat is "necessary," as is the final breakdown of the entire system. Marxists were certain that all of this would take place; only the precise date of the occurrence was in question. In the next section, I shall show that this traditional account misreads Marx and Engels. They did not provide the proof that their followers believed they had provided.

How Reliable Are the Predictions?

The Immiseration of the Proletariat

It is a matter of controversy among interpreters whether Marx and Engels believed that the working class would grow progressively poorer. There certainly are passages, such as the one cited above and similar ones, particularly in the *Communist Manifesto*, in which they predicted the progressive impoverishment of the proletariat.

> In proportion as the repulsiveness of the work increases, the wage decreases. (CM, T 479) . . . The proletarians have nothing to lose but their chains. (CM, T 500)

Similar passages occur in *Wage Labor and Capital* (T 215ff.). The immiseration thesis is put forward more than once by Marx and Engels.

It would be a mistake to regard this merely as a rhetorical exaggeration calculated to stir up the working class, which they regarded as the agent of social transformation. Both Marx and Engels had ample empirical information to show that the workers in England in the first sixty years of the nineteenth century lived under generally worsening conditions. Marx documented this fact in grisly detail from government documents in the middle portions of Volume I of *Capital*. Engels had documented the same facts earlier in his work entitled *The Condition of the Working Class in England in 1844.*[1] The claim about the progressive immiseration of the working class fully accorded with the facts as they existed then. Significant numbers of workers earned less than they needed to support themselves and their families; their lives were destroyed by abject poverty.

But Marx and Engels took pains not only to describe the impoverishment of workers in their own time (that was obvious to anybody who wanted to look) but also to assert that the same condition would continue with only minor changes in the future. In order to establish that contention, they argued another thesis—namely, that wages tended toward subsistence. We encountered that thesis and their argument for it earlier, in Chapter 8. As workers are exploited, their employers are compelled by competition to drive down wages as far as possible, to a level at which they barely suffice to keep workers alive and able to work.

It is not clear that Marx and Engels managed to establish that latter contention. But even assuming that we have good grounds for believing that wages tend toward the subsistence level, it does not follow that workers will get poorer and poorer.

As we saw in Chapter 2, Marx claimed that capitalism rests on exploitation. This implies that the *value* of wages tends to decrease. But that occurrence would clearly be compatible with an actual increase in the amount of goods consumed by workers and, hence, with an improvement of the "standard of living." Capitalism brings with it a phenomenal increase in productivity: The amount of time needed to produce a given commodity constantly decreases, so that fewer and fewer workers produce more and more goods. Marx was well aware of that:

> The development of the productiveness . . . of capital sets in motion an ever increasing quantity of means of production through a constantly decreasing quantity of labor. . . . Every single commodity . . . also contains less materialised labor. . . . This causes the price of the individual commodity to fall.[2]

But as goods get cheaper, the total volume of goods increases. Thus the value of labor power, measured by the value of goods that labor needs to subsist, may well go down, while the total amount of goods that workers' wages can buy may well go up. If productivity increases faster than wages fall, then increasing exploitation may well go hand in hand with a rising standard of living.

Workers today have cars, whereas a hundred years ago they walked to work. But that does not tell us anything about the *value* of wages. It takes a lot less work to make cars today than it did when they were first being produced. The quantity of goods consumed by the average worker tells us nothing about the value of those goods.

There are ample passages in which Marx recognizes that even if one managed to establish that, due to exploitation, wages tend to fall to the subsistence level, it does not follow that workers will have a progressively lower standard of living, or even that their standard of living, defined by reference to the quantity of goods consumed, will not rise. Marx and Engels sometimes seemed to assert that workers will become poorer in absolute terms; at other times they recognized that their theory did not support such a claim. The prevalence of exploitation implies, however, that when the standard of living of workers rises, the total amount of capital owned by the capitalists rises even faster.

> If capital is growing rapidly, wages may rise; the profit of capital rises incomparably more rapidly. The material position of the worker has improved, but at the cost of his social position. The social gulf that divides him from the capitalist has widened (WLC, T 211).

While wages go up, the total mass of capital controlled by the capitalist class increases even more rapidly. As a consequence, workers may not get poorer in terms of their consumption of goods because their standard of living is, in fact, going up. But their "social position"— that is, their power in relation to their employer—shrinks. Where formerly they dealt with the owner of their factory, whom they perhaps knew personally, they now work in a much larger company and they deal with "management," a faceless bureaucracy.

This thesis is often referred as the "relative immiseration thesis."[3] But that is a misnomer. Immiseration refers to the suffering of the working class. It is not clear that the working class, given the improvement in its standard of living, suffers from the fact that the total investment in raw materials, machines, buildings, and so on, increases even more dramatically. Marx's point is not primarily a prediction that the standard of living of workers would fall, but that they would face a capitalist class whose economic power grew day by day.

We must conclude that Marxian economics provides no support for the claim that the working class will become progressively more impoverished. What it implies, instead, is that the economic and hence political power of the working class shrinks before the growing economic and political power of the capitalists.

The Falling Rate of Profit

Marx called this the "Law of the Falling Tendency of the Rate of Profit" because he realized that there were conflicting tendencies with respect to the rate of profit. On the one hand, according to him, there is a long-term tendency for the rate of profit to fall. But there are counteracting tendencies on the other hand.

This "Falling Rate of Profit" is undoubtedly central to Marx's thinking about the development of capitalist society. We noted earlier that he expected capitalism to come to an end when the relations of production— the private ownership of means of production—became "fetters" on the productive process.

> The *real barrier* of capitalist production is *capital itself.* . . . The means— unconditional development of the productive forces of society—comes continually into conflict with the limited purpose, the self-expansion of limited capital.[4]

Capitalists pursue profit, in part, through ever-increasing mechanization, the "unconditional development of the productive forces of society." But that increases the ratio of capital invested in machinery to capital invested in labor required to produce any given commodity—what Marx calls the "organic composition of capital." A change in the organic composition of capital depresses the rate of profit because it reduces the amount of labor that is capable of generating surplus value.

Marx symbolized surplus value by s, the amount of capital laid out to pay wages by v, and the amount of capital going toward machines and raw materials, and so on as c. The organic composition is accordingly symbolized by v/c and the rate of profit is

$$\frac{s}{v + c}.$$

Because surplus value is produced by labor, according to Marx, as the ratio between v and c changes in favor of c, a smaller proportion of $v + c$ will produce surplus value, and hence

$$\frac{s}{v + c}$$

will tend to become smaller—unless compensated for by a corresponding change in s/v, the "rate of surplus value." This fall in the rate of profit removes the incentive for the capitalist to invest in further technological advances.

Suppose a capitalist invests $2000.00—$1000.00 in wages and $1000.00 in machinery. Suppose further a rate of surplus value of 100 percent. Then the rate of profit is

$$\frac{\$1000.00}{\$1000.00 + \$1000.00},$$

or 50 percent.

Now if our capitalist buys a new machine that requires an additional investment of $1000.00, the rate of profit drops to 33.33% unless compensated for in a corresponding change in the rate of surplus value from 100% to 150%, or

$$\frac{\$1500.00}{\$1000.00 + \$2000.00},$$

or 50 percent.

The fact that capital is privately owned and must yield private profit thus interferes with the development of productive forces. Competition, at first, spurs capitalists on to invest in new labor-saving devices. But these investments depress the rate of profit and thus discourage further investment. The pursuit of private property becomes a "fetter" on those forces of production. The anarchy of the marketplace, the lack of conscious coordination of the actions of individual entrepreneurs in the market, proves an obstacle for the further development of the productivity of industry.

But what reason do we have to think that the organic composition of capital is increasing? It is quite evident that capitalist production uses more and more complex machinery and that the *volume* of capital goods per worker increases. But that does not suffice to demonstrate a change in the organic composition of capital. That ratio is expressed as the ratio of the *value* of constant capital to the *value* of variable capital. The mere increase in the quantity of such goods does not prove that there is more constant capital, *in value terms*, per worker than there used to be. The rising productivity of workers, as well as technological advances, may well serve to cheapen capital goods, so that their value decreases even as their quantity increases. The fact that production is more and more mechanized does not suffice to prove that the organic composition of capital has changed. We need to show, instead, that more and more work goes into producing machinery. But that is not readily proved. The increasing productivity of capitalist society might well have the result that machinery is produced more cheaply—a possibility that Marx was fully aware of.[5]

The rate of profit is expressed as

$$\frac{s}{c + v},$$

the ratio between surplus value and total capital, variable and constant. If the ratio of constant to variable capital increases, the rate of profit tends to go down, unless that change is balanced by an increase in the ratio s/v, that of surplus value to variable capital—the rate of surplus value. Abstractly speaking, it is possible for the decrease in the rate of profit to be forestalled by a compensatory increase in the rate of exploitation, due perhaps to the continual cheapening of the goods consumed by workers, or to the fact that new machines make it easier to control the labor force and thus to make workers work harder, or to the fact that new machines require less skilled workers whose labor is therefore less expensive to reproduce in value terms.[6]

Marx acknowledges the existence of these countervailing tendencies. He therefore speaks about a *tendency* of the rate of profit to fall, but he still believes that this tendency exists. His reasons for that, however, are questioned by many commentators.

Add to that the fact that the preceding argument presupposed the Labor Theory of Value, which, as we saw in the Chapter 11, remains incomplete. The inescapable conclusion is that the Law of the Falling Tendency of the Rate of Profit has not been established conclusively.

The Concentration of Capital

There is no question that capital has become much more concentrated over the last 200 years. Marx was clearly right about that. But less clear is the extent to which the centralizing trend has contributed to the stagnation of capitalist economies. Many people believe that this has occurred to a significant degree, but Marx has no well-worked-out theory to prove it.

Increased Frequency and Severity of Economic Crises

Similarly, there is no question but that capitalism is subject to periodic crises. Marxian theorists have derived these crises from the Falling Rate of Profit, or from the immiserization of the proletariat. But inasmuch as these two theses are not fully demonstrated, the claim that crises will be more frequent and more severe also remains unsupported.

The first four of the seven predictions listed earlier are thus open to doubts. The remaining three are not of a purely economic nature. The increasing unity and organization of the proletariat cannot be predicted on purely economic grounds, but they are clearly presupposed by the prediction that capitalism will collapse and that a proletarian revolution will take place. I will discuss these predictions in the fourth part of this book.

These claims about the inevitable collapse of capitalism are unsupported by a fully developed economic model. By the same token, Marx's theory of crises remains undeveloped—albeit full of fruitful suggestions.

It is true, of course, that Marx and Engels' central claim turned out to be correct—namely, that capitalism is not an unchanging order but, like all other human societies, is subject to constant change. The economists and social theorists, then and now, who regard capitalism as eternal are clearly mistaken. Nor was Marx wrong about all of his characterizations of the changes involved. There has been an enormous increase in total capital, in mechanization, and in the concentration of economic power. The relative economic power of capital in relation to the workers has increased, as has the size of the large economic units. But will all these changes in capitalism sooner or later bring about a total transformation of the system? That still remains to be seen. The collapse of capitalism, thought by Marx and Engels to be inevitable, has not occurred. We have seen that they did not have adequate support for that prediction.

Traditional Marxism claims that it has scientific proof that capitalism will fall victim to crises of increasing severity and frequency. This claim is false. Although it may well be true that capitalism will not last, Marx and Engels did not establish that fact, and their conception of the process of transformation is not entirely persuasive.

Political Implications

In his eleventh Thesis on Feuerbach, Marx proclaimed that "philosophers have only *interpreted* the world . . . ; the point, however, is to *change* it" (T 145). Accordingly, Marx and Engels were not content to develop a theory of capitalist society and of history. They proposed a political program—that the working class, with allies among the intellectuals, should organize itself with the end of taking power in its own behalf.

The prediction that capitalism will fail and be replaced by socialism obviously adds considerably to the persuasive power of this political program. But what if that prediction turns out to be dubious? Interpreters disagree about the extent of the damage done to Marx and Engels' political program by the failure of their economic predictions.

In the traditional Marxist view, the political program is unacceptable if the economic analysis and predictions turn out to be incorrect. Rosa Luxemburg, the most gifted leader of the German Social Democratic party before World War I, stated this explicitly in her polemic against Eduard Bernstein, the leader of the moderate wing of that party:

> Bernstein began his revision of Social Democracy by abandoning the theory of capitalist breakdown. The latter, however, *is the cornerstone of scientific socialism*, and with the removal of that cornerstone, Bernstein must also reject the whole socialist doctrine.[7]

Luxemburg makes a strong claim: The Marxian political program for organizing the working class with a view to replacing the capitalists in power and installing socialism ("Social Democracy") is acceptable only if Marxian economic theory is firmly established. That view was not hers alone but, on the contrary, was widely shared. Economics was considered the "cornerstone of scientific socialism." It was in relation to social policy what mechanics is in relation to engineering: Mechanics allows us to build bridges and buildings and machines that stand up for a long time. In analogous ways, economics was thought to offer a firm foundation for social policy making, and Marx's economics was proven sufficiently valid to play that role. The phrase "scientific socialism" implies both claims: that social science is capable of the same degree of certainty as physics, and that the Marxian theory of socialism had reached, or was close to reaching, that degree of certainty.

But such a view of Marx's economics is no longer acceptable for the reasons explained in this chapter and the one preceding it. Marx's economics does not have the requisite degree of certainty.

Does that concession force us to give up Marxian politics? That depends. If we believe with many interpreters of Marx that exploitation is not directly experienced by workers, then the Marxian political program requires the solid foundation in science that Luxemburg claims for it. If such a claim turns out to be unjustified, we need to suspend political action until further research has yielded a more solid foundation for political action. If exploitation is not directly experienced, the failure of Marx's and Engels' predictions of an inevitable collapse of the capitalist system requires that one give up working for socialism in the Marxian sense.

In the reading presented here, the failure of the prediction of inevitable economic collapse is not as damaging to Marx and Engels' political program as it would be according to the traditional interpretations. In order to understand that, we need to return to the distinction, drawn in the chapter on fetishism (Chapter 9), between the experienced reality, which is not fully intelligible, and the underlying reality, which a complete economic model explains to us.

We do not need the economic model in order to know, at first hand, that there is exploitation and class struggle, that capitalism is inherently unstable (twenty years of uninterrupted growth and stability seem to be a near miracle in the history of capitalism), that the power of the capitalists becomes more and more overwhelming, that there is a continuing tendency in capitalism to make work more routine, that the important decisions in the economy of what should be produced are made not in the interest of the society as a whole but in the interest of the greatest profits for capitalists. Daily experience provides many reasons for agreeing with the political program of Marx and Engels.

These experiences alone, however, do not suffice to support the Marxian political program. The experiences of exploitation, of economic and social malaise, are open to alternative interpretations. Along with Marx and Engels, we can explain them as signs of the gradual collapse of capitalism. But we may also see them in a religious framework as punishment meted out by a god to an impious nation, or from the capitalist perspective as minor malfunctions in a system that is, all in all, the best that human intelligence has managed to develop.

These experiences require interpretation in the light of theory. But as we saw in Chapter 9, Marx also insists that economic theory must be supported by these experiences. However useful many of the models of bourgeois economics may be, they are ultimately inadequate because they imply that there is no exploitation, or that capitalism is able to provide jobs for all, or that crises are not endemic to capitalism. Social theory serves to interpret experience; experience supports the theory.

It turns out, then, that the failure of Marx's and Engels' predictions has very different political implications depending on whether one believes that some of the defects of capitalism are directly experienced. Marx, I argued earlier, believed that working people see before their own eyes some of the shortcomings of capitalism. The failure of his predictions leaves one with the obligation to develop more adequate theories to shed light on these shortcomings and to make them unambiguously understandable. But it does not imply that workers are possibly not exploited, or that alienation is only in the workers' minds.

The economic model is, of course, important for political action: The surface reality, experienced by all, is confusing. Workers are exploited, but equivalents exchange for equivalents. Workers move freely from job to job, but exploitation rests on coercion. Social structures seem governed by prices, but these social structures are human creations. All of these contradictions provide openings for the apologists of the capitalist system who try to convince us, for example, that capitalism is stable and will last forever, that there is no exploitation and no class struggle. It is therefore important to understand capitalism, and to do that requires the theory that Marx left incomplete. But the reasons for adopting the political program of Marx and Engels in the first place are there for everyone to see.

The socialist revolution that Marx and Engels wrote about was meant to be a revolution of the majority of people. It is fought in response to the failures of capitalism that are experienced by everyone. One need not be a scholar, an economist, or a philosopher to understand the weaknesses of capitalism. Technical knowledge may be needed to understand why capitalism works that way and how to fight it, but not why it needs to be replaced. The process of replacing capitalism will occupy us in the remainder of this book.

Notes

1. Frederick Engels, *The Condition of the Working Class in England in 1844* (Moscow: Foreign Languages Publishing House, 1962).

2. Marx, *Capital*, Vol. III (New York: International Publishers, 1967), p. 226.

3. Ernest Mandel, *Marxist Economic Theory*, Vol. I (New York: Monthly Review Press, 1971), pp. 150ff.

4. Marx, *Capital*, Vol. III, p. 250.

5. Ibid., p. 236.

6. Ibid., p. 232.

7. Rosa Luxemburg, "Social Reform or Revolution," in Dick Howard, ed., *Selected Political Writings* (New York: Monthly Review Press, 1971), p. 123. My italics.

For Further Reading

Andrew Gamble and Paul Walton, *Capitalism in Crisis: Inflation and the State* (London: Macmillan, 1976), Chapter 4.

PART THREE

The Theory of Society

12

What Are Classes?

THE CONCEPT OF CLASS is central to the thought of Marx and Engels. Unfortunately, they never provided a systematic account of what they meant by "class." The third volume of Marx's *Capital* breaks off in the middle of a sentence about a page and a half into the chapter on classes. All we have, aside from that, is a collection of single sentences or short paragraphs in their various writings from which their conception of class has been reconstructed. Little wonder, then, that there is a wide range of interpretations of their theory of class.

Capitalism develops, as we saw in Chapter 7, when the society divides into owners of means of production and "free" laborers—workers who are neither slaves nor serfs, who own nothing but their ability to work.

> In themselves, money and commodities are no more capital than the means of production and of subsistence. They want transformation into capital. But this transformation itself can only take place under certain circumstances, that centre in this, viz. that two very different kinds of commodity possessors must come face to face and into contact: on the one hand the owners of money, means of production, means of subsistence, who are eager to increase the sum of values they possess, by buying other peoples' labor power; on the other hand free laborers, the sellers of their own labor power, and therefore the sellers of labor. (CI, T 432)

The "control of the capitalist [viz. over the worker] is in substance twofold" (CI, T 385). The capitalist functions like the conductor of an orchestra by coordinating the different activities—"A single violin player is his own conductor: an orchestra requires a separate one" (CI, T 385)—and the capitalist owns the means of production. The capitalist owns the means and controls the process of production. The worker does neither.

Capitalist society here appears to be split into two major classes; the owners of labor power and the owners of capital. Passages like these have yielded the conception of the nature of classes that has dominated traditional Marxism: Classes are groups of people characterized by their relation to the means of production: The capitalists own the means of production; the workers do not.

The classical formulation of this conception of class was provided by Lenin and has since then been repeated over and over again:

> Classes are large groups of people, differing from each other by the place they occupy in an historically determined system of social production, by their role in the social organization of labor and, consequently, by the dimensions of the share of social wealth of which they can dispose and the mode of acquiring it.[1]

This conception of classes has three distinct aspects. Classes are (1) groups of individuals (2) who are united by having the same relation to something, and (3) the relations that serve to define a group of people as a class are economic relations.

But the precise nature of the economic relations that define the different classes has been the subject of intense debates. Classes have been said to consist of all the people who have the same ownership characteristics, of all those who have the same positions of power, of those who have a certain function in the production process, or of all those who have one of these characteristics plus specific ideological positions.[2] But these debates are misguided. When we consider what Marx and Engels actually said about classes, we find that it is class struggle, not primarily the relation to the means of production, that forms people into a class.

> The separate individuals form a class only insofar as they have to carry on a common battle against another class; otherwise they are on hostile terms with each other as competitors. On the other hand, the class in its turn achieves independent existence over against the individuals. (GI, T 179)

Here class struggle is cited as a necessary condition for people to form a class. Classes thus are not merely groups of people who have the same relation to the means of production; rather, they are groups of people in a "common battle." That battle ebbs and flows. In the lull between engagements, the members of a class compete with each other—that is true of both capitalists and workers.

In addition, the class develops and changes in the course of class struggle. As time goes on, it acquires permanent organizations (e.g., in the form of business organizations in the case of the capitalists, and labor unions in the case of workers).

> The small peasants form a vast mass, the members of which live in similar conditions, but without entering into manifold relations with one another. Their mode of production isolates them from one another instead of bringing them into mutual intercourse. . . . In this way, the great mass of the French nation is formed by simple addition of homologous magnitudes, much as potatoes in a sack of potatoes. Insofar as millions of families live under economic conditions of existence that separate their mode of life, their interests and their culture from those of other classes, and put them in hostile opposition to the latter, they form a class. Insofar as there is merely a local interconnection between these small-holding peasants, and the identity of their interests begets no community, no national bond and no political organization among them, they do not form a class. (18th, T 608)

A group of people has the *preconditions* for forming a class when they "live under economic conditions of existence that separate . . . [them] from . . . other classes," but they form a class in a genuine sense only once their "identity of interests" generates "community" or a "national bond." People who are subject to the same economic conditions can form a class if they unite and form a national organization. Specifically, as long as they have not formed a "political organization," they are not a class in the full sense. Relationships to the means of production do not make them into a class; they are necessary conditions but not sufficient. Also necessary are similar "interests" and "culture." More important, a "national bond"—specifically a "political organization"—is required.

> The proletariat goes through various stages of development. . . . At first the struggle is carried on by individual laborers, then by the workers of a factory, then by the operatives in one trade, in one locality, against the bourgeois who directly exploits them. . . . At this stage the laborers still form an incoherent mass scattered over the whole country, broken up by their mutual competition. . . . But with the development of industry the proletariat not only increases in number; it becomes concentrated in great masses, its strength grows and it feels that strength more. . . . The collisions between individual workers and individual bourgeois take more and more the character of collisions between two classes. Thereupon the

workers begin to form combinations (Trade Unions) against the bourgeois.
. . . But every class struggle is a political struggle. . . . This organization
of proletarians into a class, and *consequently* into a political party, is
continually being upset again by competition between the workers themselves. (CM, T 480–481; italics mine)

Classes develop in the course of class struggle, on the basis of groups
of people who have similar economic conditions and hence similar
interests and culture. The full development of classes takes place in the
course of an extended and complex process in which, first, small groups
struggle locally over issues of interest to them. Those struggles give rise
to organizations that are initially quite ephemeral and only gradually
manage to last. Between struggles, the hard-won unity crumbles and
workers compete with each other once again, until a new issue sparks
a new fight. The unity of the class is a hard-won accomplishment that
slowly gives rise to stronger organizations. "The development of the
proletariat proceeds everywhere through internal struggles," Engels wrote
in 1882.[3] These organizations expand into national organizations and
then turn into, or give rise to, political organizations. Once that stage
is reached, the class struggle has given rise to classes, in the full sense
of that term.

The development of classes sketched in the preceding passages implies
that the very nature of classes changes throughout history. The word
"class" is ambiguous. In some periods, classes are no more than scattered
groups of people who work under similar conditions, who lack all
"community" or "national bond." These people are no different from
one another than "potatoes in a sack of potatoes." At other times,
national bonds and a sense of community come into being. Later still,
organizations arise—economic organizations such as trade unions, or
political ones such as parties. But then we encounter a new phenomenon.
A split opens up between the organization and its individual members,
who feel that their specific interests are not properly represented by the
leaders of their organizations: "The class in turn achieves independent
existence over against the individuals" (GI, T 179). In this last case, a
class is obviously no longer merely a collection of individuals, living
under the same "economic conditions of existence." Now a class is
organized, even though competitive strains may exist between individual
members and conflict may arise between the organizations and their
membership. Only when they have achieved enough unity to form
political organization have these groups become classes in the fullest
sense of that term.

Classes are "groups of individuals," if ever, only very early in their
histories. After awhile they form groups that are aware of themselves

as living under distinct conditions. They now form a community, such that they are connected to each other not only through economic conditions but also through ties maintained deliberately through community organizations such as schools, churches, country fairs, and celebrations, as well as through shared ways of looking at and doing things—all examples of what Marx and Engels call "practical consciousness" (see Chapter 6). Now a class is not a collection of individuals who all have some relation to something else, (e.g., the means of production); rather, it is a network of people connected to each other through common ways of thinking and acting.

Accordingly, the *Communist Manifesto* has assigned communists the task of promoting the "formation of the proletariat into a class" (CM, T 484). The proletariat, earlier described in terms of their economic conditions—working for wages, and owning no property besides their ability to work (CM, T 478–479)—do not constitute a class by virtue of these common conditions. Only political activity, in which communists are exhorted to participate, will bring the class, in the fullest sense of the term, into existence.

The conception of class that emerges from these passages differs from the standard Leninist conception. Classes are not mere collections of individuals sustaining similar economic relations; they are the organizations that working people build in the course of class struggle. Classes therefore do not arise *automatically* when the first groups of landless laborers begin to look for work. Classes, as described by Marx and Engels, *create themselves*. They do not suffer their history passively but make it. They create their common way of life, their common understanding of themselves as a distinct group, their economic organization, as well as their political parties—always in opposition to and struggle with the bourgeoisie. Classes thus do not just happen to arise as the economy changes. Classes create themselves in struggle with an opposing class.

But these struggles are not only struggles between classes. The unity of each class is also struggled for, as when the organizations forged by that class now take on an independent existence separate from, and sometimes in opposition to, its members.

The existence of a group of individuals having the same economic conditions of existence is thus only one of a number of preconditions for the formation of a class. The traditional Leninist conception of class describes classes only in their earliest, most primitive form. It ignores the all-important fact that classes are human creations, that classes exist only to the extent that they organize themselves in the course of their history, during which the very meaning of the concept of "class" undergoes transformation. The unity of the class does not flow automatically from the common economic conditions but is a hard-won accomplishment.

But classes are not the only groups that fit that general description. Racial, ethnic, gender, and religious groups—all seem to fit the same pattern. How do classes differ from these other groups? This chapter has not provided the concepts to answer that question. Inasmuch as Marx insisted that classes come to be and organize themselves in the course of class struggle, we must find out what that struggle is about in order to see what differentiates classes from other groups that are similarly self-created in the course of their own histories.

Notes

1. V. I. Lenin, *Selected Works*, Vol. III (Moscow: Progress Publishers, 1970/71), p. 231. This conception of class has received a powerful defense in recent years by G. A. Cohen, *Karl Marx's Theory of History* (Princeton, N.J.: Princeton University Press, 1976), Chapter 3, section 5.

2. For an interesting overview of contemporary interpretations of Marx on class, see Frank Parkin, *Marxism and Class Theory: A Bourgeois Critique* (New York: Columbia University Press, 1979), Chapter 2. See also Jon Elster, *Making Sense of Marx* (Cambridge: Cambridge University Press, 1985), Chapter 6, section 6.1.

3. Marx and Engels, *Selected Correspondence* (Moscow: Progress Publishers, 1975), p. 334.

For Further Reading

Bertell Ollman, *Social and Sexual Revolution* (Boston: South End Press, 1979), Chapter 2.

T. B. Bottomore, *Classes in Modern Society* (New York: Vintage Books, 1966), Chapter 2.

13

Class Struggles

A LOOK AT HUMAN HISTORY shows us wars, conflicts over religion or territory, over national pride and integrity, over wealth and its control, and over political institutions. It appears that the history of human societies is the history of religious, racial, ethnic, gender, economic, and other struggles. But Marx and Engels make a much more restricted claim:

> The history of all hitherto existing society is the history of class struggles. (CM, T 473)

What shall we make of this assertion? At first, the point seems to be that all struggle in history is class struggle. But surely Marx and Engels cannot mean that. If their assertion is to make sense at all, we need to read in it a lesser claim—namely, that class struggles are fundamental in human history. What gives class struggle that preeminent position in history? We cannot hope to answer that question unless we can state clearly what Marx and Engels meant by "class struggle."

What Is Class Struggle?

At first this question seems an easy one to answer: Class struggle is a struggle between classes. But if we adopt the reading of Marx and Engels put forward in the preceding chapter, according to which classes create themselves in the course of class struggle, we are committed to the view that there is class struggle in which some of the participants, at least, are not classes in a full sense but instead are groups that are on the way toward developing into a class. As we saw in the preceding chapter, that reading certainly finds support in the writings of Marx and Engels.

Every movement, in which the working class as a *class* confronts the ruling classes and tries to constrain them from without, is a political movement. For instance, the attempt by strikes, etc., in a particular factory or even a particular trade to compel individual capitalists to reduce the working day, is a purely economic movement. On the other hand the movement to force through an eight hour, etc., *law* is a *political* movement. And in this way, out of the separate economic movements of the workers, there grows up everywhere a *political* movement, that is to say, a *class* movement.[1]

Class struggle includes a wide variety of struggles, and not all of them have a fully formed working *class* as their protagonist. Groups develop into classes only in class struggle; when that struggle begins, a group on one side of the struggle, at least, has generally not yet organized itself into a class. Such a struggle is a *class* struggle only because classes come to be in the course of it, not because the participants are fully formed classes.

If class struggle cannot be defined by reference to the participants, we may be tempted to define it by reference to the issue struggled over: Class struggle, we may want to say, is struggle over exploitation. But Marx and Engels seem to use the term "class struggle" in a much broader sense:

The Communists fight for the immediate aims, for the enforcement of the momentary interests of the working class. (CM, T 499)

They provide a wide range of examples of fights over "immediate aims": "With the bourgeoisie . . . against the absolute monarchy" (CM, T 500); against the deskilling of workers (CM, T 479); in support of workers abroad, such as support by British workers for the Union forces during the American Civil War (T 519); against what today would be called "urban renewal," which destroys workers' housing;[2] for Irish Independence;[3] and so on.

It seems difficult to say what is *not* an instance of class struggle, once we look at the large number of different issues that Marx and Engels regard as examples of it. Almost any conflict over any topic, not just conflicts over exploitation, are called class struggles by them. It begins to look as if almost any conflict could be regarded as an instance of class struggle, and that would make the quote from the *Communist Manifesto*, which seemed problematic, trivially true. If all struggles are class struggles, then the history of society is indeed the history of class struggles.

Clearly, Marx and Engels were trying to say something more significant. We may try to explain their intention as follows: In any given conflict, whether between individuals or between groups, there is a bone of contention—namely, what the participants, if they are still talking, talk about. In a wage conflict the subject is wages. Offers and counteroffers concern wages; wages are the subject talked about in the negotiating sessions. But there is more at stake than what is being talked about: If the employer gives in to workers' demands, the union will gain in prestige among the workers and gain more members and more support. That will tend to make it more powerful and thus enable it to press harder for future demands. What is at issue, in that case, is not just wages but power, the power to exploit workers and to maintain exploitative arrangements. Class struggle takes place where such power is at issue, whatever the overt subject of discussion may be. Conversely, wage demands and working conditions do not give rise to class struggle if the demands are explicitly framed to leave power relations unaffected.

Marx draws a distinction similar to this one when he warns German workers about the pitfalls of alliances with petty bourgeois organizations. The subject of the struggle may be the same: Both groups may "desire better wages and more secure existence for workers," but the petty bourgeois, being themselves small capitalists who hire labor, are not interested in putting an end to the institution of wage labor. They are not interested in challenging the power of employers to exploit; they just want to make exploitation less painful (T 504). The subject of the struggle, working conditions, is the same for petty bourgeois and worker, but the underlying issue is quite different. The petty bourgeois seeks some reform of the existing capitalist system; the workers engage in class struggle.[4]

In some struggles, that issue—the power to exploit—is out in the open; sometimes it is only implicit. Throughout history, "oppressor and oppressed . . . carried on an uninterrupted, now hidden, now open fight" (CM, T 474). In actual cases the distinction between class struggles and other struggles will not always be easy to draw. But in principle, the distinction is clear: Whatever the subject openly discussed between the protagonists in a struggle, it is class struggle only if the power to exploit is at issue in it.

But if class struggle is a struggle over the power to exploit, who will actually participate in that struggle? One would think that the answer must be: Clearly only those members of the society who are actually engaged in wage work. But that, it would seem, leaves out children and students, older and retired people, the chronically ill, the unemployed, and everyone who works but not for wages, such as women who work in the home. The class struggle, then, would seem to include only a bare majority of the population, on the side of the working class.

Marx and Engels do not take up that question. One might point out, however, that clearly not only those people who actually work at any particular moment should be counted as participants in the class struggle but everyone who has at one time taken wage work, or could do so at some time, is a participant in that struggle on the side of the working class, because his or her interests are those of the workers.

Having reached that answer to the question of what class struggle is, and who participates in it, we can now go on to examine why Marx and Engels claim that all struggle in history is class struggle.

The Primacy of Class Struggle

The role of classes, according to Marx and Engels, is more central, more fundamental than that of other kinds of groups of a similar type. Class struggle plays a role in history not played by, say, racial struggle or the struggle between men and women.

But what does that mean? Surely history provides examples of all sorts of struggles: religious wars, tribal conflicts, contests for colonies. There are also the continued divisions along race lines, as well as the struggles over domination of women by men. What can be meant by saying that class struggles are "fundamental" to these? In Northern Ireland, for instance, it would appear that the religious divisions, paired perhaps with different national allegiances, are the fundamental divisions. In some of the civil wars in African nations, the basic irritant appears to have been tribal rivalries that have a very long history. The oppression that whites inflict upon blacks unites whites of different economic classes against blacks of all economic classes. In similar ways, women of all economic classes are dominated by men of all economic classes. It is not at all clear, therefore, what Marx and Engels had in mind when they claimed that class struggles are fundamental in human history.

Here are different interpretations of this claim:

1. Class struggle is fundamental to other struggles in the sense that other struggles are brought about by class struggle.
2. Class struggle is fundamental in that other struggles cannot be won unless class struggle is won first.
3. Class struggle is fundamental in being the most important of all the struggles being fought out.
4. Class struggle is the most inclusive.
5. Class struggle is the only source of revolutionary change in society.

1. This first version of Marx's thesis asserts that, for instance, black oppression and sexism exist *because* there is class struggle between the working and ruling classes of capitalist countries. Racism and sexism, according to this view, are said to be caused by capitalism because racism and sexism divide the working class and thus make exploitation easier for the capitalists. Without capitalism they would not exist.[5]

Marx is, of course, aware of the divisive role played by ethnic dissension in the formation of the working class. He notes that

> every industrial and commercial centre in England now possesses a working class divided into two *hostile* camps. English proletarians and Irish proletarians. The ordinary English worker hates the Irish worker as a competitor who lowers his standard of life. . . . He cherishes religious, social and national prejudices against the Irish worker. . . . This antagonism is artificially kept alive and intensified by the press, the pulpit, the comic papers, in short, by all the means at the disposal of the ruling classes.[6]

This is a complex statement: The Irish workers, working for less than the English, tend to depress the wages of the latter and compete with them for jobs. Hence the English workers hate the Irish. But, *in addition*, they hold all kinds of "prejudices" against the Irish having to do with religion, nationality, or way of life. Capitalism, and the class struggle that is endemic to capitalism, is by no means the cause or "root" of those prejudices, but it tends to keep them alive both because it pits worker against worker in competition for jobs and because ethnic (or racial, or religious) biases are actively and deliberately encouraged by the employers who find racial divisions in the working class to be to their advantage. Class struggle fosters racial and other conflicts, but it does not cause them.

Marx's theoretical formulation of class struggle does not imply that class struggle in capitalism is the cause of racism. In his analyses of concrete situations he clearly recognized that the causes of racism lie elsewhere. Historical evidence is on Marx's side in this instance. The history of racism reaches far back, long before the beginnings of capitalism.[7]

2. Where class struggle has been considered fundamental in the sense of being the struggle that needs to be won before any other can be won, oppressed groups have been admonished to postpone their struggle for equality until the socialist revolution had abolished capitalism. Only in a socialist country, it was said, can one hope to end oppression. Capitalism must therefore be toppled first.

That was clearly not the understanding of Marx and Engels. In England, in the 1860s, the Irish played a role not unlike that of Puerto

Ricans in the United States today. They had the worst jobs, they were looked down upon by the English, whether bourgeois or working class, and their country was nothing less than an English colony. In this context, Marx and Engels have said the following:

> The English working class will *never accomplish anything* until it has got rid of Ireland. . . . And this must be done, not as a matter of sympathy with Ireland, but as a demand made in the interest of the English proletariat. If not, the English people will remain tied to the leading strings of the ruling classes because it will have to join with them in a common front against Ireland.[8]

Here Marx and Engels insist that the class struggle between English proletariat and bourgeoisie cannot progress unless the Irish question— in our language the issue of "racism"—is addressed and settled first. Settling a racist division must not be postponed until after the socialist revolution; indeed, the development of the working class is impossible unless the racist division is settled first.

3. Is class struggle the most important struggle? As we have just seen, the answer to that question has varied over time. In the late 1860s, when the letters just quoted were written, Marx and Engels obviously thought that the struggle against the oppression of the Irish was the most important struggle, because without it the English proletariat could "never accomplish anything." In a letter to Marx written in the same period, Engels expressed regrets that the Irish had failed to understand that their "sole allies in Europe" were "the socialist workers,"[9] but he does not insist that the Irish join the class struggle of the socialist workers, let alone postpone their own struggle for the sake of that of the socialist workers of Europe. He clearly did not believe that the class struggle was fundamental in the sense of being the most important struggle.

4. Class struggle is fundamental to all societies because there is always class struggle of some sort, whereas the other conflicts that color and shape class struggle differ widely from one society to the next:

> The history of all past society has consisted of the development of class antagonisms, antagonisms that assumed different forms at different epochs. But whatever form they may have taken, one fact is common to all past ages, viz. the exploitation of one part of society by the other. (CM, T 489)

The many different kinds of conflicts in any given society can be better understood if they are seen against the background of and in connection with the struggle between classes. The converse is, of course, also true: Class struggle is affected by the existence of, for instance, racial or gender struggles. But although all societies experience class struggles, no other kind of conflict is universal to the same degree. Class struggle is therefore fundamental inasmuch as all divisions in societies are played out against the background of such struggle, which itself is colored by those other divisions. Class struggle is the most inclusive struggle of all.

Women have responded to this claim by pointing out that there are more societies known to us in which women were oppressed than societies that exploited labor.[10] Marx and Engels' answer to this objection is contained in Engels' later work, *The Origin of the Family, Private Property and the State* (T 734ff.), which essentially argues that the oppression of women in the family is a consequence of the development of the institution of private property—that is, some form of exploitation. Engels argues that class struggle is, indeed, the most inclusive struggle.

It is not clear whether he is right about that. The anthropological evidence is scanty and open to different interpretations. At any rate, this is not the only sense in which Marx and Engels regard the class struggle as fundamental.

5. Class struggle is the source of revolutionary change in societies: The flourishing and decay of different cultures is due to class struggle.

Marx and Engels classify historical periods by their mode of production and specifically by the way in which, in the societies known to us, the product of the many has been taken and used by the few. The "glory that was Rome" flowed from the hard work of slaves who did not share in that glory. In feudal society, the work of the serfs supported a class of largely idle landowners and soldiers. The surplus produced by the serfs allowed the Church to erect monumental cathedrals. The productive wealth of capitalist countries is produced by workers who do not own or control the wealth they have produced.

> Freeman and slave, patrician and plebeian, lord and serf, guildmaster and journeyman, in a word, oppressor and oppressed, stood in constant opposition to each other, carried on an uninterrupted, now hidden, now open fight, a fight that each time ended, either in a revolutionary reconstitution of society at large, or in the common ruin of contending classes. (CM, T 474)

The great transitions in human history occur when one mode of production replaces another—transitions that are a long time in coming and have their effect for long periods of time afterward. But these transitions, as well as the processes that lead up to them, are the effects of class struggles, because the very essence of these transitions is the replacement of one class, with its characteristic mode of production, by another class with its different mode of production. To date that has also meant the replacement of one form of oppression and exploitation by another.

All societies known so far have been exploitative. By virtue of their superior political, military, or economic powers, members of one class have forced the members of the other to hand over part of what it produced. This exploitation has been a constant source of friction. There have obviously been other sources of conflict, such as religious or cultural differences. But only class struggle finally put an end to the ability of a given ruling class to exploit and thereby ended the rule of that class. (The centrality of the power to exploit to the entire political structure will be discussed in Chapter 17.)

Class struggle, of all the struggles in history, is the one that overturns modes of production and classes and puts different classes with different modes of production in their place. It is for that reason more fundamental than the other struggles and, by the same token, differentiated from them.

This is one of the most central claims in the thought of Marx and Engels. They presumably derived their evidence for it from the study of history. But it is not clear how reliable that evidence is inasmuch as they never developed a detailed interpretation of that history.

But is class struggle even fundamental in the fifth sense, under capitalism? The revolution, when it comes, will bring an extended democracy, which in turn, will require full equality for all members of the society. Can class struggle, struggle over the power to exploit, give rise to a more equal society unless, *at the same time*, it is a struggle against all oppressions within the respective classes? This question has stirred up an enormous amount of controversy, but little agreement has been reached on answers thus far.

Notes

1. Marx and Engels, *Selected Correspondence* (Moscow: Progress Publishers, 1975), pp. 224–225.
2. Marx, *Capital*, Vol. I (New York: International Publishers), p. 659.
3. Marx and Engels, *Selected Correspondence*, pp. 221ff.
4. This is the view of class struggle put forth by Geoffry de Ste. Croix, in *The Class Struggle in the Ancient Greek World* (Ithaca, N.Y.: Cornell University Press, 1981), Chapter 2.
5. See Hal Draper, *Karl Marx's Theory of Revolution*, Vol. II (New York: Monthly Review Press, 1978), pp. 66ff. Draper argues that capitalism is a

necessary condition for racism, sexism, and so on, whereas John McMurtry, in *The Structure of Marx's World-View* (Princeton, N.J.: Princeton University Press, 1978), p. 87, n. 19, claims that capitalism is a sufficient condition for racism and sexism.

6. Marx and Engels, *Selected Correspondence*, p. 222.

7. Cedric J. Robinson, *Black Marxism* (London: Zed Press, 1983), Part I.

8. Marx and Engels, *Selected Correspondence*, pp. 216, 218.

9. Marx and Engels, *Selected Correspondence*, p. 218.

10. See Michelle Zimbalist Rosaldo and Louise Lamphere, eds., *Women, Culture and Society* (Stanford, Calif.: Stanford University Press, 1974).

For Further Reading

Zilla Eisenstein, ed., *Capitalist Patriarchy and the Case for Socialist Feminism* (New York: Monthly Review Press, 1979).

14

Class Consciousness

What Is Class Consciousness?

HUMAN BEINGS MAKE their history by arranging their lives to meet the problems of survival and procreation. They shape their ways of life based on an understanding of themselves and of the world. In Chapter 6, I called this central understanding "practical consciousness," following Marx and Engels. Any group has such a practical consciousness. As we saw, it may be quite inarticulate, because it consists primarily of ways of acting, of going about the daily business of living. It consists, in addition, of those shared traditions and values of the society that are accepted as "common sense":

> Upon the different forms of property, upon the social conditions of existence, rises an entire superstructure of distinct and peculiarly formed sentiments, illusions, modes of thought and views of life. The entire class creates it out of its material foundations and out of the corresponding social relations.[1]

The explicitly formulated *ideology* of a society, or group, is distinct from these mainly inarticulate ways of acting. More than likely, it both reveals and conceals aspects of the practical consciousness. What a group says it does may not always coincide with its actual ways of doing things.

> And as in private life one differentiates between what people think and say of themselves and what they really are and do, so in historical struggles one must distinguish still more the phrases and fancies of parties from their real organism and their real interests, their conception of themselves from their reality.[2]

Practical consciousness manifests itself in "knowing what to do" in standard situations. Having been socialized into their society, people act in predictable ways in the ordinary, oft-repeated situations of everyday life. They also apply these traditional understandings to new situations and to the solution of problems. Practical consciousness consists of ways of being and acting even if these have never been put into words. Ideologies, by contrast, describe, explain, and defend the practical consciousness of a given group. These ideologies, especially when they are elaborated into philosophical systems by full-time intellectuals, may well be one-sided and distorted representations of the practical consciousness embodied in practice.

Most societies are split irreparably by the class struggles in which classes develop, and which, sooner or later, will put an end to each society. In most societies there exist opposing groups, with opposing experiences of the order of that society, whose ways of life and understandings of the world are therefore sharply opposed. They have different points of view, anchored in opposing roles in the society.

The identity of classes, or of groups that are developing into classes, rests in part on their shared practical consciousness and on their ideology. Beginning as loose associations of people who are in similar economic positions, they slowly form political organizations in the course of many struggles both within and between classes. An important achievement in that long history is the creation of practical consciousness and its articulation into a class ideology. A rising class coalesces around new ways of producing and new ways of organizing itself. In the early stages of this process, the group develops its own characteristic way of producing necessities and of arranging its life. Only afterward are the principles governing the new ways of living and producing put into words, in the form of political and economic maxims, and of a whole new outlook on the world in which those maxims make sense. This self-understanding of the class, which consists of practical consciousness as well as class ideology, is often also called "class consciousness."

Class consciousness encompasses the shared practices and sayings of a class, of what we see most members of a class do in given situations or what we can hear them say regularly. Thus class consciousness is the consciousness of individuals, but not necessarily of every individual, in all situations. It is what most people tend to do and say most of the time in ordinary situations, what usually seems self-evidently right and true to them and what they therefore depart from only with difficulty or under serious pressure.[3]

The rising bourgeoisie first developed the new capitalist ways, the pursuit of profits, the hiring of wage labor, and the restless search for the self-expansion of capital. But it was only after that process of capitalist production had developed to some extent that the new world outlook and its specific politics—the class consciousness of the bourgeoisie—found its way, for instance, into the liberal theory of John Locke, at the beginning of the eighteenth century.

Now consider the situation of the workers. They are members of the society at large and are socialized into it. They thus share the "ruling ideas" of the age that "have ever been the ideas of its ruling class" (CM, T 489). The two classes share a world, of industrial capitalism, of technology and science, of ever-increasing productivity. In this world, individualism, individual freedom, democracy, and equality of opportunity are treasured concepts. The outlook and ways of life of the working class—its class consciousness—thus share important elements with bourgeois ideology, both in its practices and its ideas.

At the same time, because they are not members of the ruling class, workers go about their lives in ways very different from those of the capitalists. They do not invest capital and hire workers. They hire themselves out and are exploited. The explicit ideology as well as many of the practices of the ruling class sit uneasily with the workers' implicit understanding of their own world. For instance, the idea of equal opportunity—that everybody can be a capitalist if only he or she works hard enough—has a very different meaning for young workers as compared to what it means for the sons and daughters of the capitalists. Given that political campaigns cost large sums of money, and that "money talks" loudly in politics, the idea of democracy has a different meaning for working people and for capitalists—witness the low voter turnouts in elections. And so it is with the other ideas associated with the bourgeoisie. These ideas are one of the starting points for the class consciousness of the working class that slowly develops in opposition to the bourgeois outlook, as the class itself develops into a class in the full sense. The class consciousness of the working class never becomes completely separate from the bourgeois ideology. Instead, it gives new meanings to the concepts that play an important role in bourgeois ideology but are very imperfectly realized in bourgeois practice. Thus, for instance, socialist democracy has a different meaning from bourgeois democracy, for the latter applies only to politics whereas the former embraces all aspects of the society. The development of a proletarian class consciousness is not complete until the working class has become the dominant class and has abolished class distinctions.[4]

Class consciousness is the accomplishment of a class that gains a clearer and clearer class identity as it develops. In becoming a class, it works out its specific way of organizing the world. Class consciousness is nothing more or less than the way of acting in and understanding the world that surrounds a given class.

The development of class consciousness is complicated by class struggle. The ruling class is always attempting to retard the development of a working-class ideology. Thus ideology is a weapon in the class struggle. The small disagreements that occur continually are always in danger of growing larger. There is, in a class society, always the danger that full-fledged class struggle will erupt in ways that would seriously interfere with production and the perpetuation of existing social arrangements. One strategy for forestalling such serious conflict is to mask, as far as possible, the proper ideology or outlook of the workers and to cover it over with ideas more favorable to the employers. Marx and Engels were aware of this strategy and hence devoted Part III of the *Communist Manifesto* to unmasking these deceptive forms of socialism. One target of their criticism were the so-called "bourgeois socialists":

> The Socialist bourgeoisie . . . requires that the proletariat should remain within the bounds of the existing society, but should cast away all its hateful ideas concerning the bourgeoisie. (CM, T 496)

The bourgeoisie appropriated the language of socialism but turned it into a defense of the status quo in order to slow the development of the proletarian class and its class consciousness.

As I read them, Marx and Engels insist that human beings always act in the light of thinking and of their understanding of themselves and the world. Similarly, groups that are developing into classes always have their own understanding of themselves and their world—an understanding that is not necessarily put into words, however. This understanding, in the case of the proletariat, includes the knowledge that socialism is possible and necessary and that the socialist revolution is its task. But the working class reaches that knowledge only when it is fully formed and the impending demise of capitalism has become obvious for everyone to see. The class consciousness of the groups on the way to that point may well be reformist rather than revolutionary, more interested in purely economic gains than in contesting the capitalist's power to exploit.

This interpretation of Marx and Engel's idea of class consciousness departs from that of traditional Marxism. Many readers of Marx think of class consciousness in very different ways. From one perspective, class formation is the result of the formation of large-scale enterprises. In these enterprises workers organize to fight exploitation. This development is an objective process, distinct from the development of class consciousness. Revolution thus has "objective" conditions (the presence of an organized working class in a decaying capitalist system) and a "subjective" condition (class consciousness). Because the development

of the two kinds of conditions are distinct processes, one can take place
without the other. Interpreters who read Marx in that way have been
known to say that sometimes the objective conditions for revolution
exist while the subjective ones are missing.

According to this alternative interpretation, class consciousness does
not develop throughout the history of the class. Its development is
independent of the economic and social conditions under which the
class develops and may therefore fail to develop at all. This interpretation
is associated with the work of Wilhelm Reich.[5] It appeals to a well-
known passage by Marx:

> Economic conditions had first transformed the mass of people of the
> country into workers. The combination of capital had created for this
> mass of workers a common situation, common interests. This mass is
> thus, already, a class against capital, but not yet *for itself*. In the struggle,
> of which we have noted only a few phases, this mass becomes united
> and constitutes itself as a *class for itself*.[6] (Italics mine)

In this passage Marx says that the working class will understand itself
as a *political* actor, which struggles for power against the ruling bourgeoisie, only when it matures fully. But he is noncommittal as to whether
class consciousness has been developing all along as an integral part
of the history of the class. He definitely does not assert that class
consciousness develops independent of the economic and political development of the class.

In other passages, Marx is more explicit in suggesting that class and
class consciousness develop in one and the same process. In *Class
Struggles in France*, he suggests repeatedly that the program advocated
by the working class was not revolutionary, *because* the class was not
ready to act as a separate class against the bourgeoisie: "The Paris
proletariat was still incapable of going beyond the bourgeois republic."[7]
The Paris proletariat did have its own class consciousness, one that was
sharply opposed to the outlook of the capitalists. The Paris proletariat
also had its own political program, but it was not a revolutionary one
because, according to Marx, the working class was not sufficiently
developed and neither, therefore, was its class consciousness. The class
consciousness of the working class develops apace as the class develops
and corresponds closely to the social conditions. It does not develop
independent of "objective" conditions.

The Origins of Working-Class Consciousness

Where does the working class get its class consciousness?
This question becomes important when class consciousness is thought

to develop independent of the objective conditions. It is widely held that, according to Marx and Engels, class consciousness is brought to the proletariat from the outside by bourgeois intellectuals (such as Marx and Engels themselves). In this connection, Lenin quoted with approval the views of Karl Kautsky, the leading theoretician of the German Social Democratic party before World War I:

> Socialism and the class struggle arise side by side, and not one out of the other; each arises out of different conditions. Modern socialist consciousness can arise only out of profound scientific knowledge. . . . The vehicle of science is not the proletariat but the *bourgeois intelligentsia*.[8]

Again, there are certainly passages in the writings of Marx and Engels that tend to support this reading:

> Finally, in times when the class struggle nears the decisive hour, . . . a portion of the bourgeoisie goes over to the proletariat, and in particular, a portion of the bourgeois ideologists, who have raised themselves to the level of comprehending theoretically the historical movement as a whole. (CM, T 481)

Against this reading speak two important views of Marx and Engels:
1. They disagree that "socialism and class struggle . . . arise out of different conditions," as Kautsky and Lenin believed, if by "socialism" is meant the theory guiding working-class political action:

> Just as the *economists* are the scientific representatives of the bourgeois class, so the *Socialists* and the *Communists* are the theoreticians of the proletarian class. So long as the proletariat is not yet sufficiently developed to constitute itself as a class . . . these theoreticians are merely utopians who, to meet the wants of the oppressed classes, improvise systems and go in search of a regenerating science.[9]

Not everyone is a good theoretician. Marx agrees with Kautsky and Lenin on that. It takes a good deal of training to develop good political theory, and that training, in a capitalist society, is a privilege of middle-class intellectuals. But to be valid, a theory requires more than that it be competently framed and argued for. Theories framed in isolation from an active, fully developed working class—precisely the sort of theory that Kautsky and Lenin thought was to be brought to the workers "from the outside"—"are merely utopian"; they are mere pipedreams, too distant from actual political conditions to be of any use to the developing class. The class consciousness that Kautsky and Lenin spoke of is not only useless, Marx believed, but positively harmful.

2. When the proletariat is ready to act in its own behalf, it does not frame theories, in that sense of "utopian" theories, because it already knows what to do. Class consciousness consists, above all, of *knowing what to do, not in having a "correct" theory*:

> A class in which the revolutionary interests of the society are concentrated, so soon as it has risen up, *finds directly in its own situation* the content and material of its revolutionary activity; foes to be laid low, measures, dictated by the needs of the struggle, to be taken; the consequences of its own deeds drive it on. *It makes no theoretical inquiries into its tasks.* (Italics mine)[10]

Knowing what to do does, of course, involve a complex understanding of the world, a practical consciousness that, once put into words, takes the form of a theory. But this is theory that arises directly out of the experiences of an active workers' movement. It is not imported into the proletariat from the outside by bourgeois intellectuals, because its development is integral to the development of the class.

These different theories about the genesis of class consciousness yield different explanations of the fact that the proletarian revolution, which Marx and Engels expected a long time ago, is still waiting to be made. According to Reich's reading of Marx, the failure of the European working classes to make a revolution was due to their failure to develop proper class consciousness when the objective conditions for revolution were ready, because they were the dupes of bourgeois ideology (as a consequence of pervasive sexual repression). Kautsky's interpretation of class consciousness implies that when revolution was objectively possible, the working class failed to accept the correct theory offered by bourgeois intellectuals and therefore did not take revolutionary action. In Lenin's understanding of class consciousness, there was no proletarian revolution in Europe because the communist parties, which had the correct theories, did not manage to persuade the working class to take revolutionary action when that was called for by objective conditions. According to the reading of Marx presented in this book, the working-class revolution has not yet occurred because the working class has not been ready. Capitalism has not reached the end of its rope and, therefore, the requisite class consciousness has not yet developed.

Political Implications

The differences between my reading of Marx and the various readings in the tradition are quite complex. Central to all these differences, however, is the disagreement about what class consciousness is. Traditional Marxism tends to take class consciousness as a set of beliefs that have been articulated in speech or writing. Class consciousness is "science" (Kautsky) or "revolutionary theory" (Lenin). Such a theory is produced by bourgeois intellectuals and "arises out of different conditions" than the class struggle. In my reading, by contrast, class consciousness arises, first and foremost, from the *practices* of people, from what they do habitually in given situations. Class consciousness is therefore as much a product of class struggle as is class organization.

According to the traditional view, class consciousness, viz. correct theory, will direct the proletariat to take power once the capitalist economic system is close to collapse. In my interpretation, class consciousness is formulated by people who go around solving their own problems. They will develop revolutionary practices to the extent that the existing practices clearly fail. The failure of capitalism must be perceived by large numbers of people, and large numbers of people—not just bourgeois intellectuals—must develop ways of living that avoid those problems.

These disagreements reflect clearly on the role of the intellectual in the radical political movement. In the Leninist view, the intellectual functions as the expert who gives leadership to the organizations of the workers. In my view the intellectuals' role is to articulate in theoretical terms the understanding held by the working class of its own situation. Intellectuals serve as mirrors to the working class rather than as expert leaders. (This does not take away from the critical importance of intellectuals).

Class consciousness, as understood in my reading of Marx, is much more complex than traditional Marxism believed it to be. Hence we might also expect the revolution to come after a much longer period than traditional Marxism had predicted. It takes a long time for a class as a whole to emancipate itself from the ideology of its ruling class and to shape its own ways of doing things. People tend to do what they have always done under given circumstances. Old ideas die slowly, as Marx realized full well. Change

> takes place only very slowly; the various stages and interests are never completely overcome. . . . Within a nation itself the individuals . . . have quite different developments . . . and an earlier interest remains for a long time afterwards. . . . (GI, T 195)[11]

The new outlook and patterns of action of an entire class that are required before major social transformations can take place only slowly replace older outlooks and ways of going about daily activities. But a genuine revolution can take place only in the process of the self-creation of a class. New institutions will work only if they are seen by significant numbers of people as a solution to a problem that is widely perceived. A class ideology imposed from above remains just that. It never becomes the class consciousness of the class on which it is imposed.

Notes

1. Marx, *The Eighteenth Brumaire of Louis Bonaparte* (New York: International Publishers, 1968), p. 47.
2. Ibid.
3. Lukacz, in *History and Class Consciousness* (Cambridge: MIT Press, 1971), pp. 50–51, interprets Marx in the opposite way on this point: Class consciousness has nothing to do with what people actually think.
4. The central role of bourgeois ideology in capitalism was emphasized by Antonio Gramsci in *Prison Notebooks* (New York: International Publishers, 1971), pp. 1–14.
5. Wilhelm Reich, *The Mass Psychology of Fascism* (New York: Farrar, Strauss and Giroux, 1970), Chapter 1.
6. Marx, *Poverty of Philosophy* (New York: International Publishers, 1971), p. 173.
7. Marx, *Class Struggles in France 1848–1850* (New York: International Publishers, 1964), pp. 42–59.
8. V. I. Lenin, *Selected Works* (Moscow: Progress Publishers, 1970), p. 150.
9. Marx, *The Eighteenth Brumaire*, p. 125.
10. Marx, *Class Struggles in France*, pp. 42–43.
11. Marx is inconsistent on this point. Sometimes he stresses the complexity of social change and how much time it will take. More often he is excessively optimistic and expects revolution within the near future (see Chapter 16).

For Further Reading

Bertell Ollman, *Social and Sexual Revolution* (Boston: South End Press, 1979), Chapter 1.

15

Alienation

THE CONCEPT OF ALIENATION appears very early in the writings of Marx, but its full significance cannot be appreciated without an understanding of capitalism and class struggle. Having discussed both of these, we are now ready to talk about alienation.

Alienation in Marx's Early and Mature Works

Marx's essay on "Alienated Labor" (EPM, T 70–81) begins with some of the aspects of capitalism discussed in Part Two of this volume: the division of labor; exchange value; the tendency of workers to grow poorer, or of capital to become concentrated in fewer and fewer hands; and the fact that

> the whole of society must fall apart into the two classes—property owners and the propertyless workers. (EPM, T 70)

These and other features of capitalism are associated with the concept of "private property." (Marx means by that the private ownership of the means of production, not consumption goods such as the house you live in, the car you drive, or the clothes you wear.)

How did private ownership of the means of production come about? Political economy—the nineteenth-century precursor of what we call "economics"—does not have a satisfactory answer to that, Marx complains, for it either ascribes the existence of private property to human greed or derives it from events in prehistory (EPM, T 71). We saw in Chapter 1 why Marx is not convinced by the claim that capitalism is the result of human greed: He does not believe that there are human character traits, such as greed, that exist unchanged throughout human history. Hence, if today in the capitalist era, human beings are greedy, capitalism is at least as much a cause of the prevalence of greed as greed is a cause of capitalism.

What, then, is Marx's explanation for the existence of private ownership of the means of production? His answer is "alienation": "Private property is . . . the necessary consequence of alienated labor" (EPM, T 77). He then realizes, as he continues to pursue this train of thought in his notebooks, that this is not a satisfactory answer because it lays him open to the perfectly appropriate criticism that he, like all the other economists, leaves central questions unanswered—in this case, the question: Why is there alienation? He raises that question too (EPM, T 80), but the manuscript breaks off before he attempts an answer.

It seems clear that Marx—in 1844—was looking for a *philosophical* answer to the question: Why does capitalism exist? He wanted to derive the nature of the existing system from a set of concepts.

But on *analysis of this concept* it becomes clear that though private property appears to be the source, the cause of alienated labor, it is really its consequence. (Italics mine) (EPM, T 79)

The project is to understand capital by providing, much as Hegel had done, an analysis of the relevant concepts. Marx wanted to demonstrate "how they [the laws of capitalism] arise from the very nature of private property" (EPM, T 70). In his mature work, he replaced this philosophical method of explanation, in which a situation is explained by making connections between concepts, with the different method of explanation in which one explains a social fact (e.g., capitalism) by writing its history. The method of the *Economic and Philosophical Manuscripts* is not the method of *Capital*. Marx and Engels rethought their method of explanation in the course of writing *German Ideology*. The philosophical explanation of "private property" was never completed; rather, it was replaced by the historical explanation provided in *Capital*.[1]

In recognizing this transformation in Marx and Engels' method, some authors have classified the *Economic and Philosophic Manuscripts* as immature works that throw no light whatsoever on the views of the mature Marx and Engels. It would seem to follow that the concept of alienation plays no role in Marx's and Engels' later works.[2]

This reading has left many interpreters of Marx unconvinced. A change in method does not inevitably compel one to surrender all the insights won with the old method. The change in Marx's method of explanation is widely recognized. But this change does not make Marx's discussion of alienation completely irrelevant to the economic and political analyses of the later writings. On the contrary, it is widely believed that alienation is an integral aspect of capitalism. But inasmuch as the essay fragment on "Alienated Labor" is one of the few pieces of writing by Marx in which he tries to develop a key concept systematically, many readers of Marx and Engels limit their discussion of the concept of alienation to an exegesis of this essay and assume that the concept reappears in the later work just as it appears in the relatively early writings. But capitalism is approached differently in the works written after the *German Ideology* (i.e., after 1845), and so is alienation. We therefore need to consider alienation first as it is discussed in the *Economic and Philosophical Manuscripts* and then as it reappears in a somewhat different form in *Capital*.

The Early Concept of Alienation

What is this condition of alienation? Marx distinguishes four aspects of it:

1. Human beings are alienated from the objects of their work. What workers produce does not belong to them; it belongs to their employers. But why is that a problem? Suppose workers in an automobile plant were paid not in money but in kind—that is, they received an automobile every so often; would they then not be alienated?

> The alienation of the worker in his product means not only that his labor becomes an object . . . but that it exists *outside him* . . . and that it becomes a power of its own confronting him. . . . (EPM, T 72)

The product of the worker at issue here is surplus value. The worker produces the money needed to pay wages and to reproduce buildings, raw materials, and so on. But the worker also produces surplus value that belongs to the capitalist. The more a worker works, the more surplus value s/he produces and the more s/he therefore increases the power of the capitalist. The capitalists reinvest surplus value and thus strengthen their economic position and with it their position of power in relation to other capitalists and to the workers. The alienation of the workers consists in the fact that in doing their work, they strengthen the power of the opposing class.

2. Why do they do that? We already know the answer to that. Because they have nothing to offer in the labor market except their ability to work, they must work in order to live. They must work whether they want to or not; they must therefore also work to strengthen their enemies whether they want to or not. Marx presents this point in discussing the second aspect of alienation, the worker's alienation from the activity of

working. "His labor is therefore not voluntary, but coerced; it is *forced labor*" (EPM, T 74). Work is not something people choose freely, for that implies the possibility of refusing to work. It is to that extent not something that is "theirs"; "it is not [their] own but someone else's" (EPM, T 74), and hence it is not something in which the worker affirms him- or herself. As a consequence, the worker "is at home when he is not working" (EPM, T 74).

3. But human beings, as we have noted repeatedly, define what it means to be human not directly but by shaping their world to be a certain way. It is in work that human beings create what it means to be human. To the extent that that is a deliberate process, human beings are actually free (EPM, T 75). But what shall we say of people who work whether they want to or not, who have no control over what they do and how they go about it, and who therefore have no control over the sort of world that is created by their work? Industry is a major source of pollution, to give just one example of what is at issue here. Insofar as people must work industrial jobs because this is all that is available to them, they are forced to produce an environment they would not choose if they had a choice.

The implication is that the activity of working, which is potentially the source of human self-definition and human freedom, is here degraded to a necessity for staying alive. Work could be the source of a genuinely human life; but here it comes to be no more than the prerequisite for maintaining biological existence. Alienation "makes individual life in its abstract form" [viz. mere biological survival] "the purpose of the life of the species" (EPM, T 75). Questions of what sort of life people actually lead, or would like to lead, or believe they ought to lead, become secondary; survival is everything.

But what distinguishes human beings from animals is precisely the fact that we can choose to live in different ways. Because we can shape our lives, what life should be like is an intelligible issue for us. But for the person who has no say over work, whether to work or not and how to work and at what, the ability to shape life is curtailed. Hence the question "What should life be like?" loses its meaning. The life of human beings comes to be little different from that of animals. In that sense, alienation is dehumanization.

4. Human beings are, finally, forced not only to work in ways and under conditions not of their choosing but also to compete with one another for work; they are thus separated from their fellow humans.

The Later Concept of Alienation

It is not difficult to see the form in which these aspects of alienation return as dominant themes in *Capital*. The doctrine of "relative immiseration" asserts that as workers keep producing profits for the capitalist class, the total mass of capital—and with it the power of capital over the working class—grows faster than the wealth and power of the working class itself.[3] The worker's alienation from the product of his or her labor, described in the early essay as the situation of individual workers, here returns as the lot of the entire working class under capitalism; that is, it works only to strengthen its opponent, the capitalist class.

What in Marx's early piece is called the worker's alienation from the activity of production recurs later as the defining characteristic of capitalism—namely, that there is a large class of workers who have nothing to sell in the marketplace besides their ability to work and who, therefore, *must* sell their ability to work. Machines, raw materials, and buildings become "capital" only when that propertyless class has come into existence and is ready to be exploited.[4] Once sold, that ability to work is under the control of the employer, thus opening the way to exploitation. "Forced labor" becomes the precondition for forcible exploitation.

Capital stresses the divisiveness of the capitalist labor market as explicitly as does the essay on "Alienated Labor": Workers must compete against one another.

Alienation is often understood as a psychological condition; the word is thought to refer to how individual people feel.[5] Such an interpretation of the concept of alienation accords most nearly with how we talk now, when the word "alienation" has to do with how people feel, not about their relations to things, activities, and other persons in the world. That reading of Marx is, of course, based on the text:

> In his work, therefore, he does not affirm himself, he does not feel content, but unhappy. (EPM, T 74)

But it is a very one-sided reading, because it ignores all the other aspects of alienation that cause of this feeling of unhappiness. *Capital* does not speak of "alienated labor," of the conditions of individuals; its focus is the alienated working class. It speaks not about the emotional states of individuals but about the social condition of the working class; whose members are forced into work they may not want. Workers, therefore, are compelled to strengthen the power of those who force them into that work, and they are weakened by internal dissension over the opportunity for work.

More plausible is the frequent reading that defines alienation as a lack of self-realization. Workers, unable to choose their work, often cannot find meaningful work, have limited access to means of education, and, certainly in Marx's day, had no meaningful leisure. Hence their work and their lives present no challenge, no opportunity for growth and personal development.[6]

But this account of Marx's concept of alienation is still incomplete. It does not do full justice to Marx's claim in "Alienated Labor" that human beings are potentially free because they are species beings, and that insofar as they are not actually free, they are alienated. The same claim reappears in somewhat different words in *Capital*, in which the term "species being" itself is no longer used; but the conception of human freedom expressed by that term remains and still plays an important part.

Human beings, unlike animals, are capable of thinking about what they are doing; they are capable of producing what they want and not only what they need. Human beings "produce even if they are free from physical need, and only truly produce in freedom therefrom" (EPM, T 76). This thought is echoed at the end of Volume III of *Capital*: "The realm of freedom actually begins only where labor, which is determined by necessity, ceases" (CIII, T 441). The realm of freedom begins where actions are chosen, not imposed on us by physical or biological necessity, and where we choose what appears valuable in its own right.

But human beings do not merely produce commodities for consumption or as means of production; they also produce their societies and themselves:

> We have seen that the capitalist process of production is a historically determined form of the social process of production in general. The latter is as much a production process of material conditions of human life as a process taking place under specific historical and economic production relations, producing and reproducing these production relations themselves, and thereby also the bearers of this process, their material conditions of existence, and their mutual relations. (CIII, T 439)

Human production is the production of society and its members. Unlike animals, human beings are *capable* of freely producing— things, society, themselves—but they do not always do so. Sometimes this process of creation is deliberate, when it is the "object of one's will and consciousness"; throughout most of human history, however, it has not been deliberate. Early on, societies and human nature were shaped by intentional human acts, but the intentions concerned the solving of particular problems; in the meantime, the longer-range consequences of the solutions chosen—what sorts of societies resulted and how that affected human nature—were not considered and thus remained unforeseen. In their time, Marx and Engels believed that genuine freedom—the deliberate and thoughtful shaping of the social order and, consequently, of what it is to be a human being—was within reach. Freedom, which once existed only as a possibility because humans did not make use of their capacity to determine what human life could be like, is now within reach, ready to be actualized.

The concept of freedom used here is quite specific: It meant being free to "make one's life activity itself the object of one's will and consciousness." But today freedom has usually a different meaning. We are accustomed to calling a person free who can do as he or she pleases. If people want to spend their time drinking, or writing thick historical novels, they are free if no one hinders them in doing what they want. This is the freedom of the individual to do as she or he pleases. Marx and Engels appreciated the importance of that sort of freedom, but insisted on its limitations:

> This right to undisturbed enjoyment, within certain conditions, of fortuity and chance has up till now been called personal freedom. (GI, T 198)

In a society, such as ours, where individuals have far-reaching personal freedom, everyone (subject to certain legal restrictions) is allowed to pursue his or her private goals. Individuals may choose to drink or to write, but they make those choices and act according to them in a social framework over which they have next to no control. The shape of the institutions under which we live is the fortuitous outcome of those individual pursuits. The shape of the capitalist system as a whole is the result not of various collectively taken decisions but of the choices made by separate individuals in competition with one another. The shape of the social system as a whole is therefore the result of "chance." Where there is only individual freedom and competition but no collective decision making, individuals have personal freedom but, at the same time, are at the mercy of forces over which they have no control.

It is possible to have "personal freedom" but to lack the other freedom that comes only with collective control over society. In this second sense, human beings are free to the extent that the group to which they belong, *together*, shapes its way of life as the group chooses. As people have different ideas about how best to fashion their lives, such collective decision making inevitably involves discussion and the weighing of different desires and outlooks. People are free, therefore, when they collectively think about what their lives should be like and try to arrange their society accordingly.

This collective decision making produces what Marx and Engels called "human freedom" because it gives the group as much control as is humanly possible over its society. Only groups that think and act together can acquire the power to shape their social settings. Only in that way do they acquire a new kind of freedom *and* enhance their personal freedom. For in a society such as ours, personal freedom is everywhere bounded by institutional restrictions. Our personal freedom ends where the power of the separate individual ends. By joining with others for collective control, we enhance the power and thus the freedom of each of us.[7]

In a capitalist society, human beings act consciously, but not to the fullest degree; they are therefore not free. The reasons for that claim are familiar. The workers are forced to work; they cannot choose not to work, even for a limited period. How the work is done is not under their control because they have sold their labor time to the capitalists and thus cannot use that time as they please. But the capitalists, too, are not free to choose how or whether to work. The economic system leaves them only two choices: to maximize profits or to get out. Hence both worker and capitalist are alienated under capitalism.

> The propertied class and the class of the proletariat present the same human self-estrangement. But the former class feels at ease and strengthened in this self-estrangement, it recognizes estrangement as *its own power* and has in it the *semblance* of a human existence. The class of the proletariat feels annihilated in estrangement.[8]

Capitalism grants a wide degree of personal freedom but does not permit human freedom, because it does not permit human beings to plan their production processes with a view to what sort of society it will create and how it will affect human nature. Under capitalism it is not possible for people to adopt some and reject other production techniques, for instance, on the grounds that they do not like what certain techniques do to the people who use them. Profit maximization is the only acceptable criterion for choosing production techniques. In the *Early Manuscripts*, Marx simply makes this assertion. Only in the economics does he provide any reason for the assertion. Under capitalism "the process of production has mastery over the human beings instead of being controlled by them" (CI, T 327). Inasmuch as capitalism allows only separate, individual actors—the capitalist system is not deliberately chosen and maintained by a collective decision, but results from and is preserved by myriad individual choices—capitalism itself cannot be actively questioned. We can *talk* about the merits or faults of capitalism, but as individual agents we cannot do anything about it. We could change it only if we all participated in changing it at the same time. Hence it is only with the abolition of capitalism that genuine human freedom can flower, for only then will human beings consider together what they want to produce and how to shape their lives as human beings.

As long as the individualism intrinsic to capitalism is taken for granted, the possibility of genuine human freedom as well as the shortcomings of the existing system remain hidden from view. Alienation under capitalism is compounded by the fact that capitalism misrepresents itself due to the fetishism of commodities.

This life process of society, which is based on the process of material production, does not strip off its mystical veil, until it is treated as production of freely associated human beings and is consciously regulated by them in accordance with a settled plan. (CI, T 327)

We shall return to this vision of the future. For now we need to summarize our discussion of alienation: Human beings are capable of being genuinely free, of producing themselves as they choose to be rather than from necessity. But that can happen only if decisions are discussed and made collectively about regulating the production process. In the competitive capitalism that Marx and Engels studied, such collective decision making is impossible. Hence all people under capitalism are not fully free, and are therefore alienated.

Notes

1. For an interesting account of the shifts in Marx's methodology, and one more complex than mine, see Jean L. Cohen, *Class and Civil Society* (Amherst: University of Massachussetts Press, 1982), Chapter 1.
2. See Louis Althusser, *For Marx* (New York: Vintage Books, 1970). pp. 21ff.
3. See Chapter 11 of this volume.
4. See Chapter 7 of this volume.
5. Erich Fromm, *The Sane Society* (New York: Fawcett, 1955), p. 111.
6. See, for example, Allen W. Wood, *Karl Marx* (London: Routledge and Kegan Paul, 1981), Chapters 1 and 2. I have discussed this conception of alienation and its problems in more detail in my *Alienation and Class* (Cambridge: Schenkman Publishing Co., 1983), Chapter 5.
7. For a more detailed discussion of Marx's concept of freedom see George Brenkert, *Marx's Ethics of Freedom* (Boston: Routledge and Kegan Paul, 1983).
8. Karl Marx and Frederick Engels, *The Holy Family* (Moscow: Progress Publishers, 1975), p. 43.

For Further Reading

Wood, Allen W., *Karl Marx*, Chapters 1–4 (London: Routledge and Kegan Paul, 1981).
Schmitt, Richard, *Alienation and Class*, Chapter 5 (Cambridge: Schenkman Publishing Co., 1983).

PART FOUR

The Politics

16

Utopian and Scientific Socialism

MARX AND ENGELS DID NOT invent the term "socialism." It was in vogue before they began writing and was used by people with political outlooks quite different from theirs. In the third section of the *Communist Manifesto* they differentiate their view of socialism from a variety of other contemporary or earlier versions. They admired some of these a great deal, particularly the socialisms of Claude-Henri Saint-Simon, Charles Fourier, and Robert Owen, but were nevertheless critical of them for being "utopian":

> The economic situation as they [viz. Saint-Simon, Fourier, and Owen] find it, does not, as yet, offer them the material conditions for the emancipation of the proletariat. They therefore search after a new social science, after new social laws, that are to create these conditions. Historical action is to yield to their personal inventive action, historically created conditions of emancipation to fantastic ones, and the gradual, spontaneous class-organization of the proletariat to the organization of society specially contrived by these inventors. (CM, T 497–498)

Marx and Engels called these three thinkers and reformers "Critical-Utopian Socialists"—"critical" because they attacked "every principle of existing society" (CM, T 498). But why did they call them "utopian"?

Utopian Socialism

In current English usage, proposals are called "utopian" if they appear unattainable. Any serious suggestion that people travel to the moon was utopian before the invention of rockets because there was no known means of propulsion for such a distance beyond the earth's gravitational field. Similarly, thinking is called utopian if it proposes unrealistic goals.

If we look at the passage quoted above, we see that Marx and Engels use the term in a rather different way. They do not criticize the utopians for their choice of goals—the destruction of capitalist society—but on the contrary praise them for attacking

> every principle of existing society. Hence they are full of the most valuable materials for the enlightening of the working class. (CM, T 498)

The problem concerns the means chosen to transform society. The utopians neglect "historical action" and substitute "personal" action; for "historically created conditions of emancipation" they substitute "fantastic" (i.e., purely imaginary) ones; and they substitute themselves, the inventors of these new schemes for a more humane society, for the "class-organization of the proletariat." In addition, the proposals of the utopians are offered as "absolute truth . . . independent of time, space and the historical development of human beings" (SUS, T 693).

In general terms, Marx and Engels criticize their great socialist predecessors for failing to see that societies are historical creations and that, therefore, changes in societies must take account of the history and stage of development of each society in question. Historical change can be successful only when the requisite conditions prevail. One of those is the existence of large numbers of people ready to make a change. New societies are not brought into being by great leaders alone.

More specifically, Marx and Engels raise four criticisms:

1. Since capitalism was very undeveloped around 1800, when Fourier, Saint-Simon, and Owen worked and wrote, the utopians did not understand capitalism.
2. As a consequence, they did not understand class struggle.
3. They therefore substituted the actions of a great leader—usually themselves—for the concerted action of the proletariat.
4. The utopians were idealists, in Marx and Engels' sense of that term. They did not understand the connection between what people think and the material conditions under which they do their thinking.

Let us examine these criticisms, one by one:

1. The utopians were critical of the inequality, exploitation, and poverty characteristic of the bourgeois society that was just taking shape before their eyes, but because they did not understand capitalism, they

also could not understand how these evils were connected with capitalist society.

> The socialism of earlier days certainly criticized the existing capitalistic mode of production and its consequences. But it could not explain them, and, therefore, could not get mastery of them. It simply could reject them as bad. (SUS, T 700)

They therefore also did not understand that the solution to the socio-economic problems before them required the abolition of the capitalist system; they did not see the problems as elements in a very complex system that needed to be abolished as a whole.

But capitalism, like all other social systems, has a natural life span. It needs to mature before it is abolished. Capitalism cannot be replaced as soon as people understand that it is the source of their suffering; rather, it has to run its course and develop fully before a socialist revolution is possible.

The utopians had a very inadequate understanding of the process of social change.

2. Since the utopians did not understand capitalism, they did not understand that the evils they were trying to remedy—exploitation, inequality, poverty—were the inevitable accompaniments of the rule of the bourgeoisie. Thus, they also did not know that a revolution was necessary in which one class, the proletariat, would take power from another, the capitalists. But this change could only be brought about by the proletariat as a class. In the utopian view of social change, there was no room for class struggle, nor was the working class identified as the agent of social change.

> Hence they [viz. the utopians] reject all political, and especially all revolutionary, action; they wish to attain their ends by peaceful means, and endeavor, by small experiments, necessarily doomed to failure, and by the force of example, to pave the way for the new social Gospel. (CM, T 498)

Marx and Engels insisted, by contrast, that "the emancipation of the working class must be the work of the working class itself" (T 555).

3. The utopians, accordingly, also misunderstood the role of the farsighted individual reformer, thinking that one such person could be the leader to build a new world. Instead, such individuals can do no more than to "fight for the immediate aims of the working class" (CM, T 499). They may try to be helpful to the working class in the work

that it alone can do, but they cannot hope to do its work for it. The utopians did not understand who was to be the agent of social change.

4. They thought that our understanding about the world depends exclusively on how well we use our minds.

> If pure reason and justice have not, hitherto, ruled the world, this has been the case only because human beings have not rightly understood them. What was wanted was the individual man of genius, who has now arisen and who understands the truth. (SUS, T 685)

If previous generations had not developed the proposals of Saint-Simon, Fourier, or Owen, that failure must be attributed to their not thinking as clearly about the world as these three reformers did. But such a view ignores the insight of materialism, that what we know depends to a considerable extent on the world in which we live. It is impossible to understand capitalism before it has developed sufficiently to be observable, it is impossible to understand the historical role of class struggle before classes are sufficiently developed to become active politically, and so on. Of course, one must think well. Marx and Engels did not underestimate the contribution they themselves made by virtue of their own scholarly efforts and exceptional abilities. But they also believed, as we saw in Chapter 14, that socialist theory can be adequate only if its originators do not only think well but think under the requisite conditions—namely, when capitalism is ripe and socialism is just around the corner.

The utopians ignored history. They failed to see that as history changes, so do the concrete problems of human beings. They did not study their immediate environment to see what, precisely, the problems were and what it took to remedy them. Hence they misdiagnosed problems; they did not understand what was possible to do in their time and what needed to be deferred for the future. Most important, they did not understand who was going to bring about all these transformations.

Scientific Socialism

In calling their socialism "scientific," Marx and Engels were making the claim that it is not utopian; at the same time, they were making additional claims about the character of their own work—namely, that it constituted "science." Science explains the observed reality. It explains why there is widespread poverty under capitalism and, by implication, shows that in different social systems poverty has different causes. It links the observed evils, such as poverty, to the capitalist system by showing that exploitation is at the root of poverty under capitalism. It also explains the general structure of capitalism and thus can show who supports and who tends to oppose the perpetuation of capitalism.

Utopian and scientific socialists agree that the widespread poverty of working people must be remedied. The differences between them consist in how they plan to go about that. Scientific socialism knows that the evils to be remedied are due to the capitalist system. They also know that economic systems have historical careers that cannot be curtailed at will by human beings. Hence scientific socialism is more patient than its utopian precursors. It does not go out to build the better society as soon as the ink is barely dry on its blueprint for such a society. Understanding that social transformation is a long and slow process, it tries to understand what the next step is and then attempts to take it. In addition,

> in the foundation of their [viz. the utopians'] plans they are conscious of caring chiefly for the interests of the working class, as being the most suffering class. Only from the point of view of being the most suffering class does the proletariat exist for them. (CM, T 498)

The emancipation of workers is sought, not because they are exploited but because they are poor. But abolishing poverty is a very different goal from creating a society without exploitation. In a society without exploitation, the power over the workplace and over the investment of social surplus is not reserved for a minority but is shared widely. The abolition of poverty is an economic goal, the abolition of exploitation a political one. These different goals require different means for their realization.

Socialist theory is also needed to identify the supporters and the enemies of reform. For Saint-Simon,

> the antagonism between the third estate and the privileged classes took the form of an antagonism between "workers" and "idlers." . . . The workers were not only wage workers, but also the manufacturers, the merchants, the bankers. (SUS, T 688)

Saint-Simon had some understanding of class divisions and hostility between classes but completely misperceived the identity of the protagonists in the class struggle. Hence he thought that the workers and the employers they worked for belonged to the same class. By the same token, he only dimly recognized and completely misinterpreted the nature of exploitation. Socialist theory is needed in order to clearly identify not only the adversaries in the drama of social change, but also its goals. In understanding that it is not up to them alone to build a new world, the socialists, said Marx and Engels, take a role different from that taken by the utopians. They "support every revolutionary movement against the existing social and political order of things" (CM, T 500). Their immediate aim is "the formation of the proletariat into a class" (CM, T 484). They are able to make a contribution precisely by virtue of their scientific knowledge. They have

> the advantage of clearly understanding the line of march, the conditions, and the ultimate general results of the proletarian movement. (CM, T 484)

The misery of the workers as well as their lack of power, which manifest themselves in exploitation and the instability of the economic system, are there for all to see. Scientific socialism allows us, however, to understand these phenomena by explaining how these different complaints of working people are connected because they are all symptoms of capitalism. Knowing that, the socialists understand what needs doing; they understand "the line of march." Their analyses of contemporary capitalism give them an understanding of the "ultimate *general* results of the proletarian movement."

It is worth noting that Marx and Engels tended to vacillate about the precise role and usefulness of social science. In the passages quoted here from the *Communist Manifesto*, they suggested that scientific analysis is necessary at all stages of the workers' struggle. In other passages, we saw earlier, they claimed that before the final collapse of capitalism the usefulness of theory is more limited (see the second section of Chapter 14). In that latter view the distinction between utopian and scientific socialism becomes more difficult to draw, but it does not lose any of its importance.

Scientific socialism must be forever self-critical. Early on in their careers, Marx and Engels had criticized German philosophers for neglecting the detailed study of their own condition because they lacked this self-critical attitude:

> It has not occurred to any of these philosophers to inquire into the connection of German philosophy with German reality, the relation of their criticism to their own material surroundings. (GI, T 149)

Scientific socialists must be self-critical in two ways. They must constantly reexamine their results to see whether changed circumstances will require an adjustment in previous conclusions, and they must always be on the lookout for the intrusion of bourgeois ideology into their thinking.

If one wants to change the world, one must rest one's diagnoses of problems and prescriptions for change on a study of reality *as it is at the time*. The prescriptions, which at one time may be the best that can be had, can become reactionary when adopted by a later generation whose reality is different:

> Although the originators of these systems [viz. Fourier, Saint-Simon, and Owen] were, in many respects, revolutionary, their disciples have, in every case, formed mere reactionary sects. They hold fast by the original views of their masters, in opposition to the progressive historical development of the proletariat. They therefore endeavor, and that consistently, to deaden the class struggle, and to reconcile class antagonisms. (CM, T 499)

In the days of the utopians, the class struggle was undeveloped. Hence it was a defensible idea that poverty and exploitation could be overcome within the limits of the existing system. A generation later, when class conflict had become much more acute and its role therefore better understood, the old conciliatory stance simply retarded the necessary historical development of the working class. Similarly, as we shall see in Chapter 18, Marx and Engels initially believed that a revolution had to be violent, but they later changed their minds about that in the light of changed conditions. Scientific socialism cannot adopt the analyses of past eras because capitalism changes continually—"the bourgeoisie cannot exist without constantly revolutionizing . . . the whole relations of society" (CM, T 476)—and hence scientific socialism must reexamine its understanding of the world. It must rethink what its problems really are, what *precisely* the cleavages in the society are, and how to deal with them.

This view was expressed in the most widely read work of Marx and Engels, the *Communist Manifesto*, but it is usually ignored. The opinions of Marx and Engels have been taken as unchangeably true, very much in the manner in which the utopians took their views to be true for all times and places. A socialism that aspires to being scientific must rewrite its analyses of capitalism in every generation. Many Marxists have refused to do that and have thus lapsed into utopianism just when they thought they were being the most scientific.

But scientific socialists must not only be constantly alert to the ways in which their understanding of capitalism is rendered obsolete by changes in capitalism; they must also be on the lookout for signs that they have been misled by the "ruling ideas of the epoch"—that is, the "ideas of the ruling class." They must periodically reexamine "the relation of their criticism to their own material surroundings" (GI, T 149). This is a particularly serious worry in the case of intellectuals, who by virtue of their education and work, are not members of the proletariat. The workers' movement needs people like that, but

> if people of this kind from other classes join the proletarian movement, the first condition must be that they should not bring any remnants of bourgeois, petty-bourgeois, etc., prejudices with them. (T 554)

We saw in Chapter 14 that classes develop a class ideology in the course of their history, but that they do this in a setting where there is already a coherent ideology in use—the ideology of the current ruling class. The new and antagonistic class ideology is thus developed in the context of, in competition with, and in opposition to the reigning ideology. It is easy to get confused here; indeed, scientific socialists must again and again reexamine themselves to prevent their ideas from being taken over from the reigning bourgeois ideology, or from becoming mere mechanical inversions of such an ideology.

Scientific socialism is not utopian; it does not draw up blueprints to be executed through the efforts of gifted reformers. It recognizes the same evils as did the utopians but tries to explain them through its scientific study. These explanations bring to light the root causes of the observed problems and how they can be attacked. They are never complete but require constant reexamination in the light of new facts and further reflection.

Were Marx and Engels fully scientific socialists, or are there remnants of utopianism in their work? I shall argue in the second section of Chapter 18 that their views retain an element of utopianism.

17

The State

CLASS STRUGGLE IS THE motor of history. Dominant classes exploit the subject classes and maintain their power, as well as their mode of production, by means of that exploitation. Exploited classes, in turn, challenge the power of the dominant class to exploit them. Once they succeed, the former ruling classes lose their preeminence and are replaced by new ruling classes. A new mode of production takes the place of the previous one. The major upheavals in history are therefore brought about by class struggle over exploitation.

But class struggle, in its most developed form, is political struggle—that is, struggle over state power. Class struggle cannot be fully understood unless one understands the role of the state in capitalist society.

The Independent State

In scattered remarks, Marx and Engels describe the state as independent. If we look closely, we can distinguish three different senses in which the capitalist state is said to be independent.

1. In ancient society, particularly in the East, but also in Latin America (Mexico and Peru), production in what Marx called the "Asiatic Mode of Production" was dominated by one person who claimed divinity, ownership of all property, and state power. That supreme ruler combined in his person the leadership of the ruling class and the leadership of the state.[1] In capitalist society, by contrast, the ruling class and the state are distinct.

Capitalist society consists of two or more classes. But not all the institutions in that society are clearly identified with one or the other of these classes. In particular, the state in capitalist society is an

171

independent institution that is separate and distinct from the ruling class institutions, such as employers' associations or trade associations, or the political parties that represent the different classes.

The capitalist state is independent of the capitalist class insofar as it is a distinct institution. Capitalists do not have political office simply by virtue of being capitalists.

2. The state is independent from the capitalist class also insofar as the interests of one are not identical with the interests of the other. The capitalist class represents its private interests. The state is supposed to represent the public interest.

There is, for instance, a clear difference between public and private parks, schools, and art collections. The owners of the private institutions are free to use them according to their own interests, within legal limits. By contrast, public resources are run by the government to benefit all; the government is the guardian of the public good.

> Every *common* interest was straightaway severed from society, counterposed to it as a higher, *general* interest, snatched from the activities of society's members themselves and made an object of government activity, from a bridge, a schoolhouse and the communal property of a village community to the railways, the national wealth, and the national university of France. (18th, T 607)

The state represents the common, general interest of the nation, in opposition to the private interests of individual entrepreneurs. The publicly owned institutions are there for the benefit of all. The independence of the state consists in its being devoted to the "common interest."

3. But what constitutes the public interest is, of course, a matter of controversy and looks rather different from different points of view. What is "good for General Motors" is clearly not always good for the employees of General Motors—exploitation is good for General Motors but not for the exploited. From the capitalist point of view, however, the maxim that "what is good for General Motors, is good for the country" is a defensible view. Here the public interest is defined from the standpoint of the capitalists. From the standpoint of the people who do not own or run a business, "what is good for the country" looks quite different. "What is good" may well be full employment, affordable health care, education, and so on.

Accordingly, the definition of the public interest becomes an issue in the class struggle. The class that is most powerful will define the public interest in the light of its private interests and the state will be on its side. But the government does not always act in the interest of the ruling class. On the contrary, it often enforces laws that benefit working people against the interest and objections of the capitalists. Marx was perfectly well aware of that. He relates, in some detail, the struggles of employers against factory legislation and their various attempts to sabotage the enforcement of those acts, once they were passed.

> As soon as the working class, stunned at first by the noise and turmoil of the new system of production [viz. the factory system], recovered, in some measure, its senses, its resistance began. . . . For 30 years, however, the concessions conquered by the workers were purely nominal. Parliament passed five Labor Laws between 1802 and 1833, but it was shrewd enough not to vote a penny for their carrying out, for the requisite officials, etc. They remained a dead letter. . . . The normal working day for modern industry dates only from the Factory Act of 1833.[2]

Concessions were diffcult for the working class to get, but the workers *did* get them. Employers cannot always have it their way; the government works for both parties in the class struggle. It does appear to do more than just the bidding of the capitalists.

In general, the extent to which the state will be dominated by the ruling class depends on the relative strength of the contending classes in the class struggle. Marx notes in *The 18th Brumaire of Louis Bonaparte* that during the regime of Napoleon III in France, between 1852 and 1871, the proletariat and the bourgeoisie were equally unable to take power, so that the state of Napoleon III was fairly independent of all class pressures and could use the peasantry as its base.

> France, therefore, seems to have escaped the despotism of a class only to fall beneath the despotism of an individual. . . . The struggle seems to be settled in such a way that all classes, equally impotent and equally mute, fall on their knees before the rifle butt.[3]

In this passage we encounter a third sense in which the state may be independent—namely, if it is relatively free to operate without bowing to class pressures because the classes are equally matched and the influence of each neutralizes that of the other.

The state is therefore said to be independent if state institutions are distinct from class institutions and/or if the interests of the state are not automatically identical with class interests, and/or if class pressures are evenly matched so that the state can make policy independent of those class pressures.

The State as Manager of the Affairs
of the Bourgeoisie

The independence of the state is only half the story. Marx and Engels *also* insist that the state is on the side of the capitalist ruling class. Some interpreters therefore believe that Marx and Engels have several incompatible concepts of the state. I shall argue that these different claims about the independence of the state are perfectly consistent.

Marx and Engel's concept of the state is a flexible one. In many passages, they mean by "state" no more than what we often mean by the "government": the bureaucracy, the police, the courts, the tax office, and so on. It is

> the centralized state power, with its ubiquitous organs of standing army, police, bureaucracy, clergy, and judicature . . . [and] parliamentary control . . . the national power of capital over labor, a public force organized for social enslavement. (CW, T 629–630)

The state here refers to the legislature—"parliamentary control"—and to the familiar organs of the executive and judiciary branches. The "clergy" is added to take into account those countries, such as France, in which there was an established church. We shall encounter a broader concept of the state in the next section.

In the last quarter of the nineteenth century, the French state was "under parliamentary control," but that did not make it the organ of all the people; rather, it placed the state "under the direct control of the propertied classes" (CW, T 630). This is a claim that Marx and Engels repeat over and over, that the state is "but a committee for managing the common affairs of the whole bourgeoisie" (CM, T 475). We need to find out what that means and then see whether that claim is consistent with their earlier claim that the state is independent.

Different interpreters give rather different reasons for regarding the state as clearly on the side of the capitalists. One common interpretation asserts that the government is separate but, nevertheless, closely identified with the capitalists. The reason is that the capitalists and the upper echelons of the politicians, the military, and the bureaucrats are closely linked to each other by being members of the same class, products of the same schools, and members of the same clubs who live in the same suburbs and intermarry. Working people, by contrast, are excluded from the government because they are excluded from that social circuit of suburb, school, and country club.[4]

There is a good deal of empirical research to show that, in our day, this connection between government and the top layer of the capitalists is, in fact, often a very close one; Marx, too, was fully aware that, in his era, the role played by the government was, in part, conditioned by the fact that the people in the government belonged to the capitalist class. He discusses this connection in his pamphlet on the Paris Commune of 1870, the first (albeit short-lived) workers' government in human history. Before the establishment of the Commune, elections had served the sole purpose of "deciding once in every three or six years which member of the ruling class was to misrepresent the people in Parliament" (CW, T 633). The Paris Commune abolished the existing government and substituted one in which workers, rather than members of the bourgeoisie, did government work at workers' wages. The Commune also abolished not only the privileges of the bureaucrats but also the bureaucracy as a separate social class. An important achievement of the Paris Commune was precisely that it broke the hold of the ruling class over the government by ending the practice of staffing the government mostly with members of the ruling class.

The close class connections between the members of the governing elite and the top echelons of business ensure that the day-to-day policies of the government serve the interests of the capitalists. The connection between the ruling class and the state consists in the ability of the capitalists to use the *power* of the state to their advantage. In this view, which is often called the "instrumentalist" version of the Marxist theory of the state, the state is treated as an instrument of ruling class power.

But many interpreters want to hold that the capitalist state is on the side of the capitalists not only because they have more power, and thus can use the state in their own behalf, but also because the very structure of the capitalist state favors the ruling class. The state is the manager of the affairs of the bourgeoisie by virtue of its *structure* as a capitalist state.[5] Capitalism is perpetuated, in part, through the day-to-day exercises of state power on behalf of the capitalists; in addition, it continues to exist because the very structure of the state is supportive of capitalism, because it supports the reproduction of the capitalist system.

The instrumentalist and structuralist views of the state are widely seen as mutually exclusive. But Richard Miller has argued recently that they are both valuable, though one-sided. The contribution of each must be taken seriously in any adequate political theory.[6]

The State as Framework of Exploitation

Capital thrives on the reinvestment of profits, but profits are the products of surplus labor that workers are compelled to perform without pay. Exploitation is at the very heart of the maintenance of the capitalist system. But how is exploitation possible? Workers possess no property; they are dependent on daily work for the money to keep them and their families alive. They must accept work even if they do not like the conditions; they must submit to exploitation for fear of starving. Exploitation is made possible by the discrepancy in economic power between worker and employer. This discrepancy is the direct consequence of the fact that means of production are private property.

Thus far it seems that only the relations between individual workers and employers are necessary for exploitation to take place. But suppose that the workers want to organize to resist the demands of employers, or that they threaten to burn down the factory if their working conditions do not improve. Clearly the individual employer needs the backing of all the other employers, in the form of the state, the police, the army, and the courts, to resist those threats. Exploitation in the individual workplace is possible only within a complex social and legal order, which includes a state apparatus that formulates laws and then enforces that legislation.

The worker and the employer meet in the marketplace and strike a bargain. For that contract to be even possible, a law of contract is needed; also necessary is a social order in which people who are socially and economically very unequal are nevertheless equals before the law. The employer, because he has greater status and wealth, is not thereby entitled to break contracts or to cheat his employees. Underlying capitalist exploitation is a legal system that treats all people equally, whatever their other differences may be.

Marx gives other examples of the very complex legal and political order required as the background condition for exploitation:

> For example, the fact that surplus labor is posited as surplus value of capital means that the worker does not appropriate the product of his own labor; . . . This . . . law of bourgeois property, . . . through the law of inheritance, etc., attains an existence independent of the accidental transitoriness of individual capitalists. (CI, T 260)

In order for the reproduction of capital to occur, the law needs to guarantee that what the worker produces, including surplus value, belongs to the employer. But since employers are mortal, the continuity of capital must also be guaranteed by laws of inheritance. Exploitation, under capitalism, presupposes a complex legal order that enforces contracts and the rights of private property.

Exploitation is possible in a feudal or slave society because the property owners are also in control of the state and its power of organized violence. In feudal times, for instance, the large landowners were at the same time political leaders, and the king or emperor owed his position, in part, to the ownership of more land than anyone else. The situation was similar in even earlier times:

> In the case of the ancient peoples, since several tribes lived together in one town, the tribal property appears as state property, and the right of the individual to it as mere "possession." (GI, T 186)

Where land was owned by a community, the political and economic power of the community were embodied jointly in the state. Individuals only "possessed" their land; that is, they were allowed to use and farm it, but they could not sell it.

Under capitalism, however, exploitation occurs, even though workers and employers exchange equals for equals and the contract between them is entered into voluntarily. There is no overt threat of violence involved in capitalist exploitation.

One of the innovations of capitalism has been the sharp distinction between private and public concerns. Under capitalism, property is privately owned and each owner is supposed to consider only private interest. Private property becomes "private" not only in the sense that it belongs to particular individuals, but also in the sense that public intervention in the conduct of private economic affairs is minimized. The public is denied an interest and a voice in the sphere of private property. The state becomes quite separate from the economy, because the economy has become the realm of the purely private. The public aspects of that social order become distinct in the form of the state:

> Out of this very contradiction between the interests of the individual and that of the community the latter takes an independent form as the *State*. . . . Just because individuals seek *only* their particular interest, which for them does not coincide with their communal interest . . . the latter will be imposed on them as an interest "alien" to them, and "independent" of them. (GI, T 160–161)

The state, in this very broad sense, is independent because it is distinct from the class of owners. It is nevertheless on the side of the capitalists because it maintains the economic order of capitalism—for instance, by denying that considerations of public interest override private economic interest and by providing the requisite legal foundations for private ownership. The state supports exploitation by preserving the economic sphere as that of private ownership. It can do this only because it is independent. The capitalist order rests on the independence of the state from the economy.

The specific economic form in which unpaid surplus-labor is pumped out of the direct producers, determines the relationship between rulers and ruled . . . the corresponding form of the state.[7]

In our time, to be sure, this autonomy of the private economic sphere has become compromised. But the presumption still is that the owner of private property has a right to dispose of that property as s/he sees fit. The burden of proof is on the person who asserts that public interests should curb private enterprise. The established principle is that the public has no rights in the sphere of private property. In that way the nature of the state, its separateness from the realm of private economic enterprise, is an indispensable foundation of capitalism and thus supports the capitalist class.

Marx's theory of the state contains a clear distinction between the *power of the state*, as manifested in legislation and in the selective enforcement of legislation (e.g., the early English Factory Acts mentioned earlier), and the specific *nature of the state*. The power of the state is more or less in the hands of one class, depending on the balance of class forces in a society. But the nature of the capitalist state—its independence—will always favor the capitalist class, even when the power of the state is substantially in other hands.[8]

In the broadest sense of the concept of the state, Marx includes the following meanings:

1. The actual acts of the government and uses of state power (e.g., pieces of legislation and their enforcement);
2. Various government agencies (not only the repressive ones, but the entire bureaucracy);
3. The legal system according to which the state, in the previous two senses, acts and is constituted, and which it enforces;[9] and
4. The nature of the state, in terms of its independence from the sphere of private economic activity.

These several meanings of the concept of the state, together with those pertaining to the concept of independence, explain how Marx and Engels can claim both that the state is independent and that it is the instrument of capitalist class rule. The state is independent in the sense that the capitalists do not hold state power by virtue of being capitalists— because they operate in the private sphere, which is distinct from the public sphere, the sphere of the state. But this very independence, the *nature* of the capitalist state, gives the capitalists more power over the *acts* of the state than the workers, permits them to staff the government *agencies* in larger numbers than workers, and defines the "public interest," more often than not, in terms of capitalist class interest. The state is, accordingly, not independent in those latter respects. In addition, only a state that is independent in the first sense can enforce the legal underpinnings of exploitation in the private sphere; in that case, it would not be independent in the second sense, because its acts in favor of the capitalists over the workers.

This is only a very rough beginning for a theory of the capitalist state. Marx and Engels did not work out the mechanisms by which capitalism shaped that state. But they were aware that the connections between a mode of production and the state are much more complex than indicated so far. There is clearly no one-to-one correspondence between a mode of production and a particular structure of the state. For instance,

> the really difficult point to discuss here is how relations of production develop unevenly as legal relations. Thus, e.g., the relation of Roman private law (this less the case with criminal and public law) to modern production. (G, T 245)

Roman law developed in a mode of production very different from that of capitalism, but the revival of the Roman law of property was, as a matter of historical fact, an essential step in the development of capitalism.[10]

Class Struggle in the Democratic State

In the preceding section we saw that Marx and Engels' conception of the state was quite inclusive and that they argued that the nature of the capitalist state is an essential precondition for the capitalist organization of the economy. Private ownership of the means of production is all of one piece with the separateness and independence of the state; legislation reflects the actual economic practices in the law of property and inheritance, for instance, as does the general conception of a legal system that is supposed to treat all persons equally.

But, the reader may object, none of this suffices to show that the state in capitalist society is not impartial. In Marx's day, when working people did not have the vote, power was perhaps one-sidedly in the hands of the capitalists. But since that day, the control of the state has passed into the hands of all the voters and the vote of the owner of property counts for no more than that of the person who barely makes a living.

This is an important observation, but it does not contradict the claims made by Marx and Engels. For they distinguished two ways in which the state supports capitalism and the capitalist class. Depending on the balance of power in the class struggle, the exercise of state power will favor one class or another. The winning of the vote by working people—which they accomplished only after long drawn out struggles—clearly put the control of state power more within their reach. As a result, the capitalists cannot pass laws or enforce them completely as suits their own interests; legislators must now answer to working-class constituents.

But all of this day-to-day political activity takes place within the limits and structures of the capitalist system, in which the state is independent in the senses explained in the preceding section. The economy is still under private control; private profit is still a powerful and legitimate moving force of economic activity. Exploitation is still the source of the capitalists' profits. The nature of the capitalist state has not changed, nor has the support that this structure provides for the continuation of the capitalist system.

In the capitalist state as Marx and Engels knew it, the economy, and with it exploitation, were outside the realm of politics and thus not affected by the extension of suffrage and the development of democratic political institutions. Hence the capitalist state, by its very structure, maintains capitalism. A working class that wants to put an end to exploitation must therefore put an end to the capitalist state. Not only must the existing bureaucracy be discharged and the existing structures dismantled but the capitalist state, in the broad sense, must be abolished as well. The entire system of laws and the underlying principles must be challenged, reexamined, and, where necessary, replaced. Above all, the distinction between democracy in the political realm and exclusive control by owners in the economic realm must end. The abolition of the capitalist state amounts to the extension of democracy to the economy. Marx customarily refers to this state as "a community of free individuals, carrying on their work with the means of production in common" (CI, T 326). This is the central idea in Marx's conception of communism, which we shall discuss in Chapter 19.

Notes

1. Marx, *Grundrisse* (Harmondsworth: Penguin Books, 1973), pp. 473ff.

2. Marx, *Capital*, Vol. I (New York: International Publishers, 1967), pp. 278–279.

3. Marx, *The 18th Brumaire of Louis Bonaparte* (New York: International Publishers, 1963), p. 121.

4. Ralph Miliband, *The State in Capitalist Society* (New York: Basic Books, 1969), Chapter 3.

5. Martin Carnoy, *The State and Political Theory* (Princeton, N.J.: Princeton University Press, 1984), Chapter 4.

6. Richard Miller, *Analyzing Marx* (Princeton, N.J.: Princeton University Press, 1984), Chapters 3 and 4.

7. Marx, *Capital*, Vol III, pp. 791–792.

8. This is also a more generous concept of the state than that used by Engels, for whom the state essentially consisted of the repressive arm of the government, the police and the army. See Frederick Engels, *The Origin of the Family, Private Property and the State* (New York: International Publishers, 1972), Chapter IX.

9. Marx and Engels include a fourth aspect under the concept of the state—namely, its different forms in the sense of "democracy, aristocracy, and monarchy" (GI, T 160). The connection between the forms of the state, in that sense, and capitalism is poorly understood, and Marx and Engels have no theory that bears on it. Iring Fetscher found a fifth meaning of the concept of the state: the state as the means of legitimating the existing social order. See Fetscher, *Marx and Marxism* (New York: Herder and Herder, 1971), pp. 182ff.

10. This difficulty is developed in interesting ways in Gran Therborn, *What Does the Ruling Class Do When It Rules?* (London: New Left Books, 1978), Part II, Chapter 2.

For Further Reading

Martin Carnoy, *The State and Political Theory* (Princeton, N.J.: Princeton University Press, 1984), Chapter 2.

18

The Transition to Socialism

MARX WAS BURIED in Highgate Cemetery, London, on March 17, 1883. In his speech at the graveside, Engels said:

> Marx was before all else a revolutionist. His real mission in life was to contribute, in one way or another, to the overthrow of capitalist society and of the state institutions which it had brought into being, to contribute to the liberation of the modern proletariat. (T 682)

Thus far we have talked about Marx and Engels as philosophers and students of society. We must now turn to their thinking about fundamental social change. For them that meant talking about revolution.

The Concept of Revolution

In his 1895 Introduction to Marx's *Class Struggles in France*, Engels wrote:

> All revolutions up to the present day have resulted in the displacement of one definite class rule by another. (T 560)

Indeed, a revolution occurs when the power over the society passes from one *class* to another: "The first step in the revolution by the working class is to raise the proletariat to the position of ruling class" (CM, T 490). As long as the members of a new government belong to the same class as the members of the previous one, a *coup d'état* has occurred, not a revolution.

How does this transfer of power take place? Marx and Engels give various answers to that question, but often they describe this transfer of power as a "revolution"—meaning by that word an "uprising" or "victorious insurrection" (T 559).

Notice the two different senses in which the word "revolution" is used here. In the first instance, a revolution is defined as the transfer of power from one class to another; in the second the word refers to a particular political tactic, namely, "uprisings" or "insurrections." It is interesting to notice that Marx and Engels switch from one meaning to the other within the same page. Thus, in the *18th Brumaire*, Marx writes: "The social revolution of the nineteenth century cannot draw its poetry from the past." Here Marx refers to the coming proletarian revolution in which the proletariat will take power from the capitalists. The next paragraph begins with the words "The February Revolution. . . ." Here the reference is to an uprising in Paris that brought an end to the reign of Louis Philippe in 1848 but did not, in the end, transfer power to a new class (18th, T 597). That second revolution, in February 1848, was an attempt by the Paris proletariat to take power—but that attempt failed. The uprising was defeated. Similarly, Marx described the period from 1848 to 1849 in Germany as "revolutionary years" although in its wake the bourgeoisie that had risen up in 1848 surrendered "power once again to this feudal absolutist party" so that no transfer of power of any permanence took place (T 502–503).

Marx and Engels use the word "revolution" in these two senses because they believed that the proletariat would take power by means of an uprising, in which it would take *state* power. The proletarian revolution in the first sense, the transfer of power from capitalists to proletarians, would have to employ the tactic of revolution in the second sense—meaning an uprising—that would take political power away from the capitalists.

Marx and Engels believed this because, according to them, the proletariat could not use the same means to come to power as those used by the early capitalists.

All the preceding classes that got the upper hand sought to fortify their already acquired status by subjecting society at large to their conditions of appropriation. The proletarians cannot become masters of the productive forces of society, except by abolishing their own previous mode of appropriation, and thereby also every previous mode of appropriation. They have nothing of their own to secure and to fortify. (CM, T 482)

The rising bourgeoisie built its own alternative institutions in the interstices of feudalism. First it created its new economic institutions and thereby transformed significant sectors of the economy from feudal to capitalist ones; and only then, after it had acquired substantial economic power, did it also take political power and become the ruling class of modern society. It is true that Marx and Engels interpreted the English Civil War in the middle of the seventeenth century as a bourgeois revolution. But that, at best, was just one episode in a long process that reached its conclusion only when the bourgeoisie took full political power over English society in the middle of the nineteenth century.

But the proletariat does not own anything, and thus it cannot develop a new mode of production and a new way of running the economy while the old way—the way of the capitalists—is still in force. Some attempts at doing just that—that is, developing cooperative enterprises— were instructive, Marx thought, but

> the experience of the period from 1848 to 1864 has proved beyond doubt that, however excellent in principle, and however useful in practice, cooperative labor, if kept within the narrow circle of the casual efforts of private workmen, will never be able to arrest the growth in geometrical progression of monopoly, to free the masses, nor even to perceptibly lighten the burden of their miseries. . . . To save the industrious masses, cooperative labor ought to be developed to national dimensions. Yet the lords of land and the lords of capital will always use their political privileges for the defense and perpetuation of economical monopolies. So far from promoting, they will continue to lay every possible impediment in the way of the emancipation of labor. (T 518)

The proletariat cannot build socialist or proto-socialist institutions in a capitalist society and thus gradually overwhelm that society with its more effective institutions, because the capitalists have the economic and political power to stop these alternative institutions from becoming any kind of significant threat to capitalist enterprise. The proletarian majority needs to gain political power to protect its movement. The proletariat must take political power first, and then use state power to abolish private property in the means of production by nationalizing all property in land, abolishing the right of inheritance, and instituting a steeply graduated income tax (CM, T 490).

The foregoing, according to many interpreters, is Marx and Engels' theory of revolution.[1] But it seems to me that what we have here is not a theory, or even the outline of one, but only scattered comments, some of which are not plausible given what they meant by the "state." It seems more accurate to recognize that Marx and Engels did not tell us how the state, in their rich and complex sense of the term, is to be conquered by the proletariat, because they simply did not know.

A Theory of Revolution?

Consider the four different senses in which Marx and Engels used the concept of the state (Chapter 17). By "state" they meant (1) the power of the state (e.g., to pass laws and to enforce them), (2) the state apparatuses (e.g., the police, the courts, and the legislature), (3) the legal order of the state (e.g., the laws of private property and contract), and (4) the "form" or nature of the state (e.g., the division between the political and the economic sphere, which results in the independence of the state from the economy and the classes that run it).

An uprising, if it succeeds, can take over the state offices. The working class can occupy the police station and city hall; it can surround and then take over the television and radio stations, and begin to broadcast news of the uprising. Taking over the *power* of the state is, however, much more difficult. There is a great deal of difference between being in physical possession of government offices and being actually able to govern. A case history will illustrate this.

In 1918, at the end of World War I, the Imperial German government that had lost the war collapsed and was replaced by "Soldiers, Sailors, and Workers Councils" in different cities in Germany. The workers, many of them still in uniform, took over the government offices. In the port city of Hamburg, just four days after such a Council was set up, it

received a group of distinguished visitors in City Hall. Led by Max Warburg, director of one of Germany's most powerful banking and financial empires, these men represented the leading banking and commercial firms of Hamburg. Their business was unequivocal. It was clear, they pointed out, that the government of a city state of over one-and-a-half million souls could not be conducted without funds. . . . They generously offered to provide such necessary funds. Since, however, they were to take such large personal risks in the interests of Hamburg, it seemed only fair that they should have a certain voice in deciding how the funds were to be spent.[2]

The upshot of that negotiation was that the previous ruling elites came back into the city government and soon were running the city again, gradually squeezing out the workers. The uprising had succeeded in giving the workers control of the government offices, but not the power to run it. The various proletarian uprisings that Marx chronicled support the same conclusion: Taking over city hall physically does not guarantee the ability to govern the city. Here is what happened in Paris in 1848:

When it came to the actual conflict, however, when the people mounted the barricades . . . the republic appeared to be a matter of course. . . . Having been won by the proletariat by force of arms, the proletariat impressed its stamp on it. . . . While the Paris proletariat still revelled in the vision of the wide prospects that had opened before it . . . the old powers of society had grouped themselves, assembled, reflected, and found an unexpected support in the mass of the nation. (18th, T 600)

The revolution began with workers fighting in the streets. Their victory made them believe that they were now in power. While they were deliberating on how to reshape French society, the previous ruling groups gathered together again. The outcome was a clear defeat of the proletariat. It did not win state power.

But now consider the fourth sense of the concept of the state. Will an uprising give the proletariat control over the *nature* of the state? The class that wants to take state power must replace the bourgeois state with a different, proletarian one. A revolution requires not only a transfer of state power from one class to another but a *transformation* of state power. A new class will have a state of a new form. Marx was aware of that.

But the working class cannot simply lay hold of the ready-made state machinery and wield it for its own purpose. (CW, T 629)

Marx realized that having state power is not sufficient. The state itself must be transformed. The impressive achievement of the Paris Commune, Marx thought, was the realization by the Communards that the old form of the state was not an adequate foundation for building a new kind of society. The new society requires not only new economic institutions but new political institutions as well. The economic sphere must cease being private—that is, under the control of a small group of owners.

But what does that mean? Marxists traditionally interpreted the abolition of private ownership of the means of production as nationalization, as state ownership of those means of production. But nationalization involves not the abolition of the capitalist state but the extension of its power to the point where there is no private sphere at all, such that the state, still the representative of public interest, rules over all. Nationalization of the means of production yields not socialism but state capitalism.

A socialist society must also have its private sphere in which no one is told what to do and what to think. The abolition of the capitalist distinction between public and private thus cannot mean that the private sphere is reduced to the barest minimum. It must mean, instead, that the terms "public" and "private" are *redefined*. What is "private" will no longer be defined in terms of property ownership but will, we would hope, include the choice of what to do for work and where to do it. The "public," on the other hand, will lose its identification with a separate group of people—the government—and instead will be redefined as what all the people need, decide, and do together.

It is altogether unclear how an uprising in which the workers take over the government offices will lead to this redefinition of what is private and what is public. Marx and Engels had nothing to say about this. What seems clear is that they were wrong to reject the building of new kinds of institutions in the context of the old. The creation of the transitional state can, and must, be prepared for by changing the capitalist state from being outside the economy to being deeply involved in it. The welfare state is clearly a capitalist institution, but it may also be a step on the road to redefined public and private spheres. One of the sources of the failure of the Bolshevik revolution—one of many— to build genuine socialism may well have been that confusion between abolishing the private sphere by redefining what "public" and "private" mean, and the nationalization of industry.

In order to construct this new state, and the new society, the working class must understand that such innovations are needed; it must also understand the ways in which state and economy must change. How can the proletariat develop its own institutions, the expertise to run them, and the world outlook by which to orient itself?

Marx and Engels had very little to say about that. They claimed repeatedly that the proletariat is "organized by the very mechanism of the process of production itself . . . " (CI, T 438)—that workers learn to work together in the large factories where only the collective work of many different persons produces one product. But those lessons are ambiguous, as Marx and Engels themselves stressed over and over, for in the factory, workers are also compelled to compete with one another. The lessons learned in the factory, organized by capitalists, on capitalist principles, cannot help but be tainted with bourgeois ideology. In the writings of Marx and Engels, there is little discussion of the working class organizing itself. But they believed that the working class must organize itself for concerted political action before it becomes a class in the fullest sense and is ready to take power over the society as a whole.

Marx and Engels, occasionally, claimed that the required understanding is the product of revolutionary struggle itself:

> The alteration of men on a mass scale is necessary, an alteration which can only take place in a practical movement, a *revolution*. (GI, T 193)[3]

But whatever insight is hidden here still needs to be worked out. We need to know how the proletariat will gain the understanding needed to prepare itself for a revolution, specifically for transforming the state. To be told that the necessary understanding will arise in the process of revolution itself is not helpful.

As we saw in Chapter 14, many interpreters of Marx and Engels believe that the required understanding will be provided for the working class by theoreticians in the working class movement. But we also saw that these theoreticians have a very limited role. They are able to formulate the correct theory only when the revolution is near at hand. Prior to that, they are condemned to being utopians. Hence they cannot be the educators of the proletariat. The proletariat must educate itself. How that will happen Marx and Engels did not tell us.

The truth is that Marx and Engels did not have a very clear idea of the way in which a revolution will take place. They found themselves very much in the position of Saint-Simon and the other utopians, who started to think about socialism before it was possible to understand the process by which socialism would come about. Marx and Engels thought about a proletarian revolution long before the proletariat was ready to undertake it.

The rebellions that Marx and Engels observed at first hand in the fifty years between 1840 and 1890 played an important part in the transformations of nineteenth-century Europe. But there were no proletarian revolutions. Marx and Engels regarded these uprisings as revolutions—albeit failed ones—because they believed that the proletarian revolution was near at hand. They thought so first in 1848 and again in 1850. Engels still thought so in 1895 (T 562). Whatever they observed was, in their eyes, the revolution prefigured. They believed that they could discern the signs of the coming transformation. Unlike the utopian socialists, they did not make up plans and then put them into practice without studying concrete conditions. On the contrary, they studied conditions in great detail and from them discerned the shape of the changes to come.

But they misread the conditions as revolutionary when they were not, because they did not examine the question of how one could tell, concretely, that capitalism was ripe for being replaced by a revolution. They continually insisted that a proletarian revolution could not take place before capitalism was ready to be replaced. But when is capitalism ready? That question was never discussed in detail. If we look to Marx and Engels to tell us what will be the unmistakable signs of an imminent capitalist collapse, we get nothing more useful than formulations such as this:

The monopoly of capital becomes a fetter on the mode of production.
. . . Centralisation of the means of production and socialisation of labor
at last reach a point where they become incompatible with their capitalist
integument. This integument is burst asunder. The knell of private property
sounds. The expropriators are expropriated. (T 438)[4]

or this:

The whole of the particular industry is turned into one gigantic joint-
stock company; internal competition gives place to the internal monopoly
of this one company. . . . But in this case the exploitation is so palpable
that it must break down. No nation will put up with production conducted
by trusts. (SUS, T 710)

Obviously Marx and Engels thought that the concentration of capital
could go no further. But they had no clearly articulated reason for that
belief. In fact, in the France that Marx studied and described repeatedly
between 1840 and 1870, farming was still done by peasant proprietors.
There was no such thing as fully developed capitalist agriculture.
Capitalism was restricted to some of the major industrial centers. In
his notes on Mikail Bakunin's attacks on him, Marx took explicit account
of that fact and considered what shape a proletarian revolution would
take in a country where the bulk of the population was made up of
independent peasant proprietors (T 543–544). But what reason did he
have to think that such a country was ready for a working-class revolution,
and that capitalism, in such a country, was fully developed? Marx and
Engels thought that they were being scientific and only taking note of
what was happening for all to see because they thought that capitalism
was ripe. But they clearly were mistaken about that. Hence they took
what they saw—namely, various rebellions that only by stretching a
point could be called revolutionary upheavals—to be the patterns of
proletarian revolution. Falling victim to utopianism, they failed to develop
a theory of revolution. All we are left with are fragmentary insights
that do not form a coherent whole.

The Dictatorship of the Proletariat

The conception of revolution, the revolutionary uprising,
seemed to presage violence. But was violence inevitably an ingredient
of revolution? During the earlier years of Marx and Engels, working
men often did not have the vote (for that matter, working women did
not gain the vote until much later); where they did, elections were
clearly fraudulent (T 566). In such situations, a class that owned nothing

and therefore had neither economic leverage nor access to political power through the vote was reduced to street fighting in order to make its voice heard. Thus violence seemed an inevitable component of revolution.

But later in their careers Marx and Engels envisaged that with the progressive concentration of economic power in fewer and fewer hands, the small number of owners would realize that a civil war would be futile and extremely costly. They would therefore surrender power without a shot being fired. In this case, the transition might well be peaceful, especially if it was voted on by an enfranchised proletariat.[5] Legal and peaceful changes do not, of course, necessarily go together. Social change may be brought about by legal means (e.g., an election) but not be peaceful if there is rioting connected with the election. Conversely, workers may declare the constitution in power until then to be null and void—doing that would clearly not be "legal"—but if the displaced ruling class does not resist, the transition might very well be peaceful. Marx and Engels envisaged several different roads to socialism: The transition to socialism could either be via an electoral process—and thus be legal— or be illegal, according to the standards of existing law, without however provoking violence.

But they also continued to insist that the new regime immediately following the proletarian revolution would be a "dictatorship of the proletariat." Clearly they meant to suggest that the transition to socialism would not be effected democratically and, to that extent, would be coercive.

The expression "dictatorship of the proletariat" occurs only a few times in the entire body of Marx's and Engels' writings (e.g., CGP, T 538). Some commentators have thus argued that Marx and Engels are not committed to the use of coercion in a revolutionary transition.[6] Lenin, on the contrary, believed that the coercive nature of the socialist revolution was of the essence of Marxism.[7] The intermediate position, which is supported by the most extensive research, holds that Marx and Engels expected the transition to socialism to take place legally and peacefully in some countries. But they also thought that in places where democracy was not established under capitalism (e.g., Prussia, which was an absolute monarchy until the end of World War I), only extralegal means would be available. In such places the transition to socialism would have to take the form of a "dictatorship of the pro-letariat."[8]

But this, too, is an extremely general point. The "dictatorship of the proletariat" implies that power in the society will shift as a result of coercion. What form will that coercion take? In an early letter, Engels talks about "a democratic revolution by force."[9] Some interpreters (e.g., Lenin) thought this meant that after the revolution the former bourgeoisie would, for a time, be deprived of political rights. But it is not at all clear that this is what Engels had in mind. Perhaps the phrase referred to the old picture of socialism as being established by an uprising and, with it, democracy for everybody.[10]

The extended debate over the "dictatorship of the proletariat" rests on a number of misunderstandings. For us, who remember Stalin, Hitler, or Idi Amin, the word "dictatorship" has a much more ominous ring than it had for Marx and Engels. For them, dictatorship is compatible with democracy. They could therefore call bourgeois democracy a "dictatorship of the bourgeoisie" because even where universal suffrage existed, the capitalists had a great deal more economic and political power than the workers. Calling a newly established socialist government a dictatorship of the proletariat thus indicated that it was, initially, as democratic as a capitalist democracy. Such a new socialist government would equalize political power only after a while and then become much more democratic than a capitalist democracy could ever be.

In addition, Marx and Engels used the phrase "the dictatorship of the proletariat" in order to distance themselves from the political program that they called "Social Democracy":

> The peculiar character of Social Democracy is epitomized in the fact that democratic-republican institutions are demanded as a means, not of doing away with two extremes, capital and wage labor, but of weakening their antagonism and transforming it into harmony.[11]

Marx identified this political program with the German petty bourgeoisie, who lived under political conditions that excluded the possibility of an electoral transition to socialism, and called it "petty bourgeois socialism" (see CM, T 492, and "Address to the Communist League," T 504).

The goal of this political program was not to abolish the classes of capitalist society but to reduce the tensions between them. The socialism it talked about only softened the harsh realities of capitalism. It tried to reform capitalism, not to abolish it. Hence it did not want to use coercive measures against capitalists but preferred instead to employ the vote to introduce reforms, as that option would not challenge the fundamental structure of the capitalist system. For obvious reasons, Marx and Engels rejected that program.

They did not, however, reject the notion of working for short-term reforms. On the contrary, they believed that communists

> fight for the attainment of the immediate aims, for the enforcement of the momentary interests of the working class. (CM, T 499)

They only objected to limiting the political program to nothing but short-term reforms. Reforms are essential, they believed, but they must be undertaken within a revolutionary perspective.[12]

We shall see in the next chapter that proletarian revolution represents the opening to a more democratic society—a society that would move in the direction of ending all class oppression. Hence the dictatorship *of* the proletariat was never intended to stand for the dictatorship *over* the proletariat by a party or a state bureaucracy.

The Inevitability of Revolution

Marx and Engels were quite certain that revolution was inevitable, but in different contexts that claim has somewhat different meanings.

Inasmuch as a revolution consists of one class taking power from another, it is a necessary episode in the transition from capitalism to socialism. In this sense revolution is inevitable because capitalism cannot be overcome on the terrain of capitalist class and power relations. Replacing capitalism means replacing the capitalist class—and that, by definition, involves a revolution. Thus revolution is inevitable *if* capitalism is to come to an end.

But is revolution also inevitable in the sense that we can confidently expect capitalism to come to an end? That claim has earned Marx and Engels a good deal of criticism and ridicule. Readers have talked about Marx and Engels' inclination to play the prophets. But those criticisms are undeserved.

We saw in Chapter 7 what "capitalism" meant for Marx and Engels: a social system in which all goods and services are commodities, including labor power. But labor power can be a commodity only when some people own the means of production and others do not. Capitalist society is therefore a class society. The propertyless workers in such a class society are more or less on the margin of destitution; the owners are always threatened by other owners with whom they are in competition and thus are under constant pressure to increase their capital. Together with the capital owned by many different owners who compete with each other goes a state that is quite distinct from and outside the economy. The competitive economy is free from state control. Politics and economics are clearly distinct spheres.

That system, Marx and Engels were certain, will not last. The general reason for this was discussed in Chapter 5: Social systems form organic wholes, and in the process of reproducing themselves, such systems tend to go out of equilibrium and therefore change. This general feature of societies is highlighted by the dialectic.

In Part Two, we saw some of their more specific reasons for the claim that competitive capitalism cannot last. The internal incoherences produced by the insatiable desire of privately owned capitals to grow lead to economic crises that sooner or later paralyze capitalism to such an extent that it will need to be changed fundamentally.

There is no question that Marx and Engels were correct in that prediction. The competitive capitalism of the nineteenth century, plagued by economic crises, is no more. Instead we have a capitalism that is carefully nurtured by the state, which sees to it that crises are avoided and the harshest social consequences of capitalism are ameliorated. There is no reason to ridicule Marx and Engels for predicting the demise of competitive capitalism, for that prediction has come true.

But Marx and Engels also held that even state-run capitalism is a form of capitalism—"state ownership of the productive forces is not the solution" (SUS, T 712)—and that it too would collapse. Time will tell whether they were right about that. Marx and Engels did, however, provide some good reasons for considering the abolition of capitalism, particularly the state-supported kind—a very difficult project. In Chapter 11, we encountered Marx's "relative immiseration" thesis, which holds that in relation to the proletariat, the economic power of the capitalists will continue to grow. We need only to look at the modern multinational corporations with their farflung international operations to see that this is a plausible expectation. But it is also clear that the growing economic power of the capitalists will make the replacement of capitalism by the workers more and more difficult. What are the sources of a comparable growth in working class power? Marx and Engels do not tell us. This is one more question left open.

The claim that a revolution is inevitable, however, implies not only the end of competitive capitalism but also the inauguration of socialism. Marx and Engels thought that the world was on the brink of socialist revolution and that they could see the future prefigured in the present. Their reason for believing this cannot be fully discussed until we have explained what they meant by communism.

To this discussion we must now turn.

Notes

1. Hal Draper, *Karl Marx's Theory of Revolution*, Vol. II (New York: Monthly Review Press, 1978), pp. 28ff. This interpretation is contested by Shlomo Avineri in *The Social and Political Thought of Karl Marx* (Cambridge: Cambridge University Press, 1968), Chapters 7 and 8.

2. Richard A. Comfort, *Revolutionary Hamburg: Labor Politics in the Early Weimar Republic* (Stanford, Calif.: Stanford University Press, 1966), p. 47.

3. Paul Sweezy stresses this point in *On the Transition to Socialism* (New York: Monthly Review Press, 1971), pp. 107ff.

4. Richard W. Miller, in *Analyzing Marx* (Princeton, N.J.: Princeton University Press, 1984), Chapter 5, provides a very interesting account of this "fettering" metaphor. But even thus interpreted the metaphor will not allow us, at any particular time, to say that *now* is the time of the final and decisive breakdown of capitalism.

5. See Engels' "preface to the English edition" of Marx's *Capital*, Vol. I (New York: International Publishers, 1967). See also T 523.

6. Avineri, *Social and Political Thought*, p. 204.

7. Lenin, *The State and Revolution*, in *Selected Works*, Vol. II (Moscow: Progress Publishers, 1970), p. 310: "Only he is a Marxist who extends the recognition of the class struggle to the recognition of the dictatorship of the proletariat" (italics omitted).

8. Richard Hunt, *The Political Ideas of Marx and Engels*, Vol. I (Pittsburgh: University of Pittsburgh Press, 1974), Chapter 9.

9. Marx and Engels, *Selected Correspondence* (Moscow: Progress Publishers, 1975), p. 27.

10. This is the reading offered by Jon Elster, *Making Sense of Marx* (Cambridge: Cambridge University Press, 1985), p. 447.

11. Marx, *The 18th Brumaire of Louis Bonaparte* (New York: International Publishers, 1966), p. 50.

12. Ralph Miliband, *Marxism and Politics* (Oxford: Oxford University Press, 1977), Chapter 6.

For Further Reading

Shlomo Avineri, *The Social and Political Thought of Karl Marx* (Cambridge: Cambridge University Press, 1970), Chapters 6 and 7.

19

Communism

THE REVOLUTION THAT puts an end to capitalism will usher in a society that Marx and Engels called "communist." Today, in popular usage, the word "communism" is identified with the economic and political system of the Soviet Union and is frequently used as a virtual synonym for "dictatorship," whereas any kind of government intervention in the economy is liable to be called "socialistic." Marx and Engels used those terms in exactly the opposite sense: By "socialist" and "communist" societies they meant genuinely free societies.

In his 1888 preface to a new edition of the *Communist Manifesto,* Engels explained the terms "communism" and "socialism" as follows:

> By Socialists, in 1847 [the year in which they wrote the *Communist Manifesto*], were understood, on the one hand, the adherents of the various Utopian systems, . . . [and] on the other hand, the most multifarious social quacks, who, by all manners of tinkering, professed to redress, without any danger to capital and profits, all sorts of social grievances. . . . Whatever portion of the working class had become convinced of the insufficiency of mere political revolutions . . . then called itself Communist.[1]

Socialists were concerned with the "social" question—with the stark misery of the new industrial working class—but they were not critical of capitalism as a whole. They tended to be middle-class reformers. Communism found its main adherents among working people. Communists agreed with each other that private property needed to be abolished, but because of their rather diverse conceptions of "private property," they also had different conceptions of "communism." Hence Marx, in his essay "Private Property and Communism" (EPM, T 81ff.), classified different versions of communism according to the different understandings its advocates had of private property.

Both within and outside the Marxist tradition the meanings of these two words have changed frequently since then. Marx and Engels themselves vacillated in their usage, calling themselves communists at some times and (as we saw in Chapter 16) "scientific" socialists at other times, in order to differentiate themselves from the utopian socialists (SUS, T 683ff.).

Communist Society

Because they were scientific socialists, Marx and Engels knew better than to draw up detailed plans for future, better societies. But as critics of capitalism and revolutionaries who worked for its overthrow, they knew what about capitalism needed to be abolished and what needed to be retained. However opposed they were to utopianism, they were able to characterize communism insofar as they knew what aspects of the present society needed to be replaced in the proletarian revolution. The central features of capitalism that they expected communism to abolish were the means of production—raw materials, machines—which become capital only in the context of a society in which labor power is a commodity. As we saw in Chapter 7, this transformation of means of production into capital makes possible a system in which the search for profits becomes a major economic motive and competition between capitals becomes a standard feature of economic life. The productive wealth of the society is owned by individuals who decide what to produce solely in the light of expected profits. What is produced is determined not by what the society needs but only by what people are able to buy. Production is for exchange, rather than for use. The guiding ideas of capitalist private property are profit, expansion of capital, and economic growth.

Insofar as there is no overall plan and no coordination of the efforts of individual capitalists, this economic system is "anarchic." The marketplace and its prices determine the choices made by capitalists, but this coordination through the market leads to repeated crises of overproduction and/or underconsumption, stagnation, and bankruptcies.

From its very inception, capitalism was torn by inner tensions: The way in which goods are produced is at odds with the way in which the profits are appropriated. Goods are produced collectively: A number of different people are required to produce any particular commodity, and more people still are needed to get it to market. But the means of production are privately owned, and the profits are therefore also the property of private persons. The result of this collective productive effort does not accrue to the collectivity but is acquired by individual capitalists.

In the early stages of capitalism, this discrepancy between the social nature of production and the private appropriation of its products gives rise to an impressive growth of productivity by calling forth capitalist competition. But as capitalism matures, small firms are absorbed by large ones and capital becomes concentrated at the same time as the production process becomes more and more intricately organized as a collective process. The capitalists' pursuit of private profit begins to interfere with the smooth functioning of the economy. Economic crises become more frequent and more acute, and finally lead to the overthrow of capitalism.

With the end of capitalism comes an end to the private ownership of capital. "The knell of capitalist private property sounds" (CI, T 438). The productive apparatus remains, but changes are made in the way it is run and the way its products are distributed: "Machines will not cease to be agencies of social production when they become, e.g., the property of associated workers" (G, T 293). What will also change is that the workers will now be owners, albeit not individual owners, of the machines.

It is important to note that it is not all private property but *capitalist* private property that comes to an end. Communism does not interfere with private ownership of consumption goods—one's house, car, clothes, boats, stereos, and so on. More important, the change envisaged does not consist merely of a transfer of legal title from particular individuals to, say, the state. Expropriation of some capitalists, for instance, by nationalization of their capital is only the beginning of the abolition of capitalist private property. Much more important is the transformation of the entire socioeconomic system, as discussed in the second section of the preceding chapter.

In abolishing capitalist private property, then, the proletariat abolishes classes and class struggle, exploitation, production exclusively for private profit, competition between capitals, and the anarchy of the marketplace.

The condition for the emancipation of the working class is the abolition of every class, just as the condition for the liberation of the . . . bourgeois order was the abolition of all estates and all orders. The working class in the course of its development will substitute for the old civil society [i.e., the capitalist economic system] an association which will exclude classes and their antagonism, and there will be no more political power properly so-called, since political power is precisely the official expression of antagonism in civil society.[2]

Under communism, there are no classes because there is no wage labor, and therefore no exploitation and the coercion that that implies. This is not to say that the workers do not get a reward for their work— capitalists, after all, do get paid for their work. It is simply that the difference between the people who work for money and those who own and control the means of production disappears. Under communism everybody is an owner, and if that is to mean anything significant, everybody must participate in controlling the production process. What is produced is now determined by all; as in the United States, at least in principle, everybody helps to decide how to spend government revenue. But that, in turn, means the end of exploitation, the end of forcing people to work for money they will never see. Under communism workers decide how much they want to work for the common good, for money to be reinvested, or for any account other than their private consumption. Under communism, finally, the economy is subjected to planning by everybody. With the abolition of private ownership of means of production, the economy is no longer run to provide profits for individual capitalists. It is now run by the society as a whole for the good of all.

This means, in turn, that the reasons for making economic choices change. Private capitalists are compelled by the system in which they operate to choose whatever policy will yield the highest profit. They choose to manufacture goods in view of the expected market price. They produce, as Marx and Engels say, "for exchange." Under communism, price is no longer the main consideration. Instead the "associated producers" can decide what goods are most useful to the entire community and choose to produce them. They are going to "produce for use."

Central to communism, as Marx and Engels understood it, is therefore the replacement of the individual pursuit of profit and the anarchy of the marketplace with collective control of the economy. *Democracy is extended to the economy.* What disappears is the distinction, so sharp under capitalism, between the political realm, where decisions are made democratically (at least in theory), and the economy, where decisions are made autocratically by private individuals. The Paris Commune was a vivid example of democracy for Marx and Engels.[3] The Commune

filled all posts—administrative, judicial and educational—by election on the basis of universal suffrage of all concerned, subject to the right of recall at any time by the same electors. And in the second place, all officials, high or low, were paid only the wages received by other workers. (CW, T 628)

In addition, the Commune was to be a working, not a parliamentary body—an executive and legislative branch at the same time (CW, T 632). All officials were elected and subject to recall. All policy makers were to be responsible for executing the policies they themselves made. That meant, in practice, that bureaucrats were also subject to elections and thus responsible to their constituents. According to Marx, the Commune failed because it did not extend democracy to economic institutions. But he saw in it "the political form in which to work out the economic emancipation of labor" (CW, T 635). Central to communism is the democratization of the production process. In abolishing capitalist private property, the proletariat abolishes the coercive system in which the worker's contribution is paid for, as are other factors of production, but the worker has neither the right to contribute to the economic decision making nor even the right to determine how her or his labor power is to be employed. Under communism, workers are transformed from factors of production into citizens of and law givers in the economic realm.

In a communist society, all productive wealth is public property. But what is "public property"? At times, Engels thought of it as "state property" (SUS, T 713). In this connection, transfer of the ownership title to the state was apparently an important step in bringing about communism. But Engels also insisted that with the abolition of classes, the nature of the state changes fundamentally (ibid.). Whatever that means in detail, it is clear that the transition to communism involves the transfer of ownership title not to the state as it existed under capitalism but to a new and different institution. Engels occasionally went so far as to say that, under communism, "the state withers away" (SUS, T 713). Under communism, the "government of persons is replaced by the administration of things." That prediction has taken on canonical status because it was presented by Lenin as an integral part of Marxism.[4]

The communist state differs from the capitalist state in that it is genuinely the state of all the citizens. Under capitalism everybody votes, but only in the very restricted arena of politics. In the economic sphere the capitalists hold the upper hand and that, in effect, gives them the upper hand in politics also. Only the abolition of capitalist private property will provide the possibility of full-fledged democracy. But the nature of that democracy is subject to controversy. We saw that Marx was much impressed with the direct democracy of the Paris Commune. Others have insisted that parliamentary democracy, which involves the election of representatives, is still the best model. That debate began soon after Engels' death in 1895 and continues to this day.[5]

What will the communist economy look like? The view most generally held formerly was that a communist economy must be centrally planned.

Capitalism was a market economy; through central planning communist economies leave the anarchy of the market behind them. Since World War II this view has lost ground, however, and a modified form of market economy is often taken to be the closest approximation of a workable communist economy.[6]

These debates are complicated by the distinction between the lower and higher stages of communism that Marx drew in a private document, *The Critique of the Gotha Program*. This was written in 1875, when two separate socialist organizations in Germany unified and drew up a new party program (known as the "Gotha Program" after the town in which the party congress met). The lower stage consists of "communist society . . . just as it *emerges* from capitalist society" (CGP, T 529), whereas the higher stage of communism is "as it has *developed* on its own foundation" (ibid.). In other words, the lower stage consists of the transition from capitalism to communism; the higher consists of full-fledged communism, free of all hangovers from the previous society. In the former, workers are paid in proportion to their contribution; in the latter the principle obtains: "From each according to his or her ability, to each according to her or his needs." This distinction seems to lend support to the idea that the lower stage of communism—what since Lenin's day has often been called "socialism" in another sense of that word—rests on the exchange of goods and services and is therefore a market society.[7] In the higher stage, Marx and Engels seemed to have believed, the productive potential of modern industry would be developed to the point where there was enough of everything to go around. The problems of distributing scarce resources would accordingly disappear and everyone would be able to get what they needed while contributing whatever was in their power to contribute. Such an expectation does not, however, take into account the limitation of natural resources that has become so pressing in our century.[8]

Communism, Community, and Freedom

Communist society will be a free society because everyone will participate in running not only the political but also the economic affairs of the nation. This freedom is a precondition of "human freedom"— the freedom of a group of people to determine what human life and, with it, human nature will be like.

This conception of communist society follows directly from the earlier discussion of alienation (Chapter 15). Human beings are alienated insofar as they are not free, given that "freedom" refers to conscious control over one's life.

Freedom, in this field [viz. production] can only consist of socialized human beings, the associated producers, rationally regulating their interchange with nature. (CIII, T 441)

Human beings, unlike animals, are capable of shaping their own nature through the intermediary of different social orders. So far, this shaping has taken place haphazardly. Societies before ours were too poor to be able to afford the time to consider what human and social institutions would best promote human self-expression and freedom. Nor was there social science available that would have allowed people to develop a realistic assessment of their institutions or the effects of those institutions on human nature. But capitalism, with its enormous increase in productivity, has made it possible for us to think about how to shape our society. At the same time, we have developed the scientific tools to accomplish this end with confidence. Clearly this end can only be attained by the society as a whole—the "associated producers"—not by separate individuals. The individualism of the capitalist society left the most important decisions about social organization to the anarchy of the marketplace. The shape of social institutions was the unplanned outcome of the pursuit by separate individuals of their own private interests. Such a society provides personal freedom because individuals can do as they please, but it does not provide human freedom because the society is not in control of itself so far as that is humanly possible.

We encountered the distinction between personal and human freedom in Chapter 15. According to Marx and Engels, capitalism affords personal freedom in some cases (not in Nazi Germany, Franco's Spain, or Pinochet's Chile), but only communism provides human freedom because it provides a genuine community. But that claim raises an important question for the modern reader who thinks of conformism and the suppression of individual desires and differences when she or he hears the word "community." Will the human freedom achieved in the communist community be achieved at the price of personal freedom?

Marx and Engels were aware of that question, and they took it up repeatedly. They were certain not only that personal freedom need not be sacrificed under communism, as they understood it, but also that, on the contrary, full individual development and hence full personal freedom were possible *only* under communism:

Only in community [with others has each] individual the means of cultivating his gifts in all directions; only in the community, therefore, is personal freedom possible. (GI, T 197)

By "community" they meant a society in which the sorts of decisions that can only be made effectively by everyone are, indeed, made in genuinely democratic ways.

Here is their train of thought: What persons are, as individuals, is not completely under their individual control. One cannot make oneself be anything one wants. Individual persons are shaped by the institutions to which they belong. Marx expresses this epigrammatically in the sixth Thesis on Feuerbach as follows: The individual "is the ensemble of the social relations" (T 145). For instance, the

> personality [viz.of the capitalist] is conditioned and determined by quite definite class relationships. (GI, T 199)

Inasmuch as persons do certain jobs in society, they tend to acquire certain character traits, interests, habits, and so on. Without such adaptations to the demands of their particular occupations, they would not be able to do a good job. A capitalist who cannot bear to win in competition, or to outsmart someone, will not be a capitalist for long. A worker who is unwilling to take orders will not work very often. In this way we are shaped by the work environment, and this fact limits personal freedom for it limits what we can choose to be.

In a communist society we gain indirect control over that aspect of ourselves because we can choose to change the social structure and the roles in the society that need to be filled, and with it the ways in which we are shaped by the social system in which we function. The extension of human freedom under communism is therefore also an extension of personal freedom. Under capitalism, one can *do* what one wants (within definite limits). Only under communism can one also *be* what one wants.[9]

That answer will fail to satisfy the critics, however, because what worries them is not the range of one's personal choices (although that is obviously important) but personal freedom in a more traditional sense: freedom of speech, freedom of religion, and all the other freedoms guaranteed by the Bill of Rights. Marx and Engels' view on those personal freedoms is a matter of considerable controversy among interpreters.

In the *Critique of the Gotha Programme*, Marx contrasts genuine equality under communism with the "bourgeois rights" people may have in capitalist society. The latter, he believes, are very limited because they do not take into account the differences between people that result in their having very different needs. But to give the same rights to people with different needs is to give them "unequal rights" (CGP, T 530). This critique of "bourgeois rights" has often been read as an outright rejection of bourgeois rights. Hence many Marxists have believed that the traditional personal freedoms—civil rights, equality before the law, and so on—are "merely" bourgeois freedoms and need not be preserved under socialism and capitalism. If that had been the view of Marx and Engels, they would indeed have been, as is often claimed, the fathers of contemporary communist totalitarianism. Richard Hunt has found no support for that interpretation; on the contrary, he has discovered conclusive evidence that Marx and Engels were unwaveringly committed to democracy. Other, usually sympathetic readers have argued, however, that whatever their actual opinions may have been, Marx and Engels were, by virtue of the abstract theory they developed, committed to a society that left insufficient room for the private realm and thus for individual freedom.[10]

The Inevitability of Communism

We are now in a position to take up the question left open at the end of the preceding chapter: Marx and Engels believed not only that the collapse of capitalism was inevitable but also that capitalism would be replaced with communism and not by another form of class-divided society. The proletarian revolution was to end exploitation forever and to bring about the classless communist society.

Marx and Engels have at least two separate lines of argument for this assertion.

The separation of society into an exploiting and an exploited class, a ruling and an oppressed class, was the necessary consequence of the deficient and restricted development of production in former times. (SUS, T 714)

As long as human productivity was very low, exploitation was unavoidable. Today's capitalism, with its much greater productivity, has prepared the way for a society in which people do not need to compete with each other and exploit each other. Communism is possible once capitalism is fully developed. But is it necessary? The second argument tries to answer that question in the affirmative: Communism is the opposite of capitalist private property. If it is true that capitalism will come to an end, then communism must necessarily follow.

Marx here does what all economists after him have done: He builds a model and, on the assumption that the model correctly describes reality, he makes certain predictions. That is an unexceptional procedure. But there is a difficulty with the model. The characterization of capitalism has many features. Under capitalism there is private property of means of production, the anarchy of the marketplace, class divisions, and class struggle, as well as competition and exploitation. How are these features connected? Marx seems to have believed that these features of capitalism, properly described, are necessarily connected—in other words, that any capitalist society must have all of them, such that if one is removed, then all the other ones also disappear. If that is true, then communism as the negation of capitalism follows the abolition of capitalism. But the model of capitalism has not been worked out with sufficient specificity to show that all these features are necessarily connected.

For instance, it is still a matter of controversy whether market socialism is possible, or whether that is a contradiction in terms.[11] At the heart of this argument is the question of whether a market is essential to capitalism in the sense that any restoration of markets is automatically a restoration of capitalism. The incompleteness of the Marxian model of capitalism is also shown by the debates (mentioned in Chapter 17) about the precise implications of abolishing the separation between the economic and political realms. The abolition of this separation can take the form of fascist corporativism, welfare capitalism, or bureaucratic socialism, but none of these are what Marx and Engels meant by "socialism" or "communism." The abolition of competitive capitalism, we know now, can take many different forms. Many different socio-economic orders have followed the abolition of nineteenth-century competitive capitalism. Socialism and communism, as Marx and Engels conceived them, are not the inevitable successors to competitive capitalism. Hence we cannot predict with confidence what will succeed capitalism as we know it now.

Notes

1. Quoted and explained in Hal Draper, *Karl Marx's Theory of Revolution*, Vol. I (New York: Monthly Review Press, 1976), p. 97.

2. Marx, *The Poverty of Philosophy* (New York: International Publishers, 1963), p. 174.

3. There has been a great deal of controversy about what Marx and Engels actually thought about the Paris Commune. For a detailed account, see Richard Hunt, *The Political Ideas of Marx and Engels*, Vol. II (Pittsburgh: University of Pittsburgh Press, 1984), Chapters 4 and 5.

4. V. I. Lenin, *The State and Revolution*, Chapter 1, in *Selected Works*, Vol. 2 (Moscow: Progress Publishers, 1970).

5. For a concise summary of the earlier debate, see Barry Hindess, "Marxism and Paliamentary Democracy," in Alan Hunt, ed., *Marxism and Democracy* (London: Lawrence and Wishart, 1980). For a recent replay of the same arguments, see the contributions by Herb Gintis and Paula Rothenberg in Steve Rosskamm Shalom, *Socialist Visions* (Boston: South End Press, 1983).

6. For an elaborate description and defense of market socialism, see David Schweickart, *Capitalism or Workers' Control?* (New York: Praeger Publishers,

1980). Some of the traditional debates about the difference between the capitalist and the communist economies are recreated in Paul M. Sweezy and Charles Bettelheim, *On the Transition to Socialism* (New York: Monthly Review Press, 1971).

7. This point has been forcefully argued in Stanley Moore, *Marx on the Choice between Socialism and Communism* (Cambridge: Harvard University Press, 1980).

8. See Alec Nove, *The Economics of Feasible Socialism* (London: George Allen and Unwin, 1983), Chapter 1.

9. Other authors ascribe a different meaning to communist freedom. According to Iring Fetscher, communist freedom consists of the liberation of the real human being, who is a thoroughly altruistic being. See Fetscher, *Marx and Marxism* (New York: Herder and Herder, 1971), pp. 26ff. Richard Hunt gives an important place in communist freedom to the abolition of the division of labor. See Hunt, *Political Ideas*, Vol II, pp. 213ff.

10. Richard Hunt, *The Political Ideas of Marx and Engels*, Vol. I (Pittsburgh: University of Pittsburgh Press, 1974); and Jean Cohen, *Class and Civil Society* (Amherst: University of Massachusetts Press, 1982).

11. Sweezy and Bettelheim, *On the Transition to Socialism*, p. 18.

For Further Reading

Shlomo Avineri, *The Social and Political Thought of Karl Marx* (Cambridge: Cambridge University Press, 1970), Chapter 8.

Bertell Ollman, *Sexual and Social Revolution* (Boston: South End Press, 1979), Chapter 3.

Afterword

MARX DIED MORE THAN 100 years ago, and the centenary of Engels' death is approaching. The works of most of their contemporaries are forgotten outside the universities; the few whose names we remember (e.g., Georg Wilhelm Friedrich Hegel, Adam Smith, John Stuart Mill) are read carefully by some scholars, but no one feels compelled either to justify an interest in them or to justify not reading their works. Not so with Marx and Engels. Those who read Marx and Engels, and write about them, are liable to be attacked—sometimes even in state legislatures or in Congress, as happened in the 1950s. Those who do not read Marx and Engels, on the other hand, often feel compelled to refute them first, as if one needed to justify one's lack of interest in the ideas of those two. It seems difficult, if not impossible, to be neutral toward the body of work that we have just surveyed. Anyone who thinks about philosophy, economics, sociology, or politics does so in the shadow of Marx and Engels.

We cannot ascribe the continued presence of these ideas exclusively to the fact that they have become enmeshed in the Cold War. It is true that the major international antagonisms tend to be those between countries whose rulers identify Marx and Engels as their Founding Fathers and countries that do not. But the continued preoccupation with the ideas of Marx and Engels cannot be understood merely as Cold War tactics. There is no evidence that Soviet, Chinese, or Cuban intellectuals feel the need to study and refute Adam Smith, Thomas Jefferson, or John Stuart Mill over and over again. Even if there were no Cold War, the presence of Marx and Engels in our intellectual landscape would make itself felt much more powerfully than that of most other thinkers of their time.

Yet we have examined many shortcomings in their intellectual legacy. Their works are open to very different interpretations. There is no one clear set of doctrines that we can ascribe to them confidently. What is more, some of the central components of their system of thought are flawed: (1) The Labor Theory of Value is incompletely developed. Whether it can provide an adequate economic theory of capitalism therefore remains unclear. (2) The theory of classes is presented in very fragmentary form, and the outcome of revolutionary politics in the last 100 years forces us to concede that Marx and Engels' understanding of the development of revolutionary classes was defective. The diagnoses of the errors in their theories are as varied as the interpretations of the relevant texts. (3) Marx and Engels were revolutionaries above all, but their understanding of the actual course of revolutionary transformations was uncertain and quite incomplete, constricted by the limits of their experience. (4) They were working for an end to capitalism that they thought would bring socialism and, then, communism. But what goes by those names today is diametrically opposed to what they had hoped and struggled for; their confidence that socialism and communism—free societies in which the "free development of each is the condition for the free development of all" (CM, T 491)—would follow a stagnant capitalism has proven misplaced.

In the light of these and many other very serious failures (which have been described in a large and impressive literature), why does their thought remain so important?

The thought of Marx and Engels represents the bad conscience of the capitalist world.

Marx's economics forces on us the question as to why class struggle continues in all countries, why even in the most affluent countries excessive wealth is surrounded by abject poverty, why economic stability remains an elusive goal, and, finally, why a veritable army of professional economists has been unable to build models that allow accurate predictions, even in the short run. Could it be that the capitalist system, with its classes and the pursuit of private profit, is incapable of providing a good life for all? Could it be that Marx was right in his claim that such a system is inherently unstable? And is it possible that the professional economists refuse to see this because they function as apologists for a system that cannot be defended?

Whatever the faults of Marx and Engels' class theory and theory of the state, two questions remain: Why are there such striking disparities in opportunity and legal protection in countries that proclaim their guiding principle to be Liberty and Justice for All? And why, even with the growing political power of the working classes, are the governments of the Western capitalist nations unmistakably on the side of the large corporations and systematically favoring domestic and foreign policies designed to support those corporations?

However incomplete the Marxian theory of revolution, movements that oppose this ruling system keep arising. All the material wealth and comforts that capitalism provides for some cannot conceal its moral degradation and spiritual poverty.

The world in which we live—a world that abounds in products, many frivolous, but many also extremely useful—at the same time limps from crisis to crisis: crises in nutrition, in housing, in transportation, in education, in health care, in the environment, in the assurance even that the human race will survive this century. Bourgeois social science can study separate parts of each problem, but it offers no explanation as to why capitalist democracy can never quietly enjoy the fruits of a system that is touted as the most wonderful human invention. Worse, social scientists do not even ask the questions raised by Marx and Engels. Historical materialism—the doctrine that our thinking reflects our material conditions—is a constant affront to these intellectuals because it accuses their science of being blinded by their capitalist loyalties.

Exploitation and inequality, both economic and political, and constant crises are there for all to see. The theories of Marx and Engels have not provided complete or always acceptable explanations of these phenomena, but they have not swept them under the rug either. For the defenders of capitalism, who want us to believe that our social system will provide material well-being and political liberty for those who are willing to be industrious and responsible, the writings of Marx and Engels stand as a permanent reproach for their blindness to the deprivations and injustices that capitalism visits on all but a few.

The writings of Marx and Engels therefore remain the starting point for everyone who is critical of existing societies. In addition, they keep that critical spirit alive with the hope that speaks from their books— the hope for a world in which there is no need for talking continually about freedom, simply because everyone is free, and a world in which there is no time to talk grandly about justice and equality, because all available time is taken up with providing justice and equality for all.

For Further Reading

Robert L. Heilbroner, *Marxism: For and Against* (New York: Norton, 1980).

Bibliography

Althusser, Louis, *For Marx* (New York: Vintage Books, 1970).

_____, *Lenin and Philosophy* (New York: Monthly Review Press, 1971).

Avineri, Shlomo, *The Social and Political Thought of Karl Marx* (Cambridge: Cambridge University Press, 1970).

Berlin, Isiah, *Karl Marx, His Life and Environment* (Oxford: Oxford University Press, 1848).

Bottomore, T. B., *Classes in Modern Society* (New York: Vintage Books, 1966).

Brenkert, George, *Marx's Ethics of Freedom* (Boston: Routledge and Kegan Paul, 1983).

Buchanan, Allen E., *Marx and Justice* (Totowa, N.J.: Rowman and Allenheld, 1982).

Carnoy, Martin, *The State and Political Theory* (Princeton, N.J.: Princeton University Press, 1984).

Carver, Terrell, *Marx and Engels: The Intellectual Relationship* (Bloomington: Indiana University Press, 1983).

Cohen, G. A., *Karl Marx's Theory of History* (Princeton, N.J.: Princeton University Press, 1976).

_____, "The Structure of Proletarian Unfreedom," in John Roemer, ed., *Analytical Marxism* (Cambridge: Cambridge University Press, 1986).

Cohen, Jean L., *Class and Civil Society* (Amherst: University of Massachusetts Press, 1982).

Comfort, Richard A., *Revolutionary Hamburg: Labor Politics in the Early Weimar Republic* (Stanford, Calif.: Stanford University Press, 1966).

Desai, Meghnad, *Marxian Economic Theory* (London: Gray-Mills Publishing, 1974).

de Ste. Croix, Geoffrey, *The Class Struggle in the Ancient Greek World* (Ithaca, N.Y.: Cornell University Press, 1981).

Draper, Hal, *Karl Marx's Theory of Revolution* (New York: Monthly Review Press, 1978).

Eisenstein, Zilla, ed., *Capitalist Patriarchy and the Case for Socialist Feminism* (New York: Monthly Review Press, 1979).

Elster, Jon, *Making Sense of Marx* (Cambridge: Cambridge University Press, 1985).

211

Engels, Frederick, *The Dialectic of Nature* (New York: International Publishers, 1940).

_____, *Ludwig Feuerbach and the Outcome of Classical German Philosophy* (New York: International Publishers, 1941).

_____, *The Condition of the Working Class in England in 1844* (Moscow: Foreign Languages Publishing House, 1962).

_____, *The Origin of the Family, Private Property and the State* (New York: International Publishers, 1972).

Fetscher, Iring, *Marx and Marxism* (New York: Herder and Herder, 1971).

Fromm, Erich, *The Sane Society* (New York: Fawcett, 1955).

Gamble, Andrew, and Paul Walton, *Capitalism in Crisis: Inflation and the State* (London: Macmillan, 1976).

Godelier, Maurice, "Structure, Contradiction in *Capital*," in Ralph Miliband and John Saville, eds., *Socialist Register 1976* (London: Merlin Press).

Gramsci, Antonio, *Prison Notebooks* (New York: International Publishers, 1971).

Heilbroner, Robert, *Marxism: For and Against* (New York: Norton, 1970).

Henri, Michel, *Marx: A Philosophy of Human Reality* (Bloomington: Indiana University Press, 1983).

Hindess, Barry, "Marxism and Paliamentary Democracy," in Alan Hunt, ed., *Marxism and Democracy* (London: Lawrence and Wishart, 1980).

Hodgson, Geoff, *Capitalism, Value and Exploitation* (Oxford: Martin Robertson, 1982).

Holmstrom, Nancy, "Exploitation," *Canadian Journal of Philosophy* 7, no. 2 (1977).

Hook, Sidney, *From Hegel to Marx* (Ann Arbor: University of Michigan Press, 1971).

Howard, M. C., and J. E. King, *The Political Economy of Marx* (Burnt Mill, England: Longmans, 1975).

Hunt, Richard, *The Political Ideas of Marx and Engels* (Pittsburgh: University of Pittsburgh Press, 1974).

Kapp, Yvonne, *Eleanor Marx*, Vol. I (London: Lawrence and Wishart, 1972).

Larrain, Jorge, *The Concept of Ideology* (Athens: University of Georgia Press, 1979).

Lenin, V. I., *What Is To Be Done?* in *Selected Works*, Vol. I (Moscow: Progress Publishers, 1970/1971).

_____, *The State and Revolution*, in *Selected Works*, Vol. II (Moscow: Progress Publishers, 1970/1971).

Levine, Norman, *The Tragic Deception: Marx contra Engels* (Oxford and Santa Barbara: Clio Books, 1975).

Lichtheim, George, *The Concept of Ideology, and Other Essays* (New York: Vintage Books, 1967).

Lichtman, Richard, "Marx's Theory of Ideology," *Socialist Revolution* 23, no. 1 (1975).

Lukacz, Georg, *History and Class Consciousness* (Cambridge: MIT Press, 1971).

Luxemburg, Rosa, "Social Reform or Revolution," in Dick Howard, ed., *Selected Political Writings* (New York: Monthly Review Press, 1971).

Mandel, Ernest, *Marxist Economic Theory*, 2 vols. (New York: Monthly Review Press, 1971).

————, *The Formation of the Economic Thought of Karl Marx* (New York: Monthly Review Press, 1971).

Martin, John E., *Feudalism to Capitalism* (Atlantic Highlands, N.J.: Humanities Press, 1983).

Marx, Karl, *Class Struggles in France 1848–1850* (New York: International Publishers, 1964).

————, *Capital*, 3 vols. (New York: International Publishers, 1967).

————, *The 18th Brumaire of Louis Bonaparte* (New York: International Publishers, 1968).

————, *A Contribution to the Critique of Political Economy* (New York: International Publishers, 1970).

————, *Poverty of Philosophy* (New York: International Publishers, 1971).

————, *Grundrisse* (Harmondsworth: Penguin Books, 1973).

Marx, Karl, and Frederick Engels, *The Holy Family* (Moscow: Progress Publishers, 1975).

————, *Marx-Engels: Selected Correspondence* (Moscow: Progress Publishers, 1975).

McBride, William Leon, *The Philosophy of Marx* (New York: St. Martin's Press, 1977).

McMurtry, John, *The Structure of Marx's World-View* (Princeton, N.J.: Princeton University Press, 1978).

Meek, Ronald, *Studies in the Labor Theory of Value* (New York: Monthly Review Press, 1956).

Miliband, Ralph, *The State in Capitalist Society* (New York: Basic Books, 1969).

————, *Marxism and Politics* (Oxford: Oxford University Press, 1977).

Miller Richard W., *Analyzing Marx* (Princeton, N.J.: Princeton University Press, 1984).

Moore, Stanley, *Marx on the Choice between Socialism and Communism* (Cambridge: Harvard University Press, 1980).

Nicolaus, Martin, "The Unknown Marx," in Carl Oglesby, ed., *The New Left Reader* (New York: Grove Press, 1969).

Novak, George, *An Introduction to the Logic of Marxism* (New York: Merit Publishers, 1969).

Nove, Alec, *The Economics of Feasible Socialism* (London: George Allen and Unwin, 1983).

Ollman, Bertell, *Alienation: Marx's Conception of Man in Capitalist Society* (Cambridge: Cambridge University Press, 1971).

————, *Social and Sexual Revolution* (Boston: South End Press, 1979).

Parkin, Frank, *Marxism and Class Theory: A Bourgeois Critique* (New York: Columbia University Press, 1979).

Plamenatz, John, *German Marxism and Russian Communism* (London: Longmans, 1954).

Rader, Melvin, *Marx's Interpretation of History* (New York: Oxford University Press, 1979).

Reich, Wilhelm, *The Mass Psychology of Fascism* (New York: Farrar, Strauss and Giroux, 1970).

Robinson, Cedric J., *Black Marxism* (London: Zed Books, 1983).

Roemer, John, "New Directions in the Marxian Theory of Exploitation and Class," *Politics and Society* 11 (1982):253–287.

Rosaldo, Michelle Zimbalist, and Louise Lamphere, eds., *Women, Culture and Society* (Stanford, Calif.: Stanford University Press, 1974).

Ruben, David-Hillel, *Marx and Materialism: A Study in Marxist Theory of Knowledge* (Sussex, England: Harvester Press, 1977).

Sayer, Derek, *Marx's Method* (Sussex, England: Harvester Press, 1979).

Schmitt, Richard, *Alienation and Class* (Cambridge: Schenkman Publishing Co., 1983).

Schweickart, David, *Capitalism or Workers' Control* (New York: Praeger Publishers, 1980).

Shalom, Steve Rosskamm, *Socialist Visions* (Boston: South End Press, 1983).

Sweezy, Paul M., *The Theory of Capitalist Development* (New York: Monthly Review Press, 1942).

Sweezy, Paul M., and Charles Bettelheim, *On the Transition to Socialism* (New York: Monthly Review Press, 1971).

Therborn, Gran, *What Does the Ruling Class Do When It Rules?* (London: New Left Books, 1978).

Timpanaro, Sebastiano, *Materialism* (London: New Left Books, 1980).

Tucker, Robert C., *Philosophy and Myth in Karl Marx* (Cambridge: Cambridge University Press, 1972).

_____, ed., *The Marx-Engels Reader*, 2nd ed. (New York: W. W. Norton, 1978).

Venable, Vernon, *Human Nature: The Marxian View* (New York: Merdian Books, 1966).

Wolff, Robert Paul, *Understanding Marx* (Princeton, N.J.: Princeton University Press, 1984).

Wood, Allen W., "The Marxian Critique of Justice," in Marshall Cohen et al., eds., *Marx, Justice, History* (Princeton, N.J.: Princeton University Press, 1980).

_____, *Karl Marx* (London: Routledge and Kegan Paul, 1981).

Wright, Erik Olin, *Class, Crisis and the State* (London: Verso, 1978).

Index